AN INTRODUCTION
TO THE PHILOSOPHY OF EDUCATION

AN INTRODUCTION TO THE PHILOSOPHY OF EDUCATION

Albert J. Taylor

Department of Foundations of Education
Glassboro State College

UNIVERSITY
PRESS OF
AMERICA

LANHAM • NEW YORK • LONDON

Copyright © 1983 by

University Press of America,[TM] **Inc.**

4720 Boston Way
Lanham, MD 20706

3 Henrietta Street
London WC2E 8LU England

Copyright © 1975 by
Albert J. Taylor

Copyright © 1978 by
Kendall/Hunt Publishing Company

Library of Congress Cataloging in Publication Data

Taylor, Albert J.
  An introduction to the philosophy of education.

  Originally published: Dubuque, Iowa : Kendall/Hunt Pub.
Co., 1975.
  Bibliography: p.
  1. Education—Philosophy—History. I. Title.
LA21.T38   1983   370'.1   83-6698
ISBN 0-8191-3265-9 (pbk.)

Contents

MAY 1 3 1987

Preface

This book is what the title proclaims, an introduction to the philosophy of education; that, and no more. There is a certain significance to this on several counts. First, it says that the intent is to lead the student of education toward the development of new skills, and to introduce the reader to what may be new and varied views. Stated simply, you will be introduced to a set of analytic tools which may be used for the examination of certain aspects of education as a discipline, and you will be made aware of a large and established heritage.

Second, the notion of introduction signifies that the topics covered will not be exhaustively treated. Much more will remain to be said than a single volume could present. Therefore, in presenting various positions, the author sketched these only briefly and in their barest outlines. To go beyond this, the student will find it necessary to go to those sources suggested in the text and in the bibliography. The latter is also introductory, intended simply to start the student on his way to attaining greater depth.

A third point should also be made clear. There are, and have been, varying and numerous views on what it is that philosophers do when they are engaged in philosophizing, and how this extends to education. It would be presumptuous to suggest that anyone has so conclusively responded to this issue as to make further inquiry unnecessary or impossible. Despite claims to the contrary, what philosophy of education is remains an open question. There is no attempt in this book to resolve that issue. What the author has attempted is to show that while philosophic skills are essential to the understanding of educational concepts, there is also a body of significant literature that is of value to students of education. While the philosophic skills may contribute to understanding, the body of literature will enhance one's appreciation of that institution and those practices called education.

I would also like to say a few words in acknowledgement of some debts. First, I owe much to the students in my classes at Glassboro State College. They have endured the pains of my slow learning, have taught me much, and have thereby contributed significantly to this book. I could not have done an introduction to the philosophy of education had they not taught me what it means to introduce students to the topic. I am also indebted to a number of other people who directly and indirectly contributed to my writing of this book without their having a conscious awareness that they did so. Inspiration comes in many forms and from many sources.

More personal indebtedness involves my wife, Mary, and my children, Carol, Marilyn, Kathleen, Alan, Jeffrey, and Marjorie, (that's right—count 'em), for putting up with what one puts up with in living with someone engaged in such a project. I suppose I must also thank a friend and colleague, Sam Micklus, who had the privilege and pleasure of listening to my ideas while we were on those fishing trips in Maine. Finally, a word of thanks to my longtime friend and colleague, Fred Detrick, who read, suggested, reread and encouraged the efforts leading to this volume. We learned much together.

Albert J. Taylor

Chapter 1

Introduction: The Traditional Meanings
of Philosophy

I

When one begins the study of the philosophy of education, he is often introduced to the subject through a definition of what he may expect to encounter in the realm which he is about to enter. This may be done by looking at the various ways in which philosophy has been defined. Such definitions are usually word-word definitions as opposed to word-thing definitions.[1]

To the initiate, philosophy generally seems to be a strange subject indeed. If one follows the traditional approach, he will find himself learning the history of the subject. This is puzzling enough in itself, since it's unlikely that one has ever before learned a subject by learning its history. But this is only a part of philosophy's uniqueness. In learning the history of the subject, you may learn what Plato, Aristotle, St. Thomas, Hume, Kant and others had to say on a variety of topics. And for what purpose do you learn this? Why, simply to be able to demolish these various and varied positions. A strange undertaking, indeed.

On the other hand, if one is taking a contemporary approach, there may be even more confusion. In the first place, it is rather shocking to be told that you are learning a subject matter with no subject matter in the usual sense of the term, no organized, ordered and orderly body of content with which we may come to correspond, or memorize. The struggle to learn what philosophy is may go on for quite some time, until the insight gradually develops that we have come upon philosophy unawares; that we have been doing philosophy all along without knowing it.

---

1. As the student of philosophy may guess, a word-word definition is one in which we use other words to define the term in question. A word-thing definition points to something in the world. Both approaches have their advantages and disadvantages.

1

With the hope of easing the difficulty of dealing with a strange subject, the approach followed here will differ from both the solidly traditional approach and the unrooted contemporary approach. Our particular position in the stream of history seems sufficient warrant for this approach. Therefore, while we will be taking the traditional positions into account, and examining them to some extent, we will regard philosophy as a tool, rather than a body of organized content.

As Bertrand Russell has told us, the only way to learn philosophy is to do philosophy. Consequently, time will not be wasted on word-word definitions, even though these sometimes appear to answer the question that beginners inevitably ask; *viz.*, What is philosophy? We will "do" philosophy and the reader may then reflect on his own experience to see what he has done.

II

Traditionally, philosophy has been regarded as the "Queen of Sciences" by philosophers. In this sense, philosophy would, and has been thought to, include superior methods of knowing, and the certain (i.e., absolutely sure) bodies of knowledge established by those ways of knowing. We will examine these claims subsequently.

On the other hand, philosophy has also been regarded, at a "homier" level, as simply a set of beliefs. We talk about having a "philosophy of life," or, at a professional level, of a "philosophy of education." If we examine what one has when he has such a "philosophy," we find that it usually consists of some "guiding principles" in the form of ceremonial statements. Or, the term "philosophy" may be used simply to name whatever collection of beliefs we may happen to hold.

In this simple sense, we could hardly be said to engage in philosophy, since there is nothing that we do. There is no method involved, no act of philosophizing. There is only a subject matter and that subject matter, *viz.*, whatever beliefs we hold, may have been arrived at by various routes and a host of methods. There would be little point in having courses in philosophy, or philosophy of education, if this were all there were to it, since there would be no methods, or skills or abilities to be taught, and the subject matter would be held already. Clearly, in courses called "philosophy" or "philosophy of education," we are not using the term philosophy in this simple sense.

Another relatively popular view of what it is that we do when we engage in philosophy is seen in the popular use of the term to label discourse that is not directly practical. In education, for example, discussions that are not about specific techniques, or actual classroom practices, are sometimes dismissed as "merely philosophical." In other areas as well, when questions are raised about matters which are not concerned specifically with the "doing" of things, they are regarded as philosophic questions or concerns.

This use of the term would describe an activity that need hardly be learned, since we engage in such discourse without being led into it. There also seems to be little concern about whether or not skills or abilities are developed here since, in this case, the term is merely serving as a label for what just happens to take place. As for a subject matter to be learned, any topic at all can serve as a vehicle for philosophy in this sense. So, short of learning about "everything," one would be hard pressed to indicate what the subject matter to be learned would be.

It is as the "Queen of Sciences" that philosophy has been most frequently and generally approached in the past. In doing philosophy, according to this formula, one engages in the acts of speculating and prescribing. This does not exhaust what one does, since analysis also constitutes one of the aspects of doing philosophy. But this latter phase has taken on such significance in recent years that it merits separate and detailed consideration on its own.

III

On what bases is such activity regarded as the "Queen of Sciences"? One basis is the claim that philosophy is extended theory-building which unifies theories into a meta-theory, (i.e., a super theory composed of or formed from lesser theories, or a theory of theories.) It is pointed out that the kind of theory-building carried out in fields other than philosophy results in seeing man, nature, or whatever is being studied, in particular and specialized parts. What philosophy does is put these parts together into a unified whole with all the parts made compatible.

What such claims overlook is the requirement that this would set for the philosopher. Obviously, the philosopher could not unify what he did not know about. Before he could unify two, or three, or several theories, he would be required to know these theories. This would require of the philosopher that he be not merely a scientist, since a scientist would know only one set of theories. To do the job set out for him in this notion of what it means to do philosophy, the philosopher would be required to be a sort of super-scientist, with knowledge at his fingertips of all the theories which he was engaged in unifying.

At a time in the history of thought when the sciences were undeveloped, one man might know the content of several fields well enough to engage in such unification of what was then known. He could really do some extended theory building. But with the sciences in their present, highly-sophisticated state, a highly knowledgeable scientist would not be expected to know all of the theories of even his own field. Therefore, with the possibility of thoroughly knowing one's own field being so remote, the likelihood that anyone would know several fields well enough to build their theories into a meta-theory is so limited as to be regarded as impossible.

Another basis for regarding philosophy as the "Queen of Sciences" has been the notion expressed by many that knowledge begins as philosophy and ends as science. The claim is put forth that philosophy is at the forefront of knowledge, that philosophers raise questions which scientists later answer. The well-defined answers to questions are all a part of the various sciences. But, as one moves from the area of the known into the region of the unknown, one moves from science to speculation; from a particular and reliable body of knowledge to philosophy.

This view is near enough being true to be thought plausible. If we were to examine the history of the sciences and of philosophy, one would indeed find this suggestion about the role of philosophy to be the case. Philosophy and science were, at one point in history, two names for essentially the same thing. Philosophy was the questioning forefront of knowledge, while science was that which was *known*, as distinct from that which was merely believed. Philosophers did indeed raise questions, the answers to which were regarded as knowledge.

There is good reason, however, for believing that that day is forever past. Knowledge has become so technical, so specialized, because of its growth that philosophers are no longer able to play the role which they once played. Any questions that philosophers might raise of scientists today would be so childlike in their level of relative sophistication that scientists could not be bothered to answer them. If the scientist did pause to answer the question, his answer would be from what he already knew. Nothing new would be added to the particular body of knowledge in response to the philosopher's questioning.

The reason for this is that in order to raise a question that would result in the scientist's providing an answer that would add to the body of knowledge in that field, the philosopher would be required to have at his disposal the sort of knowledge that the scientist possessed. In short, he would be required to be a scientist and would be raising his question as a scientist rather than as a philosopher. Philosophers simply do not, as philosophers, have the knowledge that would enable then to be at the forefront of knowledge and raise questions of scientists the answers to which would add to our body of knowledge. Perhaps an illustration would help.

When, near the end of the 18th century, the planet Uranus was discovered, astronomers believed that this completed the solar system.[2] At any rate, they began to compute the orbit of the planet on the basis of what they then knew, as though no other bodies were present than those already known. But, by the middle of the nineteenth century, discrepancies were noted between the predicted orbit and the path which the planet was actually following. The divergence was extremely slight, about 1/3600 of a right angle. No one knew why this divergence occurred; this was truly at the forefront of knowledge. The question to be raised would be regarding how we were to account for this disjoint experience (unexpected occurrence).

What we must remember is that, in the first place, it took a highly specialized and technical knowledge and tools even to predict what the path of the planet was to be. Only a scientist would have such knowledge. Secondly, it similarly took highly specialized and technical knowledge and tools to detect the divergence between prediction and observation. The significance of all this is simply that without the knowledge and tools of the scientist, (i.e., unless one were a scientist), the question would never occur to us. Unless he happened also to be a scientist, the philosopher would not know enough to be able to raise the question the answer to which would add to our knowledge.

Now, the speculations (i.e., reasoning, thinking, deliberating), of the scientists led to the hypothesis that another as yet undiscovered planet must be causing the apparently erratic behavior of Uranus. Astronomers, using methods that philosophers had not even dreamed existed, calculated the size and position of the heavenly body that would cause the apparent irregularities of Uranus. Eventually, they had their answer to the question with the discovery of Neptune. Notice that the whole process, from beginning to end, was scientific. Nowhere at all did philosophy enter in. This would seem to dispense with the notion that philosophy is at the forefront of knowledge, raising questions which scientists later answer.

2. Suggested by D.J. O'Connor, *An Introduction to the Philosophy of Education* (London: Routledge & Kegan Paul, 1957) pp. 79f.

Yet another basis for regarding philosophy as the "Queen of Sciences" has its origin in history also. According to the Greek formula, science was that which was known as opposed to, or distinct from, that which was merely believed. Philosophers claimed to have special ways of knowing which would enable them to answer questions with certainty, i.e., finally and absolutely rather than merely contingently. This is what they would do by engaging in speculation. And the certain (as opposed to uncertain) results of their speculation would enable them also to prescribe with equal certainty.

The question might well arise as to what philosophers were to speculate about. The answer in one sense is so simple as to be overwhelming. Philosophers would "speculate" about *everything*. And remember that with their special ways of knowing, philosophers traditionally promised to answer their questions not contingently, but with certainty. What is this speculation which philosophers engage in? We are told frequently that the speculative aspect of philosophy means thinking in a general and systematic way, (in fact, since philosophy is a sort of meta- or super-science, *the most* general and systematic way), about the whole of reality.

What one thinks about when he thinks about "the whole of reality" is a large question in itself. Indeed, it is not enough simply to think about the whole of reality. Philosophers must do this in some way other than the way scientists think about reality. Scientists think simply about *parts* of reality. Philosophers deal with the "whole of reality" in some way that distinguishes them from scientists. One way of doing this, of course, would be simply to think of all that all scientists think about. But this would be a tall order indeed. It would require philosophers to know at least all that all scientists know. Would anyone be willing seriously to claim that philosophers are people who know everything that is known?

Can one, in fact, think about the "whole of reality" without thinking about particulars? Suppose we approach this on a lower level of ambition. Suppose you were asked to think not about the "whole of reality," but simply about the "whole of your campus." Can you say what color the walls are in the men's lounge of the faculty dining hall or dining room? If you don't know that, can you think about it? If you can't think about that, then can you think about the "whole of your campus?" What would be required in order to think about the whole of your campus? What would then be required to think about "the whole of reality"? Yet, this is one of the claims made for what we mean by philosophic speculation.

Perhaps what is important about speculation is not what men think, but the methods used. As was pointed out earlier, philosophers have traditionally claimed to have special ways of knowing; ways that are distinct from the ways of the empirical scientists; ways that will lead to certain (i.e., final, absolute) knowledge. What are the ways that philosophers have of knowing? What sorts of things do philosophers *do* when they are engaged in the act of speculation?

One of the favored activities that philosophers have traditionally claimed will lead to knowledge is the use of reason. Knowledge arrived at on this basis is called rational knowledge. This is the kind of knowledge that we arrive at simply by logic, by reasoning, rather than by experience. In fact, experience is irrelevant here. An example of the use of reason would be: There may be two wooden chairs in the room located on one side of the room which you are now in. And there may be two wooden chairs in the room located on the other side of the room which you are now in. We don't know whether or not there are such chairs present, and only experience can tell us that. But, we know that if there are two such chairs in each room, they will total four wooden chairs. And that we know by reason.

Now, the senses may contribute to such knowledge in the form of raw data, sense experiences. But it is reason that assembles this raw data into certain knowledge. Historically, men believed that pure reason, unfettered by experience, was adequate for establishing knowledge. Indeed, sense experience was regarded as an intrusion which could upset the certainty of the knowledge established by reason. For reasons we shall briefly consider below, and again in the chapter on theories, we now see some limitations on the use of reason alone and on the type of "knowledge" that it leads to. But, at any rate, reasoning was one of the activities generally designated by the term "speculation."

Actually, reason alone seldom sufficed, because reason had to have a starting point. This starting point was with a self-evident truth arrived at intuitively or through revelation. Consequently, the process of intuition was also what philosophers sometimes referred to as speculation. Intuition is a personal way of knowing, largely related to feeling, and not intimately connected with logic. Indeed, at times, intuition may appear to be the opposite of reason, for the conclusions established may appear, if not in conflict with reason, at least to be illogical, in a sense. At any rate, there appear to be steps missing between the premises one holds, or the starting point of reasoning, and the conclusions one arrives at. It is the sudden "insight" that one develops, where he suddenly "sees the light," or understands what was not clear before without going through the steps one would normally go through to arrive at understanding.

Everyone has had such an experience. At times, it has been useful and helpful. Indeed, people of all walks of life will testify that some of their accomplishments have been the result of such apparently "irrational leaps." No one seriously denies that people have such experiences. But there are serious doubts about relying on intuition as a certification for knowledge. Questions are raised when people go beyond claiming to have arrived at knowledge intuitively, and claim that their knowledge is knowledge *because* they arrived at it through intuition. Intuition, questionable as it is as a certification for knowledge, is another aspect of speculation.

Revelation is yet another avenue to knowledge. It is difficult to imagine what activity one engages in that would guarantee that he would experience revelation. How could one be sure that what he had arrived at was the result of revelation rather than intuition, or even wishful thinking, might be difficult unless that information were given as part of the revelation. Yet, men do engage in certain activites, meditation, during which God discloses certain things to them. What is revealed is not subject to reason nor experience, but must simply be accepted. This method of speculation does not seem to be relied on as heavily as it once was, but perhaps that is merely a cultural phenomenon.

Similar to both revelation and intuition is yet another aspect of speculation, that of introspection. This process also resembles the use of reason in that it is ordered and is not the same immediate sort of experience that intuition and revelation are. Yet, like intuition and revelation, it does not require following an external logic. The process consists of the examination of the contents of one's own mind. In this, one might meditate as in revelation, but unlike revelation and intuition, knowledge does not come into the mind. Rather one discovers what was really there all along.

The speculation that philosophers engaged in, then, might result in direct apprehension of knowledge through intuition, introspection, or revelation. Such knowledge might be complete in and of itself, but complete or not, it was certain. It did not rely on contingent experience and therefore was not subject to the limitations imposed by "mere" experience. At times, what was revealed or intuited were self-evident first principles. These were undeniable, unquestionable, indubitable "truths" that the mind grasped.

One such principle might be that everything has a cause. We do not need to reason this out; it is simply obvious to us in and of itself and without further testimony, (i.e., it is *self*-evident.) More complex first principles that were regarded as being completely self-evident were the following: "Corporal substances differ essentially or accidently, according as they are individuals of different species (having diverse natures) or as they are numerically distinct individuals having the same specific nature"; and, "the good is convertible with being. . . ."[3]

Now, from such "self-evident first principles," arrived at through speculations of one sort or another, we may deduce other conclusions. Since these principles are so obviously true, we need be careful only to reason correctly and we shall be led to further truths. Indeed, whole systems of thought have been developed by these methods of speculation. Whole "philosophies" have been developed.

The problems of speculation as a method are suggested in the preceding sentence. What has been arrived at have been numerous and varied bodies of "certain knowledge." But, in the whole history of philosophy, a body of reliable knowledge on the order of chemistry or physics has never been developed. If it is not appropriate to point out that the reason for this phenomenon may be the methods employed, we can at least indicate that there are problems in the methods.

If we may begin with the last point about the use of self-evident first principles, a problem presents itself immediately. In the two complex principles suggested by Adler, above, one might note that, far from being self-evident, all the evidence we have regarding evolution denies the first assertion. As for the second, concerning the necessary connection between "being" and "good," despite all the trials and claims of philosophers through the centuries, no one has yet demonstrated this sort of connection between metaphysics and axiology. Hume has, in fact, clearly demonstrated that no such connection exists, a matter we shall take up later when we discuss value judgements. One problem, then, is that "self-evident first principles" appear to be evident to their authors only. Others do not seem to see them as such.

The special ways of knowing also exhibit difficulties. In the case of revelation, for example, we have the dual problem of having dieties reveal contradictory information about man, the world, or whatever matters are revealed. Where such contradictions occur, we have no way of resolving the conflict, since revelation is not subject to reason, or intuition, or any other checks. Also, that which is revealed sometimes comes into conflict with that which is intuited, or reasoned, and again the resolution of conflict is a problem.

3. NSSE, *Forty First Yearbook, Part I*, "Philosophies of Education," pp. 244 f.

The same thing is true of intuition and introspection. Since intuition is purely personal, two persons may (and frequently do) intuit conflicting items of "knowledge." How does one resolve such conflict? Again, if intuition is its own certification, we have no way of knowing who's "really" right. What may mislead us is that some-one using the term "intuition" may slip from one meaning of the word to another and we are misled because the form of the word remains the same. If I am steeped in a subject, I may, in my periods of contemplation, arrive at conclusions about my subject without knowing quite how I got there. I may have omitted some intervening steps in the reasoning process. But to grant that this may happen is not to grant that it is a reliable way of knowing. Intuition often leads one astray, too. And we still have that problem of how to remove conflict when two intuitionists disagree. "Reason" tells us that they cannot disagree and both be right.

But reason has its problems, too. This is not intended to depre-cate reason, nor to suggest that we eliminate it. All that is intended is to point out that reason alone may not be sufficient. It may not be sufficient because of the kind of truths that reason, used alone, establishes. Occasionally, the reasoning that we use has flaws that are not clearly evident and only after much study and effort do we see that we have been misled. Another problem is that once reason gets started it may lead to some strange conclusions.

I may say to you, "It's possible for me to fly around this room."

You reply, "Prove it."

I say, "All creatures that can move their upper limbs like this can fly; (I demonstrate by flapping my arms.) I can move my upper limbs like this; therefore, I can fly."

Now I have "proved" that I can fly around the room. If you were to say "Show me," instead of "Prove it," I'm sunk, of course. But, if all you ask for is proof, I may, through the use of reason alone, provide "proof."

The problem with the use of reason alone is that it deals simply with relations among statements and therefore gives little help in understanding the world. We shall explore this point in more detail later, when we discuss the various meanings of "truth."

That speculation has not enabled philosophy to keep its promise is revealed not only in these problems in the methods them-selves. It is made clear by what happened historically. In the first place, as will be made manifestly clear in a later chapter, rather than establish a body of knowledge that is certain, speculation has resulted in conflicting and competing systems of thought. And we have had embarrassing occurrences in philosophy such as competing metaphysical systems yielding identical systems of ethics, or a single system of metaphysics yielding competing systems of knowledge or values.

Beyond this, when reliable bodies of knowledge began to be established by the various sciences, they tended to deny or dismiss rather than support the tenets established by philosophers with their special ways of knowing. This has significance for the claims of traditional philosophers that they have special ways of knowing. It was through speculation that Aristotle arrived at the "knowledge" that heavenly bodies move in perfect circles. The methods of the astronomers led to different conclusions. The fact that even the most dedicated contemporary metaphysician no longer seriously entertains Aristotle's conclusion as an item of knowledge signifies that on this point, philosophy has surrendered to the sciences.

A study of the history of thought reveals that this instance is characteristic; that whenever, in the past, science and philosophy have come into conflict, it has inevitably and invariably been philosophy that has ceded the point. In yielding on the points of difference, some philosophers have imagined that they were simply giving in on specific items of knowledge. But more was involved than this. For, in surrendering on specific items of knowledge, philosophers were also surrendering their claims to have special ways of knowing. In inevitably and invariably acknowledging that the point established by science was the point to be accepted, philosophers were also granting that the methods of the sciences were the appropriate methods for establishing reliable bodies of knowledge. Their claims to have special ways of knowing need not be taken seriously, therefore.

A review of what has been disclosed by considering philosophy as speculation suggests that this may not be an essential part of philosophy. Doing philosophy is not necessarily engaging in speculation. If speculation is seen as "thinking about the whole of reality," this seems to come to nothing. If speculation is regarded simply as a special way of knowing, there are problems involved in this. Not only do the claimed special ways of knowing contain internal problems, (e.g., they do not enable us to resolve conflicting claims), but they have not yielded reliable bodies of knowledge, and have, in fact, been surrendered by philosophers themselves as fruitful methods of establishing knowledge. On this basis, we might say of speculation that it is an accompanying, rather than a defining, characteristic of philosophy.[4] That is to say, speculation has indeed accompanied specific instances of doing philosophy, but it is not an essential, or necessary, part of doing philosophy.

IV

Having considered the speculative phase of philosophy, we will be able to deal much more briefly with the prescriptive aspect. There are clearly connections between these two phases of traditional philosophy. If speculation involved "thinking about the whole of reality," a part of what philosophers speculated about was the subject matter of prescription.

Prescriptive philosophy involves us in what is good and bad, or beautiful and ugly, what *ought* to be rather than what *is*. This is the realm of values, as opposed to the world of facts, although certain philosophers have traditionally treated values as though they were facts, even while maintaining that there is a distinction. At any rate, philosophers have engaged in examining, and *stipulating*, what ought to be. Again, the basis for this prescription has generally been that philosophers have special ways of knowing what meaning terms like *good* and *beautiful* have. On the basis of this knowledge, they are therefore equipped to prescribe what values are valuable, or ought to be held to be valuable.

The problems with this view are the same as those concerning speculation. Despite their claims, philosophers have not succeeded in establishing reliable bodies of knowledge in the area of values. Having no body of knowledge to draw from, nor any special tools at their disposal, philosophers then are no better equipped than anyone else to prescribe values. When philosophers claim to be able to judge matters, or evaluate the facts which scientists study, one may reasonably raise questions about what equips philosophers for this sort of activity.

The claims of the philosophers to be able to prescribe must be rejected on essentially the same grounds as we reject speculation as a necessary part of philosophy. Again, certain philosophers have

---

4. A defining characteristic is a characteristic in the absence of which the word would not be applicable to the thing, e.g., having 3 sides is a defining characteristic of a triangle, whereas being large is merely an accompanying characteristic. In other words, if the figure did not have 3 sides, it would not be a triangle, whereas if it did not have the characteristic of being large, it could still be a triangle.

engaged in prescription, and no one denies that prescription has accompanied particular instances of philosophizing. All that is claimed is that prescription must be regarded as an accompanying rather than a defining characteristic of philosophy.

V

Our approach so far may strike one as being very negative and unprogressive. As the alternatives regarding what constitutes philosophy were established, each in turn appeared to be found wanting in some respect or another. It is not unusual to note this characteristic. Indeed, philosophers themselves have pondered the problem and have sought to remedy it, or at least to explain it. A part of this may be related to our view of other bodies of knowledge of a positive kind. We see these other areas engaged in methodically building systems of answers to questions as reliable bodies of knowledge are constructed. In contrast to this, we seem to have engaged in a process of destroying the arguments that have traditionally been put forward by philosophers and those commenting on philosophy.

What we have been engaging in is an activity that has characterized philosophy from its beginnings. If one examines the dialogues of Plato, for example, he will find this process going on. In *The Republic* as various efforts are made to indicate what constitutes justice, Socrates points out the flaws in the views that are offered. The point of this criticism, however, is not simply to destroy the arguments of one's opponents, although that may, in fact, occur. The activity is carried on, rather, in the interest of clarity, i.e., in order to clarify what it is we are talking about or what we can conceivably mean by various statements.

If one reflects on what has gone on so far, another view of what constitutes philosophy may begin to be seen. Certainly, at this stage, it would be reasonable to suggest that philosophy is not a body of reliable knowledge of a positive kind, like astronomy, or geology. This point will be expanded later on, but since the entire book cannot be presented in an introductory chapter, let the point as we have made it here suffice for the time being.

Further, if one looks back again at what has gone on so far, he may see that what we have been engaging in is a process of criticism and analysis in order to clarify what philosophy is. (And is not.) There are those who would say that this constitutes all there is to philosophy, that it has been the analytical and critical phase of philosophy that has been of the most enduring value. There are those who claim that this is a defining characteristic of philosophy.

Those who see this as constituting philosophy will point out that it does not involve philosophy's simply turning in upon itself; that it can be worked on any subject matter at all. On this basis, learning to do philosophy would then become a process of developing the tools and skills required for analysis and criticism. Such a process would enable the student to recognize, first of all, that he may have come upon philosophy unawares. Indeed, he may have been engaging in philosophy without knowing it, as we have gone along so far. If such an insight develops, he may already sense what the endeavor is about and begin to look for specific ways to engage knowledgeably and skillfully in that process. It is hoped that the balance of this book will serve to aid in that effort.

Chapter 2

The Traditional Problems
of Philosophy

I

It was suggested earlier that the subject matter of philosophy has traditionally been regarded as the whole of reality. Any subject matter at all might then be regarded as being in the province of philosophy. We have seen the problems in this view. Certainly, if philosophers claimed to be able to give us knowledge about everything, their delivery appears to have fallen short of their claim. No reliable bodies of knowledge in the usual or expected sense of the term have been developed.

Some have explained this curious phenomenon by suggesting that the real concern of the philosopher is the study of questions rather than providing answers. Questions constitute the "raw material" of philosophy, and it is the concern of philosophers to sort out questions and to ask the right questions. If his concern is simply with the questions themselves, then one may rightfully wonder at the point of doing philosophy. It would seem, in this view, to consist of merely musing over questions, which may be even less fruitful than the critical and analytical approach may appear to be at this stage.

More frequently, philosophy has been seen to deal with problems. That philosophers have been concerned with providing solutions to these problems is evidenced by the volumes on the shelves of libraries that purport to be answers to the questions raised of, and by, philosophers. Traditionally, all of these questions have been seen to center around three basic questions.

The first of these basic problems is represented by the question: What is real? The name of this branch of philosophy is *metaphysics*, or *ontology*. These words are often used interchangeably. However, there are those who make a distinction. Some see ontology as the more general term, with metaphysics, meaning literally "beyond the physical," being that branch of ontology concerned with "otherworldly" kinds of knowledge. In this sense, the provinces of meta-physics would be realms of "being" outside the realm of everyday experience. "This-worldly" concerns would be the province of cosmology, focusing attention on the characteristics of a universe of system and order. For our purposes, we need not make this sort of distinction and will follow the more general practice of using the terms *metaphysics* and *ontology* interchangeably.

Metaphysical problems center around the question: What is real? One aspect of this problem has been to determine the nature of reality in the sense of determining whether the totality of what exists is one, complete, unified system or, as William James has referred to it, a "blooming, buzzing confusion." Those who hold to the former view are regarded as *monists*. Those who disagree with this view are called *pluralists*. Another aspect of this concern for the nature of reality revolves around the nature and existence of the external world and whether this world exists "out there" essentially as our senses seem to indicate, (*realism*) or whether reality is "really" a mental event, (*idealism*).

Another metaphysical problem has to do with the existence of God. In this area, such questions are raised as: Does God exist? What is his relationship to the world? etc. *Atheists*, of course, deny the assertions of *theists*, while *agnostics* regard such questions as un-answerable.

A third area of metaphysical concerns is the field of human nature, with its questions relating to what it means to be human. Included in this area would be questions about body, mind, and soul.

The theory of knowledge, or *epistemology*, constitutes the second major branch of philosophy. This area centers around the question: What is knowledge? The question is sometimes stated as: What is truth? or, What do we know to be true? Questions are raised regarding the nature of knowledge and truth themselves. Aside from this, there are concerns about how we know. In response to this concern, there are those who suggest that we come to know through largely unaided reason. (The only "aid" granted is the starting point: intuition, or revelation, which grants us first principles from which to start.) Such claimants are called *rationalists*. Among those opposed to rationalists are those who claim that we can "know" only through the physical senses. *Empiricists* rely on the senses for knowing.

The third branch of philosophy, *axiology*, centers around ques-tions of values. Although it is regarded as a single branch, two ques-tions really characterize the field. The first of these general questions is: What is good? Questions revolving around this general question would be: What is the good life? What is right conduct? What is moral? Such questions are considered *ethical* problems. *Ethics*, being concerned with values is related to but separate from *esthetics*. Esthetics deals with the general question: What is beauty? or, What do we mean by "beautiful"? Esthetics (or aesthetics) would also consider the question: What is art? and related questions.

This sampling of philosophic problems is simply by way of introduction. Each of the three branches of philosophy will be considered in greater detail in order to provide a full understanding of the traditional problems of philosophy. It might be pointed out, however, that there is nothing sacrosanct about this organization. The traditional problems of philosophy could be examined on the basis of a completely different organization. For example, one might as readily study wholly different "branches" of philosophy, as philosophy of art, philosophy of religion, philosophy of science, etc. But it will be instructive to follow the more common procedure of examining the content of traditional philosophy on the basis of the way it has most generally been organized.

II

Metaphysics is the study of the nature of ultimate reality. To many, the question, What is real? seems silly or inane. When an instructor in philosophy first raises this question, a very common, if guarded, response is: If he doesn't know what's real, he can't teach me anything. It is the tendency to regard such questions as so much nonsense that leads people to regard philosophy as a useless and ivory-towered pursuit.

One basis for considering such questions is to see what it is that we might mean by certain of our assertions, and to follow out what these assertions might come to. Often, we are not clear about our use of certain terms. Even the most common terms, like the word "real" itself, are often used vaguely, with the user himself not clear about the content of his assertion.

What does it mean to say of something that it is real? One might consider the following situation. Suppose I were to set up on a table before you an imaginary pot. I reach into my pocket and pull out some equally imaginary tree seeds. I "plant" the seeds in the pot and stand back. Within a few moments an imaginary tree sprouts and grows. Soon, it has reached the ceiling of the room with its branches spreading out above the table. Is this a *real* tree? The most obvious answer is "no." I have suggested that it is imaginary. Now what we may consider is what the differences are between this tree which I have "grown," and the ones outside the building where you are now, that would cause you to refer to the trees outside as real, but would induce you to avoid using that term to describe the tree which I have "grown".

"I can see the trees outside, but I cannot see the tree which you have grown," you may say.

But, if "seeing the tree" is the only criterion for assigning the label "real" then I would have to label the mirage which I see on a hot summer day as "real" water.

"But I can also touch the real tree, whereas I cannot touch the tree which you have grown."

This would seem to take care of distinguishing between "real" things and mere mirages. But can you, on this basis, distinguish between hallucinations and real things. In hallucinations, I may both see and touch the thing in question.

"Well, let's see. I can enlist the help of others. Not only can *I* see and touch the real tree, but others can see and touch it also."

Ah, but suppose I find someone besides myself who can also see and touch the tree which I have grown. Is it then real?

"No, because most people cannot see and touch it."

How many people would you then require in order to determine whether or not my tree, or any tree, is real? Would we take a vote on it and decide on the basis of the result whether or not the tree is real? If most people vote in favor of its being a real tree, then it is a real tree. If most people vote against it, then it's not a real tree. But suppose someone leaves the room, or other people enter the room, and the vote changes. Does the tree change then from being a real tree to being unreal, or *vice versa*?

"No, it's a real tree, or not a real tree, regardless of how people vote."

But, what do you mean by *real*? Why are you willing to attach the label to one tree but not the other?

And so it goes, with even the most common words not always being clear, even to their user.

Traditionally, it has been asserted that metaphysics goes beyond this concern with the meaning of certain terms and statements. Usually, the claim is made that metaphysics deals with or examines the nature of reality, which includes those general areas mentioned earlier.

Doubt may arise over the most common things as we begin to

examine the nature of reality. (Here, it is assumed, we are not talking about the word "real" and what it means, but about what reality is "really" like.) Again, let us take a common object, such as a desk in your room. Common sense would tell us that the desk is really as your senses reveal it to you. It is solid, of particular and measurable dimensions, of a certain color, and able to support my weight if I sit on it.

The chemist, however, may view the chair in a different fashion. If it is a wooden desk, it is a body of hydrocarbons associated in a certain way, subject to certain alterations as I submit it to various conditions of heat, or cold, or bring it into contact with certain other materials. The physicist, on the other hand, would see it differently from this or the preceding view. To him, the desk is "really" a system of electrons and protrons with space in between, (More space, in fact, than electrons and protons), and the "particles" are in rapid motion. Such a conception naively viewed would make one wonder how it could hang together or support my weight.

What we need to consider, the metaphysician suggests, is which desk is the "real" desk. Or, stated differently, what is the desk "really" like? i.e., What is the nature of its reality?

The questions might be pushed back even further than this to the point of asking: Is the desk really there?

"Of course," you reply, "I can see it."

No, what you *see* is simply a patch of extended color. In fact, one might say that what you are doing is simply having a particular sensation called "seeing a desk." Is the real desk, then, merely your sensation of it? Is your assertion that the desk is really then merely an inference from the sensation you had?

"No, I am not talking about my sensation. I am talking about that desk out there. That's really out there. At least, if it's a real desk its there whether or not I'm having a sensation called "seeing a desk."

If the desk is really to persist independently of being seen by us, then it must be more than a sensation in our mind. (Whatever "in our mind" means.) Indeed, most people would commonly assert that there is even more to it than simply "an extended patch of color" that I see. In asserting its permanence, they generally invoke notions of substances. The desk is a substance, or a composition of substances, which is permanent and capable of *causing* sensations. These are metaphysical beliefs which operate in the inference from having sensations, to the chair as viewed by the chemist or physicist.

But we still have not gone back far enough, some will assert.

When we say, "The desk exists," (or, The desk *is*), we are classifying the desk, asserting its identity as a member of the class of things that *are*. We have given, the claim goes, the most basic characteristic of the desk. We have said that the desk has *being*. If we really want to examine the nature of reality, what we must get at is the nature of *being*, and what we mean when we say of a thing that "it exists."

One other aspect of the nature of reality might also be considered. This centers on the problem of purpose. We all have purposes in our individual lives and these purposes serve to guide our conduct and direct our ways. Much of what we do involves adhering to at least informal plans to move us in the direction of achieving our purpose.

To extend this, we might also consider whether life, not just our individual lives, but *life* itself has, or serves, some purpose outside of or beyond itself. Indeed, one might raise the question of the whole universe: Is the universe expressing some cosmic purpose, serving some absolute or divine will? Is there some grand plan behind the whole of reality? Is the universe not only an orderly but also a determinate universe? Or, is it an open cosmos? Beyond this are questions of how we can determine whether or not there is such a purpose, and if the universe does have a purpose, what is the purpose and how can we come to know it?

Such considerations generally lead into questions regarding the existence of God. If there is some grand scheme behind the universe, some cosmic will, then does not this entail the existence of some entity who devised this scheme, or possesses this will? The possibility of such an entity has led to several uses of the term "god." *Pantheists* have suggested that the universe and God are one. Such a use of the term, however, renders the word meaningless, since if God and the universe cannot be distinguished, then one might as well use the term "universe." There is less chance of being misunderstood.

Among those who distinguish between God and the universe, disagreements arise concerning the nature of God's relationship to the universe. *Deists* claim that God merely created the universe and then left it on its own. Prayer, miracles, or any suggestion of divine intervention are all rejected. Opposed to this view are the *theists*, who see God not only as the creator, but as one who sees to the running of the universe, causing miracles, responding to prayers, revealing his will to some, and being interested in human affairs, particularly those related to morality. Opposed to all these views are the *agnostics*, who declare that it is not possible for man ever to know whether or not there is a God. More positive (some say negative) opponents are the *atheists*, who deny the existence of God.

Recently, a new voice has been added by those who declare such arguments to be not merely true or false, but meaningless. The sentence, "There is a God," is meaningless, they assert because it cannot be verified. Since it cannot be verified, no one can know what is being asserted. Since "There is a god" is meaningless, then "There is no God," or God is unknowable," or any such assertions are equally meaningless.

This latter group has also suggested that it is not meaningful to ask about the purpose of the universe. It makes sense, the argument goes, to ask the purpose of specifics, but it does not make sense to ask for the purpose of the universe. As Bertrand Russell has argued, while it makes sense to ask "Who is the mother of . . . ?" for any individual, it does not make sense to ask, "Who is the mother of the human race?" Similarly, when one talks about cause, it makes sense to talk about the causes of specifics, but not to talk about the cause of the universe. If I say X causes event A, Y causes event B, and Z causes event C, it does not then make sense to ask: What causes ABC?

Much metaphysical talk about God also revolves about the giving, and refuting, of proofs of the existance of God. Such proofs as St. Anselm's purely logical ontological proof, or St. Thomas's well known five proofs pretty well cover the proofs that have been offered. All such proofs have been refuted either by demonstrating that there are flaws in the logic, or that such arguments merely make assertions about the uses of the word "god."

A third area of metaphysical concern mentioned earlier was human nature, or what it means to be human. Here, it is purported, we are not talking simply about the peculiar biological characteristics which distinguish man from all other species of living creatures. What we must talk about inevitably is what is truly distinctive about man, *viz.*, his mind and his soul. Any reference to man's biological characteristics, of course, places us in the physical realm. What we will be dealing with will be the *meta*-physical, that beyond the physical.

This gets us into immediate difficulty since there is disagreement about what we can possibly refer to when we refer to the *self* or the *mind*. There are some points about which we seem to have some degree of certainty, *viz.*, that I can identify my *self* on the basis of what distinguishes my body from other bodies. For example, I cannot get away from my body; I always see it from the same perspective; my experiences with it are of kinesthetic and other somatic sense experiences, whereas with other bodies I have visual and tactile experiences; I can directly control my body, or at any rate, much of it.

The problem arises with determining whether, when I talk about a *self*, I am talking merely about a body, or about the various experiences which I undergo, or about relations among these experiences like memory, or about dispositions or tendencies to act and react in certain ways. There are those who would claim that the self is more than these, something above and beyond these. Clearly my body is different than when I was a three-year-old, yet I am still myself. Similarly, I am in a sense a bundle of experiences, yet there must be something to *have* those experiences. Also, memory or such relations are inadequate to fully explain *self*, because something must have the memory or the tendencies.

The problem is that though one may assert that there is something which is a self, which maintains some sort of continuity and identity, it is never made clear precisely what this self is. Yet, interestingly enough, there are those who claim to be able to educate the self, even though they can't identify it. Not being able to identify what a self is precludes our being able to verify its existence. On this basis, the term remains meaningless, unless it be merely a convenient summation symbol for whatever bundle of experiences, or conglomeration of tendencies, which we happen to be talking about at a particular time. But, if this is all we mean, then what can conceivably be meant by educating a self? And what would such currently popular terms as "self-realization" come to?

Similar problems plague discussions of *mind*. Some claim the existence of minds as entities. They are clearly not physical entities, however, since we could never perform an operation that would expose a mind, as we might expose a muscle, or organ, or a blood vessel. Our inability to empirically verify the presence of an entity which we could label as a mind has led some to deny the existence of any such entity. They assert that when we talk about minds, we are inevitably and invariably talking about experiences and behaviors, if we bother to check the content of such statements. Therefore, they contend, "mind" is simply a summation symbol for particular ways of behaving.

Frequently, if someone talks about mind, and we raise a question about such a reference, the response to our question will be in behavioral terms. For example, if someone says, "He has a quick mind," we may ask, "What do you mean by quick mind?" The answer will always be to describe particular behaviors or dispositions. Therefore, what is really being talked about are those behaviors or dispositions. "No," comes the reply, "What is *really* being talked about is what has those tendencies and performs those behaviors." So, the disagreements go on.

Discussions of souls have similar problems of vagueness about what is being referred to, but the problems are manifestly more difficult. In discussions of selves and minds, there are at least empirically observable manifestations of the things. (If we assume that the manifestations are not the things.) But, with souls, we do not even have such physical bases for making claims about their existence. We can claim that there is a self or mind that does the remembering or behaving. But what are we to say of the soul? How does it manifest itself?

The thing the soul does is survive the body, provide the self with immortality. If "self" cannot be made clear, then we immediately have problems. But beyond this, it is not clear what it is that survives, or indeed, what "survives" means. It is clearly not the body. What, then? The memory? But isn't a nervous system required to record memories, and isn't this destroyed with the body? And clearly, the experiencing, the dispositions all depart with the body. Arguments about precisely what really "survives" occupy much of the attention of metaphysicians in this realm.

III

Related to metaphysics is the second major area of the traditional problems of philosophy, centering around the questions of knowing and truth. Whereas traditional ontological questions cluster about "What is?", epistemology deals with "How do we know?" or, "What is true?" Such questions deal with what knowing is, how it takes place, how we resolve conflicts between competing items regarded as knowledge, what it means to say of something that it is true, and related questions.

To determine whether or not this is a worthwhile question, you might be urged to consider whether or not there are items about which you would merely say, "I believe," but you would not be willing to say, "I know." On the other hand, there may be items about which you would be willing to say "I know," not merely, "I believe." If you make this kind of distinction, then you will not be among those who dismiss epistemology by simply saying, "I know, and I know that I know." You will realize that at least one benefit to be derived from epistemological discussion might be to clarify such terms as "knowing," "knowledge," "belief," "believing," "true," "truth," and other such words.

It is interesting to note that frequently someone will be quick enough to inform us that one task of education is to transmit knowledge. Yet, when they are asked what it is that one transmits when he transmits *knowledge*, the answer is not so quickly forthcoming, and when it is presented, it is likely to be vague and confused, containing contradictions and inconsistencies.

Of course, traditionally, epistemology has been thought to deal not merely with the meaning of certain terms, but with the nature of   KNO knowledge and truth. Epistemologists have promised to give us knowledge of what knowledge is, and what truth is. Almost immediately, questions are raised about whether knowledge is something that is external to us that we come to "correspond with" or appropriate, or whether knowledge is something that is within us. Questions of truth seem to revolve around whether truth is existent, something that we discover, an attribute of certain statements, or merely what *we attribute* to certain statements.

To get at some of the problems involved in epistemology, you might simply, as suggested earlier, consider on what bases you make distinctions between knowing and believing. What does constitute a basis for your saying of something, "I know"? An examination of the kinds of statements that people list as "knowing" statements, as opposed to "believing" statements, will reveal that the former are generally in the past or present and involve empirical experiences. The latter will generally be metaphysical statements, or statements about the future.

This suggests immediately that we know only those things which we experience, i.e., have sensory experiences with. Now, this kind of experience may be necessary, but is it sufficient? For example, when I see a stick under most instances, it appears to be straight. In water, however, it appears to be bent. In this instance, I have had two sensory experiences. Do I "know" that the stick is bent, or that it is straight? Unless I wish to be arbitrary, and merely choose one situation over the other, I must introduce some other condition in order to say "I know" of one of these situations.

Perhaps the condition will be merely the addition of another sensory experience, e.g., I can touch the stick and feel its straightness. Then I "know" it's straight. But, how do I know that one sensory experience is more trustworthy than another? On what is that knowledge based? How am I to know that I know?

Some would respond to this on the basis of the method of knowing. Certain methods can be used to get at conclusions that provide the certainty that characterizes knowledge. If I have arrived at the conclusion in question by intuition (i.e., immediate and certain apprehension), or by introspection (examining the contents of my mind which already contains, or is constituted of, knowledge), or revelation, then I can be said to know. Or, if I have arrived at my conclusion through the exercise of "right reason," then I know. But, we have earlier seen flaws in all these claims to knowing. I can also know on the basis of authority, i.e., someone else who "knows" can inform me. But, we still have the problem of what it means for him to know.

Aside from the problems of how knowledge is gotten are those concerned with what it is that I have when I have knowledge. For example, I may claim that I am going to give you some knowledge. I then proceed in the following manner. I may, through the use of diagrams, explain the interior of a car to you. I will indicate the names of the various devices you will find and explain how they function. (The circular object mounted on the end of the slender column is the steering wheel. When you turn it to the right, the car turns to the right, etc., through the whole business of how to drive.) At the end of this period of instruction, I give you a paper and pencil test in which you name the parts of the car, indicate their function, and "explain" driving. Suppose that on this test you answer every item correctly. Do you know how to drive a car?

Most people would respond "No" quite readily, and yet agree that they "know" *something*. The interesting thing is that this sort of procedure goes on constantly in schools. The pupils are told things by the teacher or a textbook. They are then asked to give back what has been presented to them. If they succeed, they are said to know whatever the subject is. What we have offered, in other words, is a fairly common *model* of knowing, albeit one that is not entirely satisfactory.

Other more sophisticated models for knowledge appear to involve two different meanings for what it is to know. The older of these models is the pattern that Euclidean geometry follows. There, we have axioms, postulates, and definitions, and on the basis of these derive a number of theorems. Traditional philosophy has generally proceeded on this basis, starting with definitions and self-evident first principles and proceeding by the exercise of logic to certain conclusions. This whole body of material then becomes a body of knowledge. This knowledge is a *deductive* model.

An alternative to this is the model presented by the empirical sciences. Here, when faced by a problem, we move through a procedure of experimentation and observation in order to arrive at conclusions. On the basis of particular and specific observations, we arrive at conclusions which are generalized to cover all similar cases. The process of generalizing from particulars is called *induction*. The body of conclusions arrived at, along with the methods used, constitutes a body of knowledge. This model is the scientific or inductive model of knowledge. (There is no intention of claiming that the scientific model does not *include* deduction.)

A sort of alternative to the positions above is the view that the "inert" bodies of conclusions arrived at by whatever method does not constitute knowing. What counts, in this view, is the process. Knowledge is regarded as processes, habits of mind, ways of coming to conclusions, etc., rather than mere conclusions themselves. The point of all this is that we cannot always be sure of what a person is referring to when he speaks of "knowledge" or "knowing."

People will speak freely of truth, as well. In fact, as we will see later, there is a tendency to connect truth necessarily with knowledge. Truth is made a defining characteristic of knowledge, i.e., we can be said to know when our minds (recall the problems with that) are said to correspond with truth. Or, we can be described as knowing a proposition only if, among other conditions, the proposition is true. (This will be analyzed in chapter 7.)

One of the problems we are left with in this characterization of knowing or knowledge is exactly what it means to say something is true. What truth is customarily accounts for much of the discussion in epistemology. Truth. we may be told, is what is presented to us in such a way that we have no choice but to accept it. There are said to be items that are known with certainty by everyone, everywhere, always. These are regarded as *absolute* truths. (Or, Truth; notice the capitol *T*.) Of course, if we can only *know* what is true, and truth is what we know, we have not been carried very far along by the argument.

One of the problems with Truth is that, despite general agreement that such Truths exist, men have trouble agreeing on precisely what they are. When we do discover a truth that everyone gives assent to, it turns out to be some such statement as follows: The sum of the internal angles of a triangle is 180 degrees; or $2 + 2 = 4$; or,

My brother is a male. Such statements are *tautologies*, i.e., the predicate adds nothing that is not already contained in the subject. They mean no more than to say, "All A is A."

Another and final question concerns the locus of genuine knowledge. Does knowledge exist prior to human experience, or is human experience required to certify knowledge? Some knowledge is spoken of as *a priori* knowledge, i.e., it is knowable in and of itself outside of any checking by human experience. It does not require any checking to know that the sum of the internal angles of a triangle is 180 degrees. In fact, if we did measure the angles of any triangles and arrived at a sum of 179 degrees or 181 degrees, we should be more willing to grant that there was some flaw in our measurement than to surrender the knowledge that the sum of the angles of a triangle is anything other than 180 degrees. Such knowledge is *a priori* knowledge.

If, on the other hand, we wish to compare the sizes of two triangles, our only method is to check the sizes empirically. This knowledge is regarded as *a posteriori* knowledge. Much discussion revolves around whether or not *a priori* "knowledge" really gives us any information. Traditionally, however, *a priori* knowledge has been held to be superior to *a posteriori* knowledge because the latter is regarded as *contingent*. (Not certain or absolute.) In the moral sphere, truth has been regarded as more precarious than in other realms. Yet, it is often here that philosophers and others have claimed to provide certain, rather than contingent, knowledge.

IV

The third area of the traditional problems of philosophy is that of values and is referred to as *axiology*. The term "values" appears to be as elusive to identify as many other terms with which we've dealt. In the first place, we cannot be quite sure whether we are talking about one's tendencies when he is overtly behaving or about what one professes to value. "Actions speak louder than words," we say on occasion, generally meaning that what a person *really* values is more likely to be seen in what he does than in what he says. Further, what men do is often overlooked on the basis of what they intended. We are willing to forgive certain otherwise undesirable actions if the doer's *intentions* were "right." Also, it is not always clear whether, in speaking of values, we are speaking of what some men prefer, or what they *ought* to want. Finally, there are questions of whether values are permanent and absolute or contextual and relative.

As was pointed out earlier, axiology traditionally has been divided into two branches, *ethics*, which deals with conduct, and *esthetics*, which deals with beauty. Generally, the term *moral*, although it may describe any activity which involves choice, is reserved to the field of ethics and is associated with such terms as "right," and "good." Even the use of *good* is usually reserved for the moral sphere. Popular usage includes such terms as "good music," or "good painting." But in philosophy, the term good usually refers to right conduct. We may use the term "goods" however to mean, not material things as it is popularly used, but rather any things that are thought to have value; in other words, as roughly interchangeable with *values*. In this sense, "goods" is simply a plural form of the philosophic term "good."

The central problem of ethics is: How ought I to behave? Attempts to answer this involve us in moral problems. A part of the problem, many philosophers suggest, is that ethical judgments differ from statements of fact. Statements like "War brings about great suffering," or "Some wars have been opposed by many people," can be checked out and confirmed or refuted. But, how does one go about confirming a statement like, "All war is immoral"? How can we say that such a statement is true or false? Suggestions have been put forth as to what would justify such statements. One view says that if such a statement agrees with objective moral codes, then it is obviously true. If it is inconsistent with such a code, then the statement is false, or not justified. Others will declare that the standard for justifying such a statement is its effect on human good. If what is asserted by such a statement can be shown to be beneficial to human welfare, then the judgment is justified.

We are led by the latter claim into another problem, that of determining what is good for us. What is good, it may be asserted, is what contributes to human happiness. But, what is it that does this? Happiness, Aristotle tells us, consists in the exercise of our native faculties, or in activity in accordance with human nature. Others insist that happiness consists in pleasure, and human good derives from doing that which brings pleasure. One problem with the first view is that it presupposes that everyone has the same faculties and will derive satisfaction from the same things—a view that seems to fly in the face of what we know about human beings. The second view, called *hedonistic*, encounters the objection that there are intrinsic goods, such as doing one's duty, that can not always be called pleasures.

Another problem concerning moral goods is that some are difficult to justify on reasonable grounds. Some goods are claimed to be goods on the grounds that they produce something desirable, or at least desired. That is to say, they are "good for something." Whether or not such a good, called an *instrumental good*, is indeed good can be checked to see if it does produce the desired results. But what of goods that are claimed to be good in and of themselves?

For example, we value money on the bases of its providing us with goods and services that we want. Therefore, the value of money is instrumental. The goods and services are also instrumental, in that they lead to our satisfaction and happiness. But what of happiness? Do we value happiness because of its instrumental value, i.e., because it effectively leads to something outside of itself? No, it would probably be agreed that we value happiness for itself. Happiness, then, is an *intrinsic* good. How does one go about justifying intrinsic goods? This has created a consistent problem for philosophers.

One reason for the persistence of this justification problem may be that there is not general agreement on what has been said when something has been said to be good. Some philosophers have seen goodness as a characteristic of a thing, or a situation, much like any other characteristic. Others claim that the goodness is in us and not in the thing, i.e., that our claim that something is good is simply an expression of our approval of it, our expression of a preference.

Similar problems are encountered in esthetics, where our concern is for what is liked, rather than what is done. Esthetics, then, involves us in matters of taste. However, we generally go beyond mere taste into the realm of not merely what *is* liked, but consider also what *ought* to be liked. It's possible, some will assert, that in matters of enjoyment or appreciation, I may, in fact, select the wrong things from the world of beauty.

Hanging in my barber's shop is a calendar which is a beautiful picture. It gives me great pleasure to gaze at the picture. Few would criticize that. The objections that would be raised would occur when I identified it as a work of art and suggested that it was better than the *Mona Lisa*. The question might arise as to whether or not I was experiencing a genuine esthetic experience in the presence of the calendar art, such as that which is purported to be evoked by "genuine" works of art like the *Mona Lisa*.

What makes the problem particularly difficult is that there is no question but that the picture on the calendar gives me an enjoyable experience. The question arises over whether or not this is an esthetic experience. What are the characteristics of an esthetic experience? We know that something occurs in the presence of beauty. The problem is whether or not this is inevitably and invariably an esthetic experience. It is difficult enough to decide which is more genuinely esthetic, a painting by Monet, or one by Klee. But the experience brought on by things so similar may raise less issues than other things. Paintings, music, and such productions are generally associated with esthetic experiences.

But what of other areas of experience? What about the enjoyment which I experience in sipping an unusually fine Scotch which has been poured over ice? Or, consider the feeling that I get from making a particularly smooth landing in my airplane, really "greasing it on." Are these esthetic experiences? Are the things that produce such experiences works of art?

But, to get into an even different realm, if an esthetic experience is a particularly moving experience of pleasure and enjoyment, do sexual experiences qualify as esthetic experiences? If esthetics involves us in the "beauty" dimensions of life, may I include love experiences, which are certainly as heightened and intense and "beauty"-filled as any of man's experiences? Or, are esthetic experiences limited to our responses to human creations? Which human creations? Those only in the areas of painting, music, dance, etc.? Whose experiences are more genuinely esthetic, those of the creator, or the spectator to the creation. What constitutes genuine creativity? Such are some of the problems which philosophers have traditionally pondered over in the area known as axiology, and particularly esthetics.

Chapter 3

Points of Contact
Between Philosophy and Education

I

The proposition that philosophy of education consists of the application of formal philosophy to the problems of education would probably not encounter serious opposition from any quarter. What we could conceivably mean by this statement, however, would undoubtedly raise some points of disagreement. Alternative views of what this means will be offered in this chapter. The traditional position will be considered first. Here, philosophy of education has generally meant following out the implications for education of the traditional problems of philosophy.

Initially, the traditional philosophers of education, following the patterns established in "formal" philosophy, set out the scope of the discipline. Just as general philosophy is an attempt to think about the whole of reality, so it follows that philosophy of education "seeks to comprehend education in its entirety."[1] Even those who are embarrassed to use philosophy in the same title with education will offer a similar explanation.[2] One such philosopher uses the word "philosophy" in the title "merely to indicate that I wish to look at education as a whole and try to make as consistent and sensible an idea of that whole as I can."[3]

In common, everyday talk, people will speak of having "a" philosophy. In such usage, "philosophy" represents merely a loose

1. George F. Kneller, *An Introduction to the Philosophy of Education* (New York: John Wiley & Sons, Inc., 1964), p. 22.
2. The basis for this embarrassment is that "philosophy" traditionally has been claimed to give us absolutely certain knowledge, and consists of such a body of knowledge. "Education," on the other hand, represents *doing* as distinct from *knowing*. Not only is education a "mere art," but because it is, we can have only opinion, not knowledge. Hence, the embarrassment.
3. Sir Godfrey Thompson, *A Modern Philosophy of Education*, quoted in D.J. O'Connor, *An Introduction to the Philosophy of Education* (London: Routledge & Kegan Paul, 1961), p. 1.

set of beliefs, that may be consistent or contradictory, related or random, that simply happens to be held by a particular person. Similarly, educators will talk about having "a" philosophy of education. This, too, will usually describe a set of loose beliefs including talk about aims, children, techniques, and a scientific theory or two, all of which serve to indicate how we feel about education.

At other times, the term philosophy is used to describe statements in education that seem not to be practical, i.e., not directly applicable to what goes on in particular classrooms. Or, it may be the label for a set of statements, largely cermonial in nature, about the aims of education purported to be held by a particular school system. It's a very popular practice to develop statements of such aims for use in curriculum guides, or for trotting out at evaluation times.

When we are speaking of philosophy of education as a discipline, however, we mean something more specific than vague-sounding aims or a bundle of beliefs. We may mean a particular way of approaching educational problems, or we may mean a body of knowledge which relates the traditional problem areas of philosophy to those of education.

In the second sense, when we think of what philosophers of education do, we would be led by the logic of the opening sentence of the chapter to see philosophy of education as speculation about educational problems. Philosophers of education, then, would be engaged in using the special tools of philosophy, i.e., the special ways of knowing, to answer questions, or develop theories, about education. One way to answer questions about education would be to engage in empirical research. Consequently, there are researchers, educators, or behavioral scientists, who will conduct research aimed at answering some of our questions about educational matters.

But, such methods, it will be claimed, leaves many questions unanswered. Further, at times there is conflict among the conclusions established by such scientific studies. The sciences are not always able to establish final, universally accepted, and conclusive answers. Because of this, we turn to the methods of philosophy to find our answers.

Using methods other than those employed by the sciences, *viz.*, the various methods of speculation, educational philosophers attempt to establish a body of knowledge concerning education. Beginning with theories about the nature of reality or the nature of man, philosophers endeavor to deduce aims and methods, in fact, whole systems of educational knowledge. Educational philosophers, through their speculative efforts, will also interpret and evaluate theories, and either account for or resolve conflicts that exist.

The function of philosophy of education is also seen to be prescriptive. At the very least, this role will involve defining and explaining the aims, or ends, of education. That is, philosophy of education also deals with what we *ought* to do in education. Traditionally, in this realm, philosophers of education have discussed not simply what our aims are but what they *ought* to be, and what means are needed in order to achieve those aims. Such discussion necessarily involves the philosopher in values, for here we are talking about what policies and practices ought to be valued. Since the methods of sciences cannot be relied on to establish values, or select out appropriate, or more importantly, desireable aims, we must rely on philosophy for this. Such concerns, it is agreed, not being technical concerns, are therefore philosophic.

Philosophy as a particular way of approaching educational problems may mean that we are also engaged in philosophy of education when we are engaged in analysis, criticism, and clarification. A part of what this means is that we examine the logic of educational propositions, or determine the nature and worth of educational theories. Such examination may also reveal to us the kind of theory which we are dealing with at a particular moment, and give us some clue as to how we handle the theory. In this phase of doing educational philosophy, we may also attempt to clarify the meaning of certain terms such as "motivation," "individualization of instruction," "learning," "adjustment," "self-realization," and "accountability." We may also identify slogans and explore their meaning and worth. This aspect of philosophy of education will be explored at greater length in the final section of this chapter.

II

Since philosophy of education is the application of philosophy to education, then it demonstrates the connections between the traditional concerns of philosophy and our concerns in education. This is not simply *logically* sound. It is asserted that we really cannot proceed to outline a program in education without considering the nature of the universe, including the nature of the creature to be educated. This, then, constitutes our starting point. We do not begin with aims, as some empiricists may contend, for that is concerning ourselves with the outcomes, or consequences, of education. What we must do, it is contended, is begin at the beginning with the nature of reality and from what we determine that to be, we may then deduce educational practices. We do this by tracing out the implications for education of whatever we establish as real.

What we must do is induct the child into the way the world really is. Since there have been various accounts given of the way the world really is, then we will have different programs of education. We will see this in the next chapter. The way reality is includes not only the way the world is, but also the way man is. Therefore, varying views of the nature of human nature have also contributed to variation in programs.

What are the connections between ontological (metaphysical) views and education? There are those who, on one basis or another, conclude that the real world is external to and independent of the knower. This being the case, we may deduce that it can be known and that it is the task of educators to induct the young into this world by giving him knowledge of it.

We may deduce anything we need to know from our world view. Since the world is not only external and independent, but also orderly, knowledge of it is also orderly and logical. This logically ordered subject matter may be gathered into its logical subject matter divisions and presented to the knower. Whether this knowledge is "wrung out" or "poured in" depends on the metaphysical view of the universe. This will be dealt with as we consider the traditional philosophic positions.

The subject matter can be presented in logical fashion by lecture, or by textbook. Both are designed to give systematic accounts of their subject matter, which is one or another aspect of reality. Whether or not the procedure has been effective may be evaluated on the basis of how much the learner can give back. We can base our measurement and evaluation on either how much has actually been learned, by pretesting and posttesting, or by comparing what has been learned to what should have been learned.

Not only is the subject matter implied in our conception of reality, *viz.*, knowledge about reality, but all aspects of education can be deduced. Our metaphysics will determine that certain teaching methods are to be used, e.g., pupils are not involved in selecting the subject matter nor how it is to be learned. They will all cover the content in essentially the same manner and will acquire the same knowledge. The teacher's role is to select and present the predetermined subject matter and then test to see that it has been learned. Even the school organization is fixed, with the school administration at the top "running" the school, and the teachers responding to administrative rules and regulations.

If, on the other hand, my ontological view is that reality is not fixed and permanent, but is dynamic and relative, then this implies a different system of education, it is claimed. In the first place, I am not going to view knowledge as something fixed and predetermined and external to the knower. What is important is not acquiring fixed, organized bodies of knowledge arranged logically by content. Instead, the emphasis will be on process. Since knowledge is dynamic, we must focus on inquiry. I must be equipped to constantly acquire new knowledge.

In fact, it is rather difficult, this view would hold, to separate method and content, because the content is the method of learning, varying with each different learning situation. Sets of facts, inert ideas, are not what are important. Such things have value, but only instrumental value. Therefore, the content of the curriculum will not focus on any particular item of content, since no specific item of content is necessary. Since knowledge changes, we must constantly engage in learning, so learning how to learn is what is important. Whatever subject matter does that job is what will be used. What will do the job will vary with individuals. So, we must aim at individualizing instruction and involve the student in the selection and development of his own learning experiences.

These illustrations make it clear that one's metaphysical position has bearing on his educational program. Sometimes, we are not even conscious of what ontological view we hold, but the view will operate, even though unconsciously, on our choices, our values, our behavior as teachers. How much better then, to get it all out, examine our metaphysical views, get them into some kind of logical and consistent order so that we may develop sound systems of educational practices.

Other questions of metaphysical nature may also be considered. One which we mentioned earlier was the concern for whether or not the universe has a purpose. If the universe has a purpose, doesn't this imply that man also has a purpose? May we not learn what that purpose is? Once that is determined, the point of education then would be to help man realize that purpose. But, on the other hand, suppose our metaphysics shows us that the universe, and therefore man, is purposeless. Would it not then be education's task to help him develop meaning in his life?

Similarly, the belief in the existence of a God also has its role to play. If there is a God, and particularly if this God rules the universe, ought not education serve to help instruct the young in God's ways and God's will? Will this not have a bearing even on our treatment of whatever content such belief leads to? For example, it would seem to be reasonable that one interest of the high school biology class would be to point out God's handiwork.

One may question the purpose of the universe and consequently, of life. Or, one may reject notions of God. These attitudes will suggest alternative educational programs. But one cannot overlook the nature of human nature. Since it is human beings we are educating, our view of what it means to be human will influence our thinking about how education takes place, and how it ought to take place.

If we look for what distinguishes man from other creatures, we may see that man's mind might serve as his defining characteristic. If we conceive of that mind as an entity consisting of, or containing, faculties, the task of education is clear. It is obviously to develop man as man, which means to develop his mind. This is accomplished by promoting the growth of the faculties which constitute or are contained in his mind. The faculties are developed by exercise, e.g., if we want to train the faculty of memory, we do it by requiring memorization. The mind may be ordered by calling up, or by impressing on it, the ordered subject matters. Our sole focus in education will be on the pupil's mind and everything else will be ignored or suppressed.

Others may hold out for a sacrosanct and inviolable *self*. The "real" human is somewhere behind that face, within that skin, and beyond our view. Since the self is to be maintained at all costs, what education must do is simply, having once determined by some mystical fashion what that self is, stand by and shield it from all influences, particularly social or societal impositions, so that the self may develop unimparied, or be "realized," or "actualized."

Similar to the self, since it is invisible and is at once a part of yet separate from the apparent physical body, the soul may also be considered the focus of our educational effort. If what is distinctive about man is his soul, then promoting growth means serving the soul. Pope Pius XI tells us:

> Education consists essentially in preparing man for what he must be and for what he must do here below in order to attain the sublime end for which he was created. . . . The subject of education is man whole and entire, soul united to body in unity of nature, with all his

faculties natural and supernatural, such as right reason and revelation show him to be. . . .[4]

Not only is metaphysics relevant, the claim goes, it is essential, since the only way we can develop an educational program that is sound and not merely a matter of opinion is to begin with sure knowledge and deduce our educational prescriptions. The fact that there are different sets of educational programs attached to differing views of the universe demonstrates that there is a necessary link between metaphysics and educational practices. The first step, then, in building a philosophy of education is to sort out and order our ontological views in order that we may from these views deduce our educational patterns.

III

If metaphysics is necessary to the development of educational programs, epistemology is absolutely vital and essential. Knowledge is the schools' stock in trade. Therefore, educators must concern themselves with this aspect of philosophy. After all, it is the schools' task to transmit knowledge. As Dewey has pointed out, if every member of a society were carried off by a plague, the heritage of that society would be lost. Yet, it is a certainty that every member of a society will, in fact, depart this life. Despite this, the life of that society goes on. It goes on in the knowledge that is transmitted to each succeeding generation. One thing that must be made clear is what it is that is to be passed along.

Just as there are differences in educational programs based on disagreements about what constitutes reality, so there are various beliefs about what constitutes knowing and the programs that these beliefs lead to. In examining two of the positions offered, one should not be misled into believing that these views exhaust all views about what knowing is and, based on these views, what education ought to consist of. The examples which follow are illustrative only, to demonstrate the traditional view that there are connections between epistemology and the educative process.

Among the differences that exist in this area will be the cluster of those who see knowledge, i.e., that which is to be transmitted by the schools, as consisting of absolute certainties opposed to those who regard knowledge as relative, contextual and dynamic. In the

4. Pope Pius XI, *The Christian Education of Youth*, Encyclical Letter (New York: The American Press, 1930).

former view, we strip away the accidental, the temporal and spatial, and are left with the essential. In the latter view, we deal with whatever happens to be held as significant in the time and place in which we find ourselves.

In order to get at the essential, the permanent and immutable, we cannot rely on the senses, or mere observation of things and phenomena. Mere observation can lead only to opinion. To get beyond opinion to that which underlies the outward manifestations, we must use the special ways of knowing and, in particular, rely on reason. Knowledge is knowing reality as it really is. This is revealed to us only by the rigorous use of reason. If we are to truly know, rather than merely believe, we must move into a realm that does not admit contingency, but is fixed and permanent. If, as Bernard Iddings Bell suggests, we regard this certainty as ". . . a truth higher than may be discovered by physical experiment,"[5] then what we transmit is knowledge that will be everywhere and for all times the same. What we pass on is a body of knowledge that is final, complete, perfect, absolute.

A basic implication of this view of knowledge is that in our program of education, children will be relatively passive, either receiving or calling up completed bodies of knowledge.

> First, we need to realize again that those who teach
> small children must devise and impart ways of giving to
> those children knowledge of the basic wisdom of the race.
> They must foster a sense of identification with the tried
> and tested customs and attitudes of our forefathers . . .
> that which the past has learned about what human beings
> ought to know and do, and to persuade them they like it.[6]

At the elementary level, this requires that the children receive instruction in reading, writing, and arithmetic since these are necessary preparations for the realization of the aims of education. To these skills will later be added such subjects as history, grammar, philosophy, and whatever may constitute the fundamental disciplines. All of these have value in preparing students for more advanced study, but they are also valuable in their own right.

Having been exposed to this preparation early in their lives, the young would then be ready for continued exposure to disciplined or intellectual subjects.

---

5. Bernard Iddings Bell, *Crisis in Education* (New York: McGraw Hill, Inc., 1949), p. 100.
6. Bell, *op. cit.*, pp. 31 f.

> In a properly organized educational system, the student . . . should have been vigorously put through the equivalent of the venerable and valuable liberal arts curriculum. This was and still is a sevenfold discipline, consisting of the verbal trivium: grammar, rhetoric, logic; and the mathematical quadrivium: arithmetic, geometry, astronomy, and music. Such training is essential to sound thinking.[7]

At this level, pupils might also begin their acquaintance with the "great books," the established knowledge of the great minds of the past. They would also receive instruction in foreign languages, not only for the mental discipline which these provide, but because acquaintance with a foreign language is simply valuable in its own right. In the case of Latin and Greek, these have the added value of being the languages of many of the great minds of the past.

Throughout this intellectual training, great stress is placed on the mastery of organized content, and young minds are constantly tested to determine the amount of learning that has taken place. This is determined, of course, by measuring the amount of attunement to certain knowledge that has been effected.

For the schools to provide other than this intellectual training would place them in the position of putting training at the level of mere opinion above education which is correspondence with a certainty that is absolute knowledge. To present such studies as current events, problems of American democracy, mechanical drawing, driver training, physical education, home economics, etc., is unreasonable and undefensible. These activities may train boys and girls for doing things, but they have no part in a school program whose purpose is education.

If, to the contrary, knowledge is regarded as relative, contextual, and dynamic, then we are committed to quite a different set of goals and practices. One major implication is that the young must be nurtured in experimental inquiry. This does not mean that the customs, beliefs, ways of knowing that are represented by organized bodies of knowledge are to be thrown out. But there is an implication that these are not to be bestowed on the child by the teacher or by great books. Rather they are to be "earned" through activity and experience, by having the opportunity to do and undergo.

There are a number of reasons for linking education with experience, and the consequent rejection of the notion that educa-

7. Bell, *op. cit.*, pp. 70 f.

tion is intellectual training in the narrow sense described earlier. One basis is that knowledge is regarded as open, changing, requiring public verification. This implies that one must be equipped to constantly check knowledge; one is consistently engaged in altering and adding to whatever is known. This makes the process at least as important as whatever belief is established. Teaching children how to think becomes as important as what they think. This does not mean that children do not acquire knowledge or master skills; it means that knowledge is more broadly viewed and items of knoweldge and specific skills do not become ends in themselves.

Another reason for rejecting notions of fixed certainty and for connecting education with experiences is that the traditional bases for establishing knowledge, *viz.*, intuition, introspection, deduction from self-evident first principles, are not regarded as trustworthy ways to establish reliable knowledge. Instead, we emulate the ways of the empirical sciences, rely on the type of evidence used in scientific studies and research, i.e., on what experience reveals, to establish knowledge. Therefore, children are taught ways of ordering their experiences, rather than being required to memorize conclusions.

This tendency to rely on the methods of the sciences also has its effect on ideas about the learner. This, too, has its implications for education. In this view, the learner is not seen as a merely passive recipient into whom knowledge is poured. Nor is he seen as a completed, already perfected self, or soul. The learner is seen to grow by interacting with his environment; he is a part of it, not alien to it.

Consequently, programs are not limited to traditionally disciplined or "intellectual" subjects. Any valued activities of society may become the subject matter of the program. The subject matter will vary according to the interests, abilities, and needs of the children in particular times and places. Since none of these are constant, the program of the school will not remain constant. Therefore, our concern will not be for the mastery of the prescribed body of content. What will be taught will be the customs, habits, beliefs, activities of a particular society.

The content of the curriculum, then, along with the methods used to transmit knowledge, is closely related to how one views knowledge. The fact that we have different sets of recommendations for educational programs may be seen as the result of distinctive epistemological views. Having seen the connections between metaphysics and education, we should not be surprised to learn that similar connections exist between views of what constitutes knowledge and what we teach in education. It is almost a self-evident fact that what we teach in schools will vary with what we regard as knowledge.

Another aspect of epistemology which is seen to have implications for education is how pupils come to know things. It seems obvious that if we can be clear about how knowing takes place, we shall be in a better position to achieve our aims in the classroom. Unfortunately, as philosophers have pondered this concern, they have not come to any generally accepted conclusions about how learning is accomplished. Consequently, different philosophic "schools" of thought have different views on how learning takes place and offer various recommendations for what ought to go on in classrooms.

There are those who suggest that coming-to-know in general is a model for the way pupils come to know in the classroom. That is to say, there is a similarity between the way scholars on the frontiers of knowledge add items to bodies of knowledge, and the way students add to their own personal bodies of knowledge. The only difference, exponents of the view claim, is a difference in degree, i.e., in the level of sophistication. Consequently, this school of thinkers suggests teaching methods that come as close as possible to emulating the methods used by the scholars. Students are engaged in a "discovery" process rather than merely "coming to correspond" with preordered and completed bodies of knowledge.

In the sciences, this means that the student will not simply read about the conclusions which scientists have come to and be expected to memorize these. He will even be led beyond the formal repetition of classical experiments, which are more in the nature of demonstrations than genuine experiments. Instead, the pupil will be engaged in the solution of real problems which will call for the development of appropriate problem-solving skills in order to discover the solution to his problem. In short, he will be *doing* science rather than learning about scientific conclusions.

Similarly, in mathematics, rather than memorize ways of manipulating numbers in a largely meaningless fashion, the pupil will be led to discover mathematical principles. He will then use those principles in devising methods for solving problems. In language studies, the focus will be on discovering principles about the language through studying the language in use. This would replace the rote memorization of questionable rules of grammar that do not really fit the language.

Others hold that there are basic and significant differences between the processes of the scholar standing at the frontiers of knowledge, and the youngster coming to know. To expect the young pupil to behave in any way similar to the scholar is to impose adult and alien standards on the child. The child comes to know by appropriating to himself, (i.e., to the self which he represents), whatever has significance for him.

In this view, if we subject the child to the sorts of activities that scholars engage in, we interpose our will, and largely "irrelevant" subject matter, between the child and his developing self. We stand in the way of and impair his self-realization. What is called for, rather than concern for organizing his experiences around subject matter which society values, is to encourage self-expression from within. Instead of developing skills in language use that will mold the pupil in society's image, we must encourage him in the full and free use of his own language. In fact, all his learning materials must be related to his personal experiences.

Aside from these questions about knowing are those that are related to knowing directly and knowing vicariously. Knowing directly means knowing by personal acquaintance, by a direct and immediate contact with things in the environment. Knowing vicariously means knowing by description, i.e., knowing *about* things without having come into direct contact with whatever we are concerned about. Questions are raised about what things can legitimately be learned through vicarious experience, and what must be learned directly. For example, can children learn democratic behavior by simply reading about it in books, or is it necessary that their living experiences be imbued with democratic values so that they may learn through direct experience? We are likely to find again a variety of answers that may be connected with one's views of what constitutes knowing and knowledge.

Epistemology, dealing as it does with problems relating to the nature of knowledge, and the ways in which knowledge is acquired, is a necessary part of philosophy of education. Consequently, as is the case with metaphysics, the philosopher of education, and all who do philosophy of education, had best order his thinking in this dimension of philosophic thought. Having accomplished this, we may search out whatever sound bases for educational procedures epistemological thought has to offer.

IV

The third area of philosophic concern, axiology, brings us to the connections between values which we hold and educational practices.

There are several bases on which axiology is seen to have implications for education. In the first place, the decision to educate is itself a moral issue, and in turn involves us in a number of moral, or ethical, issues concerning who is to be educated, to what degree, for what purposes, etc. Education being a moral enterprise, we are, on that basis, involved in the implications which values have for education.

Beyond this, as will be seen, many issues in education are not technical issues, and to pretend that all issues are merely technical is to hide from more issues, and more basic issues, than we deal with technically. Finally, education's task is not merely to pass on inert bodies of content. Every position grants that an important task of education is instruction in values. This involves us in all the questions revolving around what is to be taught in the name of morality.

When our society sets out deliberately to educate the young, we are engaging in a moral undertaking. From the moment that choice is made, we are constantly and consistently involved in choosing. We would not bother to undertake this program if we did not have specific ends in mind. These ends represent preferences for particular values. Consequently, if these ends are to be realized, it is wise to make very clear what these values are, to work to reduce conflicts among them, and to search out the most effective means for the realization of the ends which we prefer.

Initially, in deciding deliberately to educate the young, we must establish what the purposes of our effort will be. Is the system of education to be established in order to preserve a particular way of life or is the point of our work with children to be the deliberate restructuring of the social order? Are we going to induct the young into the ways of our society, or is the educational system merely going to prepare the young to assume a particular place in an economic system? Is education supposed to have practical, utilitarian outcomes, or do we educate in order to provide a sort of ornamentation for those fortunate enough to participate? Are we going to make an effort to engage the interest of the young in the joy of real inquiry, or are we going to have them amass bundles of inert facts? Is the purpose of education the realization of the good life? If so, what are the characteristics of whatever it is we wish to realize? None of these issues will be solved by the collection of data nor by careful observation. These are not matters that are resolvable by the methods of the empirical sciences.

By no means have we exhausted the value problems of deliberate education. Arriving at some notions of what purposes will guide our moral enterprise, we are faced with the task of deciding who will receive the direct benefits. The question has not always been answered in the same manner. At some points in our history, education was for the sons of those landowners who could afford to pay for it.

Even when this was extended considerably, there still was a tendency for a long time to restrict educational opportunities to white males of the upper classes of society. Although we live in an era when educational opportunities appear to be extended universally, all races, creeds, both sexes seem to have the opportunity, we still have severely restricted the educational opportunities of the lowest socioeconomic class. As we move higher up the educational ladder, we still appear to be answering the question of who is to be educated on a relatively restrictive basis. This is not always done directly. Occasionally, for example, we will close the door to higher education to certain groups by prescribing entrance requirements that members of the group cannot meet. Again, this is a matter of values and not a technical issue.

Another issue involves the degree of committment to education. The favorite slogan of some communities is "I'm for education, but . . . ." Parents will espouse the value of education in front of their children, politicians will chant their praise for what education does, board of education members will tirelessly cite its advantages. But, when portions of our income are to be taken for the support of schools, we then invoke our favorite slogan.

There are also important issues regarding other questions of support, and of control as well. Is the local community entitled to whatever education it can afford, and wishes to provide? Or, is support of education to be broader than merely local? Do the members of the wealthy local community have some responsibility for their poorer neighbors in nearby communities or other states? If some of the support of local schools comes from state governments, does that remove some of the control from the local district? Should it? Just how is the support and control to be divided in order to provide the sort of school system which we want?

In one way or another, such issues must be responded to. But, having in some fashion surmounted these, we have not solved all the ethical problems of education. Problems of values are going to crop up in establishing the curriculum and in implementing our aims through the selection of particular methods. What problems are going to be selected for study in the social studies program? What novels and stories are going to be established as required reading in the

English courses? On what bases are these selections going to be made? How are we going to treat controversial topics?

Values will also show up in the way the school is organized and operated. Are teachers and pupils involved in making and maintaining the rules and regulations? Values will show up as well in the methods of grading, promoting, and otherwise rewarding efforts. What sorts of programs will be presented in assemblies, and who will be involved in making these decisions? What holidays and special events will be celebrated by the school system as a whole? What extra-curricular affairs will be permitted, what will be their relation to the rest of the curriculum, and on what bases will students and staff participate? As our values differ, so will our selections and rejections differ in these matters.

In yet another way, and even more directly, values come to play a part in what we do in education. In view of the fact that schools are supposed to develop character, we must become directly involved with morals, since character is developed through the inculcation of particular sets of values. There seems to be little quarrel with the notion that values constitute at least as important a part of the curriculum as do facts. Indeed, there are times when values seem to override all other considerations. Educators will generally frown on cheating even when this might lead to learning. Also, the bright student who lies, or steals, or otherwise violates moral codes is not excused because he learns readily.

The issue arises not over the question of whether or not values are to be taught, but rather over whose values are to be taught. Recently, this question of whose values are to be taught came to the fore as school districts throughout the country began overtly to introduce sex education into the curriculum. In many instances, communities were split, board members elected or defeated, budgets approved or rejected, on the basis of how the community responded to proposals or programs for sex education. The battles expanded beyond local boundaries and became national in scope embroiling a number of national organizations in the controversy.

There were those who claimed, foolishly, that values were not going to be taught at all, that students would simply be presented with "the facts of life." Horrified parents roared protests against this suggestion that such value-laden material would be presented like a math problem with appropriate attitudes ignored. It became apparent that in matters of sex, as in other areas, there can be no neutral ground. Neutrality is itself as much of a position on any issue as any more positive, or negative, stand. As a result of widespread disputes, what appeared to be a national phenomena, the launching of new programs in sex education, ground to a halt. In many instances, programs that had been instituted were abandoned. Perhaps a little philosophic guidance in the initial stages, with some analysis of the issues involved and some insight in the justification of value judgements would have helped to avoid much of the tension.

Occasionally, the issue of what values to teach is joined at another level. There are those who believe that morality is the peculiar province of organized religion. They would suggest that morality cannot be introduced into the curriculum without accompanying instruction in religious values. Such a view has led not only to efforts to eliminate from the curriculum anything that appeared inconsistent with the tenents of a particular organized religion, but also to the inclusion in the curriculum of the doctrines of a revealed religion.

There have been similar conflicts between leaders of various patriotic groups who have wished to teach a narrow chauvinism and those leaders of one-world movements who wished to encourage world federalist views. The former wished to have laws enacted that would guarantee the inclusion of certain patriotic exercises, their own definition of democracy, and definite kinds and amounts of instruction in American history and the responsibilities of citizenship. Their opponents wished to place limits on such requirements and to guarantee that children would be allowed to study the United Nations and its activities.

There have also been issues raised about what children should be taught concerning the American business system. One such recent dispute has centered about the conflict between the profit motive with its concomitant exploitation of natural resources and disregard for conservation on the one hand, and the champions of ecology on the other.

Our consideration to this point has dealt largely with ethical concerns. The area of esthetics also has important implications for education. Rather than dealing with "good" in the moral sense, esthetics would deal with "goods" in matters of taste. It is not hard to imagine what many of the issues are. What are the young to be taught to value in literature? What novels, plays, and poems will be held to be exemplary? Are children to be taught to value only the classics in music, or will some concern be shown for enhancing their interest in "rock"? Will their other art experiences be limited to visits to art museums, or will there be conscious effort to bring esthetic delight into children's everyday lives?

Some effort has been made in the foregoing pages to demonstrate in a very general fashion what has traditionally constituted philosophy of education. This has given a particular meaning to philosophy of education as the application of formal philosophy to the problems of education. This view follows the pattern of relating the traditional methods and content of philosophy to education through tracing the implications for education of the traditional problems of philosophy. There is another view of the possible meaning of applying formal philosophy to the problems of education. Much of this will be exhibited in chapters 5-8. However, a brief, general view will be offered now.

V

As an alternative to the traditional position regarding the connections between philosophy and education, there is the view briefly mentioned near the end of the first chapter that philosophy consists of criticism, analysis and clarification. On this basis, the view of what constitutes doing philosophy of education represents a considerable departure from the traditional view.

A little analysis reveals that the special ways of knowing claimed by philosophers have not proved very successful. Not only is there no reliable body of knowledge resulting from these methods, a point we shall develop in detail in chapter 5, but whenever the tenets of traditional philosophy have come into conflict with knowledge established by the sciences, the tenets of philosophy have been abandoned. On this basis, philosophers must relinquish any claims that relying on speculative methods will prove to be a fruitful way of handling educational problems. As for the claims that philosophy may prescribe ends and means, it may be pointed out that since philosophers, as philosophers, have no body of knowledge from which to work, they are, therefore, in no position to offer prescriptions.

If we examine the purported connections between the traditional problem areas of philosophy and the field of education, we will find problems there, too. For example, it is claimed that we may deduce educational aims and practices from metaphysical positions. How necessary is a metaphysics to philosophy of education? There are two bases for questioning the claimed connections.

In the first place, if metaphysics, or ontology, deals with questions of reality, one may question on what basis it does this. If metaphysics deals with reality in the common, popular sense of the term, then it would seem to have little to offer, since the sciences give us much more reliable knowledge about reality. It is to the sciences that we turn when we want such knowledge, rather than to philosophy.

If, on the other hand, we see metaphysics as dealing with some "ultimate" reality, then we may question what significance this has for education. For example, even if we could establish that man has an immortal soul, this would tell us nothing about how to proceed in education. We have no way of knowing whether the actions which we undertake in ordinary classrooms have any effects on souls or not. If there are any effects, we are unable to verify that there are, or what they are.

On these bases, then, that we have other, more reliable bodies of knowledge available to us, or that the connections between metaphysical truths and educational practices have not been demonstrated, we may question the value of metaphysics for education.

Similarly, in the case of knowing, we may call on the behavioral sciences for knowledge of how knowing takes place. Philosophers, as philosophers, have no such knowledge. If we are establishing what "knowledge" is, rather than dealing with how knowing takes place, we still encounter a problem. Since he has no body of knowledge to work from here either, the philosopher is still hard put to justify his claims. If philosophy is simply a process of analysis, criticism, and clarification, the most the philosopher could claim to be dealing with in this area, would be the meaning of terms like "knowledge."

In the area of axiology, we have a different matter. There is no reliable body of knowledge here since the sciences can deal on only a very limited basis with values. What that basis is we shall consider later. Let it suffice for now to indicate that this is an area for philosophy to deal with. Since values constitute a very significant role in education, there is fertile ground for the operation of philosophy. This still might seem to leave open the question of what the philosopher has to do with values in education. But, recall what this claim about philosophy has been, *viz.*, that philosophy is a process of analysis, criticism, and clarification. Apply this to the area of values and you will have a clearer notion of what, in this view, philosophy of education is.

Chapter 4

The Traditional Positions
in Philosophy of Education

I

One of the problems that new students to philosophy frequently voice is that there seems to be no answer to their questions.
They are left hanging, even about a question like: What is philosophy
of education. Their problem might be put more precisely. It would
be more accurate to state that traditionally there has been no *single*
answer to most of the questions that have been raised. But there is
no dearth of answers as we are about to see.

Philosophers have traditionally supposed that it was their task
to answer questions about everything. The problems they faced, and
the answers they provided were divided into the three bodies of
knowledge which we have just completed surveying. As one pushes
beyond this initial look at some of the problems considered by
philosophers and begins to see the responses to those problems, he
may begin to feel even more overwhelmed. What we find is that there
is such a vast body of conflicting answers to the questions raised that
it is difficult, if not impossible, to sort out all this material and come
to a single set of generally accepted responses. The closest we can
come to this is to recognize that some points of view appear to fit
together to some extent. These various views do not mesh perfectly
but they do fall into rough patterns. Consequently, it is the usual
practice in philosophy to study these patterns. The question, "what is
real?," does not have a single answer. It has many answers. The patterns into which these answers fall are regarded as "schools" of
philosophy. The large number of answers provided by philosophers
are more manageable if they are studied by schools.

The schools of philosophy which are presented here are not the
only schools. In classifying the range of answers that have been
provided by philosophers, a number and variety of divisions have
been used. For example, if we were to take one of the schools we

will deal with, realism, and examine it, we would find that there are a number of types. Different studies divide it differently into such categories as rational realism, classical realism, religious realism, natural realism, scientific realism, etc. Some scholars, in fact, will make a completely different category out of a type that another may include under realism. For example, in some studies, religious realism is not even regarded as a type of realism, but is considered a school in itself, called scholasticism or Thomism.

The schools presented here, however, are those that are most generally included in one form or another in traditional philosophy. Therefore, they will provide an acquaintance, at least, with the major positions offered by philosophy. Beyond what is presented here, there is a fertile field for the interested student to pursue. This can follow the course of studying other positions than those presented here, or delving at greater depth into the four positions considered here. The latter can be done by becoming acquainted with the writings of the individual philosophers that make up each school.

II IDEALISM

Idealism had its origin with Plato. As the allegory of the cave illustrates, the name of the school of thought might better have been *idea*-ism. In *The Republic*, Plato pictures a cave in which men are chained facing a wall. Behind them, and out of their view, is a sort of runway on which figures move. Behind this is an open fire which causes shadows of the figures on the runway to be cast on the wall which the chained men are facing. For these men, Plato suggests, reality is simply the flat shadows moving against the wall.

The allegory pictures our plight, for we are caught in a world in which our view is limited and we see only the shadows of reality. What we see is real, in a sense, but it is not *ultimate reality*. But, let us return to the cave. Suppose the men were unchained and could move about. Can you imagine how their ideas of reality would change when they were able to turn around, move about and see the three dimensional cave with its figures, and flame? But, suppose, beyond this, they left the cave and saw the real world outside. Would it not be overwhelming to them? It would simply be beyond their conception.

So it is with us and ultimate reality. All we can see with our senses are mere *appearance*, the shadow of reality as it were. For, behind each of these things is an idea of the thing, and this idea is what is ultimately real. What is "really" real is that which is permanent and immutable. Permanence and changelessness does not characterize anything in an experience. Only the ideas of these things are eternal and unchanging.

But these ideas are not just "out there." Depending on which idealist we are dealing with, these ideas either constitute or are contained in an Absolute Mind. This Absolute Mind, containing all Ideas, is therefore all-knowing, or *omniscient.* The knowledge is coupled with all power, making an omniscient, *omnipotent* Absolute Self. Man stands in relation to this Absolute Self, as an atom is to the solar system. Man is the microcosm while the Absolute Self is the macrocosm. Ultimate reality, then, including man, is spiritual.

The task of education is to develop that spirituality; in a sense, to make man God-like. The chief concern of the school is ideas, although the soul as well as the mind must be cultivated. The cultivation of the soul takes place chiefly through the route of right conduct. The mind is developed through the medium of symbols. Consequently, subjects such as languages, literature, and mathematics are very important. Although they do not constitute the entire curriculum, the idealist focuses great attention on those subjects which develop man's humanness: the humanities, literature, history, philosophy, art, languages, religion.

As for the idealist epistemology, it may be seen to flow from his ontology. Since ultimate reality resides outside of human experience in a realm of ideas, we cannot hope to come at it through ordinary, human sensory experiences. There must be some other route since sensory experience can only acquaint us with appearance. This does not rule out sensory experience entirely, as we shall see, but it does suggest that ordinary "sensing" cannot be regarded as knowing.

Seeing what man is gives us a clue to how he comes to know. Since our minds are imperfect reflections or replicas of Absolute Mind (or as some idealists claim, "participate" in Absolute Mind), our best hope of knowing ultimate reality is in the mind. Therefore, if we wish to know, we must turn our gaze inward, rather than outward, examine the contents of our own mind, so to speak. Knowing in the idealist view is introspection.

Now, this does not rule out the senses altogether, although the senses are not reliable for geniune knowing. The senses, however, can bring things to mind. What it brings to mind, of course, are the things we experience which are, at best, imperfect reflections of perfect ideas. (Or, as Hegel would view it, manifestations of the Cosmic

Idea.) The mind then imposes its order on the raw data collected by the senses. Such perceptions come to us in bits and pieces which clearly do not constitute knowledge. These perceptions are always incomplete and imperfect. It is only when the mind works on the perception that the idea behind these perceptions that have been assimilated and ordered is revealed. When, through the use of reason, the idea becomes as whole and complete as possible in my mind, I can be said to know. True knowledge is the product of reason.

Notice that in order to become knowledge, to call to mind the idea, the perceptions must be ordered. True knowledge is ordered. In fact, knowledge is valid to the extent that it *coheres*. In order to be genuine, knowledge, or truth, must be systematic and consistent. This principle is called the *coherence theory* of truth.

Recalling that the mind of man is an imperfect replica or reflection of Absolute Mind may help to give a picture of how one comes to know or grasps the truth. Truth, or knowledge are already contained in the mind; what is required is that ideas be called into consciousness. The growth or development of the mind is not the attachment or acquiring of some external knowledge. It is, rather, the unfolding from within. It is simply a growing, expanding awareness or consciousness. It is the teacher's job to "wring out" knowledge, rather than to "pour in" knowledge.

Plato's *Meno* gives one view of how the teacher operates. In the *Meno*, Socrates "withdraws" the knowledge of a geometric theorem from a slave boy who has never studied geometry. He does this simply by questioning. His questions call to mind the knowledge which is already in the mind of the slave boy; he demonstrates the boy's eternally possessed knowledge. This Socratic method of instruction has always been the ideal of idealists.

Idealists will generally grant that the scientific method can lead to knowing of a sort. What they will not grant is that it is the only way of knowing. We also know through intuition, introspection, and the use of reason. Therefore, the ability to use these methods must be taught; i.e., we must foster and develop and discipline the intuitive faculty.

The model for knowing, in the idealist view, is geometry, where we start with axioms, postulates, and definitions (self-evident first principles), and develop theorems (conclusions or truths). Subject matters modeled after this fashion are therefore important in the curriculum. The subjects which we mentioned earlier follow this model, and in addition, demonstrate the wholeness and completeness of knowledge and truth.

Traditionally, metaphysical and epistemological positions are regarded as basic because, in a sense, they establish the bases for the way we operate. That is to say, we begin with the world as it is and what we may know of it, and from what we establish in these areas we may deduce all else. This is not to say, however, that the area of axiology is any less important in traditional philosophy of education. There is a dual need for ethical considerations. When we establish our aims in education, we are making moral choices. And, it is the task of education to develop character, i.e., to instill, or inculcate, or call out, a system of values.

Values to the idealist are permanent and immutable. Being permanent and immutable, we cannot expect to find them in the empirical realm, i.e., in the sensory world. In searching for values, we are engaged in looking for "inner principles," rather than what we see in the physical world. The routes to acquaintance with these absolute values will lie in examining the contents of the mind; we get at values just as we get at truth. This can mean that we either rely on the use of reason, or we may examine the contents of the "group mind," i.e., we may see the Absolute Will reflected in the will of society. This latter approach is made possible because a society represents a "larger selfhood," a step in the direction of identification with the Absolute Self, which is perfection.

We may use reason, however, as a check on moral rules established by the society; the group mind may turn out to be merely a changeable "popular will." We need some way to justify, to validate and authenticate these glimpses of the Absolute Good. Some universal law is needed on which all laws are based. As Kant has suggested, what is called for is a categorical imperative that will serve to justify the hypothetical imperatives, morals or laws that justify particular acts in particular circumstances.

One such law which was offered was the Golden Rule: Do unto others as you would have them do unto you. This would seem to be appropriate to every circumstance, and has the additional strength of being offered as a divinely inspired rule. But Kant objected to this as a categorical imperative. The rule is too much anchored in the individual; what's good for me is to be good for all. But this would not make much of a universal law, because as Kant says, it does not tell us enough of our duties toward *ourselves*, or our duties toward others *out of love* for others. We must look for a better expression of the Divine Will.

The categorical imperative that Kant offers us is at once profound and simple. "Act only on that maxium which will enable you at the same time to will that it be a universal law." Those acts are good, Kant is telling us, which you would be willing to have enacted into Universal Legislation for all men, everywhere, for all time, to obey. All other moral prescriptions can be checked against this one.

The idealist position is neither unusual nor surprising. In a sense, we all behave like idealists at times. In the first place, we sometimes seem to assume the idealist conception of mind and look for knowledge of values to be in the mind and simply in need of being called into consciousness. As teachers, we say to children at times, "You don't need to be told what's right. You know. Just stop and think about what you did." We are, consciously or not, suggesting that he arrive at moral rules through introspection. Or, on occasion, we say to the errant child, "Suppose the whole class behaved the way you did. Would you like everyone to act like you did?" Are we not, here, invoking Kant's categorical imperative?

Despite the idealist's emphasis on introspection, values are to be actively taught in the idealist's curriculum. The child must learn to strive toward the perfection that his spiritual nature requires. He learns this through the literature and history which he studies, where heroes of literature portray the enduring values which he is to embrace, and history reveals the moral tradition of society. The teacher teaches values through these subjects. But, the "ideal" teacher also teaches by serving as a *paradigmatic self*. In striving to identify, with the Absolute Self, the pupil is presented by a model, the teacher, who through possession of a larger "Self" than the student possess, is able to lead them in the direction of proper selfhood.

As for esthetics, the position of the idealist can most likely be made clearest by calling to mind the meaning that "ideal" generally has. Aesthetic feelings are stirred by representations of the perfect, rather than portrayals of what is in the physical world. Great art is the work that comes closest to perfection. The human figure that the sculptor produces is not anyone's particular figure; it is the idealized, the perfected, human figure; the figure as it should be. Similarly, the painting of the face is a perfected face, with all blemishes, or imperfections, removed. It is, so to speak, what the Infinite Mind "sees."

In developing esthetic sensibility in the young, we awaken children to the appropriate tastes by having them view the great works of art. But it is not enough simply to have the appropriate emotional response. Therefore, the student must become familiar with the idea behind the work of art. So, we provide for him courses in Art

Appreciation, or Musical Appreciation, in which he comes to understand as well as appreciate the work of art.

It would be misleading to suggest that the preceding views represent the position of all idealists. For example, although all idealists would see man as essentially spiritual, their views on human nature would range at least from Berkeley's relatively orthodox Christian view of a human soul created by God to Hegel's view of man as a fragment of the Absolute into which he will be reabsorbed. What we have presented here may serve as a useful starting point which may be followed by reading some of the writings of those generally regarded as idealists, or idealist educators such as: Plato, Immanuel Kant, Hegel, Schopenhauer, Jonathan Edwards, Josiah Royce, Emerson, W.E. Hocking, Comenius, Froebel, Theodore M. Green, Herman Horne, Gordon K. Chalmers, William T. Harris, Robert Ulich.

III REALISM

If the term idealism is somewhat misleading, and we have suggested that it might better be called idea-ism, the title of realism for our second "school" of philosophy might be equally deceiving. The realists have not somehow cornered the market on "reality." The term is simply supposed to convey the impression that reality, for the realist, resides in the world which we encounter in our everyday experience. If you want to know what is "really" real, you will find out, not by turning your back on the world, but by looking directly at it. Your gaze is outward rather than inward as was suggested by the idealist. What you see, hear, touch, and otherwise sense is what is real.

The world is not an illusion, the realist asserts, and ultimate reality is not simply an idea. It is not even an idea in the mind of God. Rather it is that physical realm of things and energy, whole and complete, operating according to natural laws which also are a part of the constitution of reality. Not only is reality not an idea in anyone's mind; it is, in fact, independent of all minds. It does not depend on being perceived to exist. It exists independently of whether or not anyone is perceiving it. It has an existence of its own.

In what has been said so far can be seen both differences and similarities between idealism and realism. The differences of course center about the view of the former that ultimate reality is spiritual, while to the latter, it is essentially physical. The similarities lie in the fact that both see ultimate reality *objectively*. That is to say, in both views reality is essentially whole and completed, and lying wholly outside the realm of human experience. Ultimate reality, in both views, has an "out-there-ness" which creates problems for the two positions. The major problems are those of how we go about confirming the existence of such a reality, since we can confirm only our own mental events or our own sensory experiences. Yet these are not to be confused with the ultimate reality existing "out there" independent of these personal phenomena. The other problem besides that of confirming the existence of such an ultimate reality is how we may come into contact with, or "know," such reality. All that we seem to be able to talk about are our own ideas or sensations and we have no way of moving beyond these or being sure that they ever come into contact with or reflect whatever is out there completely independent of us.

As for man himself, most realists regard him as a biological organism, a peculiar extension of the "thing-ness" and "out-there-ness" of the universe. Like other things in the universe, he is organized, and subject to the laws of nature, not only biologically, but also in all his relationships. His major distinction, for most realists, is not his soul or spirit, but his ability to reason. Therefore, when the school develops his humanness, they will focus on this ability to reason. To this extent, some of the subjects recommended by idealists are looked upon with favor by realists.

The emphasis on the reality of physical existence and natural laws, however, have their influence on realist views on education. The realist does not see the educator's role as being that of developing individual *selves*, or saving souls. To most realists, the schools' function is to adjust the individual to his environment, to bring him into harmony with what is "out there." Consequently, there is heavy emphasis on bringing the mind into correspondence with what is really there in the universe by acquainting the pupil with what we know of the universe; i.e., by presenting to him as much as we can of the natural laws that govern reality.

There will be heavy emphasis on the sciences, then. In contrast to the idealist focus on the humanities, the realist program will present the "hard" subjects of chemistry, physics, astronomy, etc. These are the subjects where we really can be said to know. About the humanities, we can only have opinions. Even in areas related to the humanities, we will be scientific. The social studies will become the social sciences where pupils will learn about the natural laws that control even human events.

The study of mathematics is important in the realist curriculum not only for its effect on the development of the human mind. Mathematics, with its order and precision represents, or may be used to represent, the orderliness of the universe. Just as language represented the symbols by which learning may take place in the idealist view, so mathematics represents the symbols by which learning may take place in the realist educational scheme. That is to say, mathematics will represent a basic tool subject in the realist curriculum. It will help the student to understand the universe by helping him to quantify and measure it. This quantification and measurement will apply even in the study of human behavior.

We may get some clues to human knowing by reflecting on the realist's ontological views. The real world is "out there," independent of our ideas about it. In order to account for how we come to know it, the realist does not concoct any strange or unusual theories. He goes at it in a very straight forward manner. Man comes to know through sensory experiences. He is a spectator to reality, and the more careful he is about his "spectating," the better are the chances that he will come to know. The exercise of care does not, in this case, consist of merely fitting things together consistently; there is more to it than coherence. If he observes carefully, he need not worry about things fitting together; they will do that naturally, since the world we observe is orderly. What we must be concerned about is that our observations are careful and precise in order to accurately reflect what is really out there.

Realists rely on a different model for knowing than that used by idealists. Obviously, reason will have its part to play. But the crucial ingredient is careful observation. The model for knowing, then, is that established by the sciences. The methods of careful and precise observation used by the sciences are the best methods we have for discovering what is really "out there" in the universe. It is when our ideas about the world correspond perfectly with what is really in the universe that we can be said truly to know. This is called the *correspondence theory* of truth, or knowledge.

There is another side to this business of knowing. What we have spoken of so far is what knowing is. We can also, the realist says, know how man comes to know. By careful study and observation, we can discover how learning takes place, and precisely what it is. Study reveals that man, like other animals, has a nervous system.

This nervous system is able to gather data from the universe through stimuli provided by the environment. The stimuli thus gathered are ordered in the nervous system, representing what we mean by knowing in some realists views. This ordering then issues in overt response on the part of the organism. This response is, according to which realist we are listening to, either an overt sign of knowledge that is held, or represents or "means" knowledge.

Since man is a part of the real world, he too is subject to its laws, and we come to know and quantify these laws just as we can any others. This applies to minds and knowing as it does to anything else in the universe. Through the use of laboratory animals, and controlled learning situations, we can come to learn about learning, and this is precisely how we came to know about learning as stimulus-response behavior. Furthermore, we can quantify what it is that we come to know about learning and mind.

"Whatever exists, exists in some amount," E.L. Thorndike has said. The implication of this, of course, is that we can then measure whatever exists. Through the careful observation of various responses, we can come to know what and how much has been learned. We can even measure the "size" of the mind so to speak. By subjecting the organism to the appropriate stimuli, (carefully selected test items), we can elicit responses and through the use of measuring instruments (tests with the resultant scores treated statistically), know not only how much has been learned, but indeed, how much can be learned, and even how much *ought* to be learned. We have reached the point of quantifying mind by dividing one's *mental age* (the score on a particular test), by his chronological age and arriving at an I.Q. (Intelligence Quotient). That number is the quantification of mind, or intelligence.

Learning, then, is being provided with adequate stimuli and making appropriate responses. The pupil is seen as a kind of receptacle. The capacity of the receptacles will vary of course. But we can know about each capacity through our testing program. The teacher's role is then to "pour in" as much knowledge as the pupil is capable of holding. What gets poured in, of course, are facts, formulas, skills, habits, and all that the mind is capable of storing. The subject matters will be those mentioned earlier.

As this conceptualization has been pursued, it has resulted in some novel phenomena. In one instance, we have had "teaching" reduced to the presentation of data by machines. The machine not only presents the material to be learned but constantly tests the students on what has been learned, and then guides him to further learning. The pupil needs merely to memorize the content of the program that is presented to him. Beyond this, there are those who have urged that educators be held "accountable" for the amount of such material that is learned, or not learned by his pupils. In fact, commercial companies are now selling "educational programs" on this basis, and will be paid according to how much is "learned" by the pupils whom they treat. They will not be paid for those pupils who have not learned what they *ought* to learn. What will happen to these pupils has not been clarified. Perhaps they will become the special charges of the regular classroom teacher.

There appears to be a tendency for the realist to treat educational problems as technical problems. In fact, the most extreme of the realists do seem to brush aside questions of values as having little import for educators. Our concern must be for facts, and skills, rather than attitudes, since there is little that can be done about attitudes anyhow. Yet, this represents only an extreme view, for values obviously will have a role to play in the realist approach to educators, just as they do in any educational plans. At times, value considerations may be ignored, but they are inevitably and invariably there, influencing our choices as much as any technical or factual considerations.

In the realist view, as in the idealist position, values are permanent and absolute. They are woven into the very fiber of reality. There are moral laws operating in the universe, just as there are natural laws. Our relationship to these moral laws is to discover them and adjust to the demands of nature. We can no more violate these laws with impunity than we can violate the laws of gravity.

Rather than looking to categorical imperatives to justify our ethical decisions, we must, as in the case of factual truth, rely on the observations of nature. Moralists long told us about the evils of smoking. But, it was the Surgeon General's report of a few years ago that really "proved" the evil effects of tobacco. Similarly, the question of whether or not the use of marijuana is evil or immoral seems to center about arguments of whether or not its effects are "really" harmful.

We may also rely on the use of reason, along with observation, to discover moral laws. For example, we know wanton killing to be an evil. There are at least two grounds for such knowledge. In the first place, studies by the social scientists reveal that in every society, there are prohibitions against wanton killing. This is evidence that men everywhere know this law. On the other hand, we can reason out why there is such a law. If wanton killing were tolerated, it could lead to the extinction of the group or society. Hence, the need for moral law prohibiting it.

Such laws are not merely formal prescriptions. They are positive guides to human conduct. A reading of the Declaration of Independence lays clear the realist's view of moral laws. Our dissolution of the ties with England was not simply the manifestation of obstinate willfulness. Our forefathers were assuming that "separate and equal station to which the Laws of Nature and of Nature's God entitles them." We also learn that men are "endowed by their Creator with certain inalienable rights." Under certain conditions, men have the "duty" to change governments.

Although values are found in nature, children are not born knowing them. It becomes necessary, then, to inculcate values through education. There seems to be an unresolved question among realists as to how such education is to be accomplished. Among more extreme realists, the view prevails that values are taught through conditioning. Through the bestowing and withholding of rewards and punishments the child "learns" to respond appropriately. This view enjoys popularity not only among harsh realists, but among laymen who believe in strict "discipline." The connections among rewards, punishments, and desirable behavior patterns seem too obvious to be questioned. Other realists, however, urge following the Aristotelian model of cultivating intellectual and moral virtues. In this view, the young are not taught to respond blindly, as rats in a maze. Instead, they are taught to "see" good and evil, and to know why acts are good or evil. Virtue is the *rational* understanding of necessary moral law.

In the area of esthetics, order and that which is in nature also prevail. What stimulates the esthetic impulse is the beauty of the order which we find in nature. Therefore, art is that which reflects the beauty of order in the universe. Artistic endeavors produce genuine works of art when those products are faithful representations of what really is. Paintings, novels, poetry are geniunely artistic when they realistically recreate the order in the universe. This is what the young are to be taught to celebrate in the realm of art.

A summary view as has been presented here represents only the briefest introduction to the varied and various views of the realists. It would be well to follow this introduction by looking at the works of representative realists like Aristotle, Hobbes, Locke, Hume, Herbart, Wm. C. Bagley, I.T. Kandel, F.S. Breed, Ross. L. Finney, Ralph Barton Perry, Alfred North Whitehead, John Wild, and Bertrand Russell.

If one considers the Thomist philosophers to be among the realists then to that list we might add the names of St. Thomas Aquinas, Etienne Gibson, Jacques Maritain, Aldous Huxley, Hillaire Belloc, Mortimar Adler, and Robert M. Hutchins.

IV EXISTENTIALISM

In one sense, existentialism represents a radical departure from the other "schools" of philosophy. This deviation may be seen in the rejection of reason by existentialists. Existentialism is represented as an irrational position, for reasons which shall be seen in the discussion on existentialist epistemology. On the other hand, this school of philosophy may be seen as simply a relatively recent extension of traditional views; as merely a reformulation of certain older positions with some novel twists.

Despite internal differences and a wide range of views, those who are generally labeled as existentialists seem to agree that the central theme of their position is the statement that "existence precedes essence." The range of their views may be seen in the fact that the most widely known contemporary existentialist, Jean Paul Sartre, along with Nietzsche, Heidegger, and Camus are atheists. The father of existentialism, Soren Kierkegaard, was a theist, as are Karl Jaspers and Gabriel Marcel. Whereas Marcel is a Catholic, Martin Buber is a Jew, and Reinhold Niebuhr, Karl Barth, and Paul Tillich are noted Protestants. Nikolai Berdyaev, a Russian philosopher was a member of the Russian Orthodox Church. Other existentialist views are expressed by novelists Feodor Dostoevski and Franz Kafka and Blaise Pascal.

An understanding of the existentialist position may begin with a grasp of the meaning of the central theme. The claim is that man simply finds himself thrust into existence, incomplete, undefined; simply there. He awakens to his existence, discovers himself simply "on the scene." There is nothing to him except his existence. Being in the world he is forced to act; his acting forces him to choose from among the alternatives that are before him. Any alternative may be chosen. The only factors over which he has no choice are his existence, he simply comes into existence through no choice of his own; the fact that he must choose; and the inevitability of death.

In the process of choosing, man is also determining his own essence. Each choice that he makes is like casting a vote in favor of a particular definition of what it means to be human. The vote is cast not only for oneself, but for all mankind. For in my choice, I say not only what I am, but what man is. As Van Cleve Morris has so skillfully put it, "Reality in Existentialist language is self-operating in-a-cosmos-of-choice."[1] Not only is this self a choosing self, but it is the self itself that is among the choices.

The choosing is not limited simply to the self, however. The self is also choosing what constitutes ultimate reality. This final reality resides within the inner self of the individual human being. The existentialist makes no distinction between the external world and the internal world of the mind. Reality has its existence in the subjective states of mind. Hence, there is no purpose in the universe, save whatever purpose the self may put there. Not only is the universe without purpose, it is also without meaning, except for the meaning it may come to have to the individual.

In what we have said so far may be seen some of the similarities between existentialism and some of the older views, particularly idealism. In the first place, there is a striking similarity between the idealist *soul* and the existentialist *self*. Both are invisible, nonmaterial aspects of "being." Both constitute the essence of what it means to be human, yet both remain vague and undefined. Although both the soul and the self are metaphysical, they are still spoken of as entities. Both are what must be "saved" or maintained at almost any price. Better that one should lose an arm or a leg, or suffer from a little ignorance than that the soul or the self should be sacrificed. Further analysis would undoubtedly give additional similarities between the two views. A major difference, however, is that existentialists do not make claims about the self surviving death.

Another similarity may be noted in the existentialist's view of ultimate reality being an idea. The nature of ultimate reality is not a physical realm of things and energy operating according to predetermined natural laws. George Kneller instructs us that "The existentialist teaches that there is no difference between the external world and the internal world of the mind."[2] The similarity is there, but the existentialist adds a novel and unique twist: the idea that constitutes ultimate reality is *my* idea. Whereas the idealist's "idea" is external, absolute, and immutable, the existentialists "idea" is temporal and personal.

---

1. Van Cleve Morris, *Philosophy and the Amer. School* (Boston: Houghton Mifflin Co., 1961), p. 77.
2. George T. Kneller, *Existentialism and Education* (New York: John Wiley and Sons, 1958), p. 3.

The centrality of the individual, of the inner self of man, has its influence on the recommendations made for the education of the young. The sort of environment that should be created and maintained is one of freedom where there are no impositions on the child and he is free to develop his selfhood. Rather than design and specify and "tie down" the learner's environment, that environment should be kept as open as possible to allow for the free play of choice.

Rather than a curriculum of tightly organized subject matters to which the pupil must come to correspond, the program must consist of whatever subject matters will develop the self. The humanities clearly qualify here, much more than do the sciences, for they tend to develop the humanness of the self. In the first place, rather than focusing on "facts," these subjects encourage a response to the really important concerns of man. Whereas the sciences and mathematics encourage a coming to correspond with merely technical details, the humanities encourage a passionate encounter with life by dealing with the problems of men. Beyond that, such subjects as music, painting, poetry and other literature encourage self-expression. In these areas, the child is more likely to be able to exert his choice, to say what the world means to him. The arts are clearly the closest approach to ultimate reality, being, as they are, expressions of an individual inner self.

The central theme of existentialism, the priority of existence over essence, gives some indication of the existentialist approach to epistemology. Man finds himself on the scene devoid of any essence. He must choose himself, i.e., literally choose his own *self*. Not only must he choose what to be in choosing what to do; he also chooses what to believe. If he wishes to rely on anyone else's explanations, including those of the scientists, in order to establish his own beliefs, he is free to do so. But he does not have to choose such explanations; no one forces him.

At the very bottom, all such choices are irrational. If we are asked to state our belief about what we think it means to be human, we may recite all that we have learned about humans from books and courses. If we are asked why we hold such beliefs, we might reply that we believe these things because they are the conclusions that knowledgeable scientists have come to. But, when we are asked why we have adopted the conclusions held by scientists as our own set of beliefs, we are left without a reason. We have simply *chosen* to do so. Even the choice to be rational cannot be defended on rational grounds; it is an irrational choice. In this it is like all choices. We can push our explanations of choice back only a step or two, and then we inevitably encounter the situation of our choices being simply and purely a matter of individual choosing.

On this basis, then, we can make no distinction between knowing, believing, and feeling. All are one and the same: a matter of simply choosing what has importance, and meaning, for one as an individual. "Knowing" in existentialist terms is simply, and solely, what we mean when we use "knowing" in such a statement as, "One cannot *know* what it means to be poor, unless he has *been* poor." This is one reason why existentialism is difficult to present. It can be known, existentialists claim, only from the inside. It cannot be presented objectively, and presented accurately.

The only distinctions one may find in knowing is between objective and subjective knowing. In the case of the former, there may be a tree, and other persons, outside my window. I know they are there. But in addition to this kind of knowing, I also know that I know. I also know that I exist. This type of knowing differs from the former type, in that I can know about other existences only objectively, and can know my own existence subjectively. I can "feel" my own existence existing. This is real, true, genuine, authentic knowing. There is nothing second-handed here; there is no "otherness" about it.

Scientific knowing is objective knowing, and this is what places limitations on it. Scientific knowing is knowing about, but it is not knowing in the way I know myself, and it can never be that kind of knowing. But, objective, or subjective, I am responsible for my own knowing, as surely as I am responsible for all other choices. If I am going to remain true to myself, then I must assume that responsibility. The degree to which I shunt this responsibility off unto someone or something else, is the degree to which I become a less authentic human being.

Each individual has the experience of awakening to himself as a self, his existential moment when he realizes that he is an individual, responsible, choosing self. Somewhere around puberty, we awaken to ourselves, come to recognize that we are not simply extensions of our parents, or teachers, or others, but are independent selves. As exciting, awesome, and dreadful as this experience is, from that moment on we must assume the burden of making our own choices.

This should be reflected in the curriculum. Our pupils should be free to develop and follow their own inclinations in learning. Choice-making should be nurtured in the young. And this should be done in the most authentic manner. In the place of having children dutifully and objectively appropriate bodies of predigested knowledge, we should encourage active involvement with subject matter. Instead of teachers lecturing at pupils, the Socratic method of learning should be followed. Just as the idealist urges the drawing out of knowledge that is already there, rather than the "pouring-in" of external facts, so the existentialist urges the same kind of development from within.

The existentialist's eschewing of reason and the scientific method of knowing points up yet another similarity between the existentialist and idealist positions. Along with idealists, existentialists urge the cultivation of personal types of knowing. In fact, they, like the idealists, *insist* that real knowing can come only through intuition and introspection.

Turning from questions of what knowing is to what should I do, we find the central theme of existentialism again suggesting certain things. With its heavy emphasis on choice, this school of philosophy is clearly devoted to concern about values. Our existence is clearly not a matter of choice, but all else is. Every situation requires doing something, which in turn requires choosing, which involves us in ethical problems.

With values, as with reality and truth, man is thrown back upon himself. His values are not chosen for him. Even to adopt someone else's moral code is to make a moral decision. There is simply no getting out of it. Since values are our own choosing, strictly our own, we make our values out of nothing. Further, we make them on no rational basis; indeed, we make them on no basis at all! The individual is therefore ultimately and utterly responsible for his own values. The degree to which I am not responsible is the degree to which I am not fully authentic, fully human.

This is as true of esthetics as it is of ethics. Art is the expression of the self. Therefore, we cannot set down criteria of what constitutes genuinely esthetic productions. Some years ago at a symposium on art attended by the author, at the Museum of Modern Art, Elmer Rice, the playwright, expressed himself this way. "I don't know what art is, but I know what I like." The existentialist would undoubtedly alter this only to say, "Art is what I like."

The implications for education are clear. As for the ethical considerations, much of what has been already said would merely be repeated. Choice must become more central to the curriculum, as far as both subject matter and method are concerned. What the school must begin to be concerned about is dealing with the ultimate questions of life. As for esthetics, beyond encouraging self-expression, the teacher's chief role will be to, first establish a climate of freedom in which the child is free to express himself, and secondly, to insist that artistic productions be authentic, i.e., to see that they emanate from the inner self of the individual.

The foregoing has presented only the most cursory overview of the existentialist position. Anyone who is interested in coming to understand the position more thoroughly would do well to regard this exposition as introductory only. It should serve simply as a background for studying some of the writings of those authors listed near the beginning of this section.

V PRAGMATISM

Pragmatism represents the most recently established of the four philosophical positions which we shall examine. Whereas existentialism had its beginning in the first half of the 19th century, pragmatism was born at the close of that century. The real "father" of pragmatism, the only distinctively American school of philosophy, was the little known American philosopher, scientist, mathematician, Charles Sanders Peirce. Also given credit as co-founders, were two other American philosophers, John Dewey and William James. This trio is generally regarded as the leading proponents of their uniquely American position. Since they were bringing their thoughts to the public at about the same time, the three are considered co-founders of the school, but Dewey and James have both admitted that they were indebted to Peirce. In fact, though they regarded Peirce's ideas as seminal, he has not received the credit due him.

Peirce (pronounced *Purs*), did not enjoy the academic respect accorded his fellow pragmatists. He held academic posts only briefly, and his writings were not widely known. Undoubtedly, some of the circumstances of his private life accounted for his inability to obtain and hold academic positions. The closing years of his life were a real tragedy, and he died in the direst poverty, succumbing to cancer in 1914. Harvard University paid his widow the princely sum of $500 for his manuscripts, from which seven (7) volumes of essays have so far been published. This fact must surely delight Harvard business officials and horrify Harvard scholars.

Pragmatism avoids some of the problems that plague the other schools of philosophy. As was pointed out earlier, both idealism and realism have a problem in their ontological views of accounting for our contact with a reality that is claimed to lie wholly outside of human experience. The pragmatists avoid this by pointing out that all we can have is human experience; if human experience cannot account for reality, then there is no accounting for it. When we talk about reality, therefore, we can talk only about actual, or possible, human experiences. To talk about some realm of "ultimate" reality that lies wholly beyond, or outside of, human experience is, to the pragmatist, to engage in nonsense.

The pragmatist's approach to metaphysics, therefore, represents something of a departure from the more traditional positions. Rather than engage in discussions about matters in terms which he regards as nonsense the pragmatist's approach is to see what sense we can make of such statements. He examines what we can sensibly mean by calling things real. He accomplishes this by translating statements about reality into "If . . . then" propositions.

Suppose we were to ask the question, Is this desk real? or, Is this desk really here? The idealist would most likely respond that it certainly is a real desk in a physical sense, but since it has spatial and temporal limitations it does not constitute ultimate reality, but is simply an imperfect reflection of that reality. The realist would undoubtedly reply that the desk is indeed real. It can be seen, touched, weighed, measured, etc. In fact, it's real independently of whether or not we have sensory experiences with it. The existentialist would probably retort that its reality is a personal, individual matter; if I believe (feel) that it's real, then for me it is real.

The pragmatist's view would be to examine what we could conceivably mean by "real." *If* the desk is a real desk, *then* this means we have had, are having, or can have certain sensory experiences such as seeing it, touching it, etc. And this is all we mean by "real." It's the only way we can sensibly talk about reality.

The central theme of the pragmatist's approach to reality is Peirce's maximum from his essay on "How to Make Our Ideas Clear"

> Consider what effects, that might conceivably have practical bearings, we conceive the object of our conception to have. Then, our conception of these effects is the whole of our conception of the object.[3]

Peirce is giving us a way of dealing with questions of "reality." Our conception of reality is as close to reality as we can get, and our conception is of practical effects, of consequences. If we are going to have a metaphysics, we must name it *experience*. This neither confirms nor denies the existence of a reality "out there." It simply ignores such claims. All we can talk sensibly about is *transaction*, a

---

3. Justus Buchler, ed. *Philosophical Writings of Peirce* (New York: Dover Publications, 1955), p. 31.

doing and undergoing between man and the environment of which he is a part. Our only truck with metaphysics will be to see what sense we can make out of metaphysical statements.

Reality, then, is dynamic. As William James once said of it, it is the "universe with the lid off." In providing awareness of this kind of reality, we do not provide boys and girls with overt bodies of knowledge about an already completed and final universe. Perhaps the other names for pragmatism suggest something about the curriculum. Pragmatism also goes by the names of experimentalism and instrumentalism.

In the spirit of experimentalism, this means that the *process* of knowing is a significant part of knowing. Consequently, the pragmatist curriculum will be dynamic, concerned with process and problem-solving. Knowledge will be what serves us. In place of a purely chronological approach to history will come studies like Problems of American Democracy. The sciences will receive heavy emphasis, not as a business of learning the conclusions scientists have come to, but as a process of learning to think scientifically. All education will be, in Dewey's terms, the continuous "reconstruction of experience." No single item of knowledge is essential, for all items have merely instrumental value. Whatever engages us in the use of intelligence will serve as the subject matter of the school.

It is difficult to separate epistemology out from the pragmatist view, because pragmatism is essentially a philosophy of epistemology. In viewing reality as experience, the pragmatist is placing knowing at the center of things. Knowing is not something which we do about a world which is "out there." The notions of a knower as one entity, and a reality-to-be-known as another and distinct and separate sort of thing *creates* a problem of dualism where none need exist. Man is of and in his world. Reality is what he happens to experience. Consequently, knowing is a transaction between man and world. It is a doing and undergoing and the resultant dispositions.

Truth, then, is simply a description of this kind of experiencing. It is not a permanent and absolute attribute of the universe which man comes to discover. It is simply what he attributes to statements about his experiences. Knowledge and truth are not "things" that are discovered already existing in the universe. Knowledge and truth are what man creates; they are simply the ways in which he structures his experiences. As James has said, Truth is "what works." An idea is its practical consequences.

There are some differences in views among pragmatists on this issue. "What works" has a peculiar and personal meaning for James.

Peirce so emphatically denied this twist to the meaning which he gave the idea that he began to refer to his own views as "pragmaticism" in order to distinguish his views from those of James. In Peirce's view, as in that of other pragmatists than James, the meaning of "what works" involved public testing rather than mere personal satisfaction.

We have spoken of the pragmatist's view of knowing in terms of transaction, doing, and undergoing. The pragmatist does not see knowledge as simply "having" ideas, or coming to correspond with a reality "out there." In the pragmatic view, man interacts with other aspects of his environment. This transaction is always on the basis of past experiences and what the individual has come to anticipate. Occasionally, he has a disjoint experience, i.e., things are not as expected. One seeks to account for this. We act out our idea, this is the *doing* phase. In the process of doing, we *undergo* the consequences of our act. If things turn out as we expected, we have new knowledge; our experience has now been restructured. This process of transaction, doing-undergoing-reflecting is the process of intelligence, the epistemological process.

The model for knowing, in the pragmatic view, is the scientific method. In this sense, there is some resemblance between the epistemological views of the pragmatist and the realist. But, unlike the realist, the pragmatist does not see the process as one of discovering knowledge, or coming across Truth already in existence. He does not regard his conclusions as anything more than tentative hypotheses. Whereas the realist sees knowledge, or truth, as that which correctly reflects reality, the pragmatist sees knowledge and truth not as being "out there," but simply as ways of structuring our experience. This is the basis for the pragmatist view that learning is the reconstruction of experience.

The learner, thus, is not the passive recipient of inert ideas or content. Since learning is the progressive reconstruction of experience, it is more important to present material in a psychologically sound manner than in a logically organized fashion. This does not mean that bodies of organized content are to be thrown out. It simply means that subject matter comes at a different place. Instead of *starting* with imposition of organized content, we start with the child where he is, restructuring his present experience, and moving him in the direction of organized subject matter, which is the way the experience of the race, or society, is organized.

Learning is a procedure involving problem solving and inquiry, rather than a process of either "pouring-in" or "wringing out" knowledge. The learning process for the learner follows essentially the method that the scholar goes through in creating knowledge.

Just as truth and knowledge are relative and contextual, not permanent and absolute, so values are also relative and contextual. Therefore, we do not make judgments about acts or situations on the basis of their consistency with pre-existent moral laws or objective moral codes. Neither are values merely, or solely, matters of personal whim. When we make judgments about acts, the judgments are in terms of their consequences. To say that something is good, is to say that it has good, or valued, consequences.

Ethical questions come down to the question "What ought I to do in this context, in these circumstances?" The way we may proceed here is essentially the way we would proceed in solving scientific problems. We limit the problem, hypothesize, try out, i.e., do, and undergo. What "works" is what is good, in the area of values, as in the area of truth. This is not to be used to justify personal whims, however, since "what works" requires public testing. Also, it requires that we take into account *all* of the consequences, not just those that we fondly cherish. "What works" may seem an unsatisfactory basis for ethical justification to some. But, the pragmatists insist, it is the best guide we have. It certainly offers more hope than retreats into moral never-never lands of absolute value.

As for esthetic experiences, these are not responses to glimpses of perfection or ultimate reality. These are new insights into feelings, new feelings that enhance our experience in a particular way, namely, filling us with delight. Therefore, esthetic values are matters, simply, of personal and public taste.

The teaching of values also must be a business of reconstructing the experience of the young. The young are provided with experiences in the schools that will develop the values which we cherish. He learns democracy, by democratic living, not by reading or hearing *about* democracy, and he is taught ways of handling problems of values. In a sense, values are "caught," through his ways of living, rather than "taught" through lectures and preaching. This does not mean that the child must directly experience every possible moral situation in order to learn morality. It means simply that he learns how to handle moral problems that one encountered in the school setting in order to be able to handle himself in other moral situations.

To see the various views of the pragmatists further, one might examine such works as Dewey's *Democracy and Education*, Peirce's two essays, "The Fixation of Belief," and "How to Make our Ideas

Clear," and William James' *Pragmatism*. In addition to these, one might also read some of the works of John L. Childs, Sidney Hook, William S. Kilpatrick, W.O. Stanley, Boyd H. Bode, V.T. Thayer, and others.

Chapter 5

An Alternative View of the Nature of Philosophy of Education

I

Traditionally much has been expected of philosophers. Traditionally they have promised much. They have promised to provide answers about the nature of the universe, about man, the nature of human nature, and man's place in the universe. They have promised to answer questions about God. And we have looked to philosophers to tell us about what knowing and knowledge are, and about truth, and how we come to know. We have expected them to tell us about the Good Life, and what beauty is. Philosophers have promised to do all of this, and to do it, not contingently, but with certainty, absolutely. Philosophers have also assured us that questions in education could be answered indubitably by their special methods.

Clearly, as the preceding pages testify, there has been no dearth of answers. That, in fact, constitutes the problem in certain areas of philosophy. We are overwhelmed with answers, varied and conflicting answers, and we have no way of resolving the differences. Not only do realists disagree with idealists, and idealists with realists, and pragmatists, etc.; a little research will demonstrate that the members of a particular school do not even agree among themselves. When the question is raised: What do the idealists think about X?, it is always legitimate to ask: which idealist? The same thing is true of the other schools of philosophy.

The problem is further complicated by the fact that with the multitude of answers, there appears to be no way to establish the supremacy of one set of answers over another. While each school of philosophy, indeed each philosopher, appears to upset the conclusions and arguments of others, there seems to be no good reason for accepting any one of the positions. At any rate, the adoption of any of the views presented in the preceding chapter means the adoption of the accompanying problems of that position.

Philosophers themselves have been concerned about this problem of philosophy and have tried to account for it in various ways. One of the easiest ways, of course, is simply to regard such matters as "mysteries." Others have tried to account for this problem of not knowing which set of answers to establish, nor on what basis to establish a set of answers, by pointing out that knowledge and Truth are infinite, and man is finite, and, therefore, what we have at best, are fragmentary glimpses of reality and truth. Unfortunately, even that assertion must take its place alongside all other candidates for our attention.

It should be understood that what follows will be simply another effort at solving some of the problems which philosophers have faced. Along with those positions we have encountered so far, the one presented in this chapter must be seen as simply another alternative which, however, convincing it may seem, has not won the general assent of those who are at least equally knowledgable in the fields of philosophy and philosophy of education. At least a part of the significance of this is that one may see herein one of the fundamental problems of philosophy. A solution will be offered, but it is with no assurance that it may win any more acceptance than any other position.

A part of the solution may be seen in briefly, and superficially, tracing out the history of thought. Clearly, early thinkers in areas other than philosophy faced problems similar to those that face philosophers. We have not always had bodies of reliable knowledge in the area of mathematics. The sciences have even more recently achieved success in giving us bodies of reliable knowledge. It may be more fruitful to consider the sciences since their subject matter is closer to what philosophers have generally regarded as the content of philosophy. Such consideration might help to account for the notorious lack of success among philosophers in establishing a reliable body of knowledge. We may also be led a little way in the direction of solution.

To the ancient Greeks, philosophy was science. Indeed, as was pointed out earlier, philosophy was regarded as the "Queen of Sciences." There are a few who still maintain this verbally and emotionally, but few any longer act on this belief. At the time when philosophy and science were one, science was as notoriously unsuccessful in establishing a reliable body of knowledge as philosophy was and has been. Such "scientific" truths were "established" as Aristotle's claims that men had more teeth than women, and heavenly bodies move in perfect circles. It was not until about the turn of the 17th century that science began to establish reliable knowledge. And, strangely or not, science became emancipated from philosophy at exactly the same time, and by the same acts.

What emancipated science from philosophy was that men who no longer called themselves philosophers began to rely on other methods than those traditionally used in philosophy. These newer methods proved to be spectacularly successful, i.e., in response to questions, they provided answers to which everyone who was equally knowledgeable in an area gave assent. Similarly, much earlier than this, men learned to compute, and mathematics also enjoyed spectacular success in answering questions.

While it is a mistake to think that the sciences and mathematics will provide the answers to questions that philosophers have dealt with unsuccessfully, a look at these areas of knowledge can be helpful. In the first place, they provide us with models that we may attempt to emulate, in a limited fashion. That is to say, we may see demonstrated in these fields the possibility that questions can be answered in a satisfactory way. It is possible to establish reliable bodies of knowledge.

To get at the reason for the spectacular success of the sciences in establishing reliable bodies of knowledge, and the contrasting lack of success in philosophy, we might look at the organization of knowledge. One way of organizing what we know is by content. On this basis, what we know about heavenly bodies is generally regarded as astronomy, what we know about plants is botany, what we know about animals is zoology, etc. Whenever questions arise, we may look at what the question is about, i.e., its content, and know whom we may assign it to for answering.

But there is another way of viewing knowledge than on the basic content. We may also organize knowledge according to how new knowledge is obtained. Organized in this fashion, there is that knowledge which is established by empirical observation. There is also the knowledge that is established by calculation and deduction. Now, when questions arise, we may examine the question to see what method is appropriate for establishing an answer. If the question is to be answered by observation, it becomes a question to be answered by one of the empirical sciences. If a question is to be answered by calculation, or deduction, we may assign it to the appropriate mathematician or logician.

Unfortunately, this does not cover all questions that may be raised. While questions of fact may be answered by scientists, (or occasionally by common sense), and questions of numerical or logical nature may be answered by the mathematician or logician, there are questions that have never been answered by these methods. There is good reason for suspecting that such questions never will be, indeed cannot be, answered in such a fashion. Our problem, the problem of philosophy, then becomes that of finding an appropriate way of answering such questions. Among these questions are such questions as: Is there a god? What is the right way to live? When did time begin? What is the nature of the mind, or self? etc. What may become clear is that we have known for some time how to answer such questions. How is it possible for us to have come across the appropriate method unawares? The answer may lie in the fact that the method used has not given the answer that was desired. In fact, the answer may not have been recognized as the appropriate answer because it was not even in the form that was expected. Despite this type of disappointment, it would seem reasonable to think that once a question has been laid to rest, once we have given the only answers possible, we should regard the question as appropriately answered.

What is surprising is that despite the failure of traditional philosophy to provide satisfactory answers to questions by the methods used, we have gone on expecting those methods to yield reliable results. Every shred of evidence is to the contrary. Further, despite the lack of reliability of such answers as have been provided, we have continued to regard them as seriously as though they constituted reliable bodies of knowledge. In the realm of science, such unreliable knowledge does not receive our serious consideration and does not survive. If it does survive, it is only as an historical curiosity. Yet, in philosophy, we continue to accord respectability to knowledge that is demonstrably and clearly unreliable. If the candidates for acceptance as appropriate answers which follow are regarded as unsatisfactory it may be pointed out that while less satisfying to some, they are at least as satisfactory as any answers provided by the traditional methods.

II

The traditional philosophers were trying to do for the universe as a whole what science tries to do for limited parts of the universe which we encounter. The problems which engaged their attention looked, at least superficially, like the problems that scientists came to deal with. As has been indicated earlier in this chapter, and in preceding chapters, no alleged solution of the problems offered by philosophers has ever satisfied more than a handful of believers.

Certain problems have consistently plagued the followers of the various philosophic positions, surviving all efforts at their eradication. Some of the problems are peculiar to particular attempts at philosophizing, while others haunt the general effort to "account for" the universe. It would require several volumes to offer criticisms of the various individual attempts to do philosophy. In fact, most efforts at doing philosophy include in them the criticism of other positions. Consequently, one can preview many of the problems in the systems devised by traditional philosophers by reading the works of other philosophers. There are a few general observations that might be offered however.

One problem that has bothered traditional philosophers has been their inability to establish indubitable knowledge about the world, despite their claims to be able to do this and repeated claims that it had been done. In idealism, for example, it was asserted that reality was constituted by a realm of ideas that were forever beyond mere experience. There were variations in this theme as various idealists saw and tried to overcome flaws in the position which another had taken.

The problem which the traditional idealist faced was pretty much one of his own concoction. In positing his realm of transcendental reality, he had guaranteed that it could never be confirmed nor refuted. Not only could we not be sure of what such a universe was like; we could not even confirm the existence of it. The realists seemed to avoid this problem by labeling as "real" the everyday world reflected in our sensations. But again, despite the switch to a universe of physical existence and energy, reality was again placed outside the realm of human experience. All that human beings could have were sensory experiences, and these were not what the realist saw as reality. Reality lay beyond, and outside, and independent of sensory experience. Yet all we could confirm having were experiences which we might label as "seeing things," "feeling things," etc. But we had no way of confirming the existence of this reality that was "out there." Yet, idealists and realists alike went on insisting that reality was out there and giving varied, conflicting and unconfirmed "reports" of what it was like.

In the area of knowing, or epistemology, we similarly encounter problems that have outlived efforts at solution. In the case of the idealists, knowing is supposed to be a process of introspection. The problem with such personal ways of knowing is that they do not enable us to establish which from among competing systems deserves our attention. If one personal "account" comes into conflict with another, which is to be taken seriously? Since both have used the same method, there is no basis for choosing between them.

Realists suffer from problems in this area also. The realists purports to give us a way out of the idealist's dilemma by suggesting that we check our ideas against reality. But, as was noted earlier, we have no way of knowing what this reality is "really" like. We can confirm nothing beyond having sense experiences. The realist's theory is called a correspondence theory. Truth is said to be what corresponds with reality. One problem is in knowing what "reality" is. The other is in figuring out what the realist means by "corresponds with." Is he suggesting that an idea is identical with an object? No, he clearly distinguishes between the idea and the thing. They are not identical. Does he mean similar to, like a photograph is similar to a scene? In what sense is it similar? Does the idea look like the object? What, then, do ideas look like? Is it the same shape, size, color, etc.? Apparently not, since ideas appear to be "in us," while things are external. The test that the realist establishes, then, for distinguishing between true or false ideas, appears to come to nothing.

The existentialist is not bothered by any of this because he makes reality a personal matter; reality resides in the individual. As for knowing, he makes no distinction among knowing, believing and feeling. On this basis, the existentialist could not distinguish between what he means by "real" and such things as dreams, hallucinations, imagination, etc. Similarly he cannot distinguish between knowing and neurotic, or psychotic, symptoms or episodes. This may not bother the existentialist greatly, despite its being the height of egocentrism. But the existentialist has created problems for himself where none are necessary.

Much of his "philosophy" turns out on examination to be merely an unusual manipulation of symbols, but he is not alone in this. In the case of epistemology, for example, the content of the existentialist's position is simply that he has chosen to give such a broad definition to the term "knowing" that it encompasses a range of acts from what might generally be regarded as knowing to psychotic episodes. In other words, he has given no information, nor made any discoveries, about knowledge. He has simply chosen to use a symbol in an unusual manner. The problem that he has created for himself are that people will frequently be misled when he talks about knowing, and he, himself, will now have to coin new words when he wishes to make distinctions among what is generally regarded as knowing, believing, and being neurotic. Unfortunately, there is no corresponding gain for this loss in his ability to communicate effectively.

The pragmatist is accused of solving some of these problems by turning his back on them. Certainly he does not devote his energy to developing systems of metaphysics. He regards such problems as verbal problems, or occasionally as nonsense, and simply concentrates on trying to make his meaning clear. In the area of truth and knowledge, he holds that anything we establish is at best tentative and tenuous. He has a tendency to slide from metaphysics into epistemology, and to see knowledge not as something "out there" to be discovered, nor even as an account of what is out there. Rather, it is a tentative structuring of our own experiences. To some, those whom James called the "tender minded," such an open-ended view is hardly tolerable, particularly when one is engaged in a quest for certainty.

Such are some of the problems of traditional philosophy. Generally, they relate to the methods that have been used. These methods in turn, appear to be related to the notion that philosophers entertained that they were to answer questions in essentially the same way as questions were answered in the sciences. It was assumed that they were able to provide a body of knowledge of a positive kind like that in the sciences, and this has proved to be manifestly false.

Many efforts were made to solve these problems by solving the general problem which philosophers faced, that of arriving at an appropriate method for answering questions. Noticing that the traditional methods failed, some philosophers, e.g., Locke and Kant, attempted to solve the problem in a different manner. They wondered if such problems as those which perennially plagued philosophers might be beyond the limits of human knowledge. Therefore, they set out to explore the powers of the human mind. This proved to be as controversial as any other efforts. As some philosophers pointed out, we could not know the limit to thought unless we could think beyond such a limit.

Others, however, saw the problem in a different light.[1] They saw that what we were faced with was not attempting to carry understanding beyond the limits of the human mind. What the metaphysician was guilty of was producing sentences which failed to meet the conditions under which an utterance can be said to be meaningful. What we were dealing with, it was asserted, were problems of

1. See for example, A.J. Ayer, *Language, Truth, and Logic* (New York: Dover Publications, 1946).

meaning, verbal problems rather than genuine issues. The appropriate way to solve these problems then was through the analysis of questions and their answers. Consequently, the nature and function of philosophy changed from providing systems of metaphysics, epistemology, and axiology, to the analysis of statements.

III

Basic to the questions of meaning are the criteria by which we can determine whether or not statements are meaningful. The criterion by which we test statements for their significance (meaning), is the principle of verifiability. This criterion requires that in order for a sentence to be meaningful, we must know how to verify what the sentence expresses. That is to say, we must know what observations could lead us to accept the sentence as true, or to reject it as being false. Perhaps some consideration of conclusions that have been established about language will help to make this principle clear and also indicate its connection to those problems that have traditionally plagued philosophers.

To begin at the most basic level, we may see that words are symbols. Their being symbols means that they stand for, or represent things, but are not the things themselves. It is we who assign the sounds and printed symbols to things; words do not choose themselves. This means that meaning does not inhere in words. Words have no meaning beyond what we give them. On this basis, it would be more accurate to say *"We* mean," than to say *"Words* mean."

Since words have only those meanings which we give, we are free to give any meaning we wish. Philosophers call this our "freedom of stipulation." In stipulating meanings for words, or choosing those meanings that have been stipulated, we sometimes disagree about meanings. In the event that this occurs, we can generally resolve such disputes by checking to see how the words are usually used. This is called *referring to the standard of common usage, or the appeal to the standard example.* This is not the same thing as looking a word up in a dictionary. It means checking to see what sort of things words are usually about.

An example of this may be seen in the case of Susan Stebbing's "correcting" the amateur philosophizing of Sir Arthur Eddington, English physicist. In *The Nature of the Physical World*, Eddington pointed out that things like tables and floors were not really solid after all. They were composed of particles separated by space; indeed there was much more space than particles, and the particles were all in motion. It was really remarkable, he asserted, that they supported our weight. Stebbing refuted this piece of linguistic naivete by pointing out that the word "solid" takes its meaning from its application to things like tables and floors; that the use of the term solid in no way denied the physicist's description of matter; and, that if these things were not solid, then nothing is, since it is by reference to such things that we assign its meaning to solid. If it did not apply to these, then it had no application at all and no meaning at all.

Now, this also illustrates that when people deal with meaning, we cannot always be sure, in advance, of what they are dealing with. When someone asks the question: What is the meaning of . . .?, we cannot always be sure of what he is asking for. If someone raises a question about the meaning of life, he might be asking for a list of characteristics which define the term, or he might be asking about the use of the words, or he might simply be trying to elicit some statement of consecration and sanctification.

The same thing may be said of "What is . . .?" questions. Generally, however, when people raise questions such as "What is X?," they are simply asking for a definition of the term. This is true also of statements like: What is the nature of X? or, What is the essence of X? In fact, the addition of the terms "nature of" or "essence of" adds nothing to the cognitive content of the question: "What is . . .?" A simple check will reveal that all three forms of the question are answered in identical fashion. Such questions are always answered by giving the defining characteristics of the term. Let us review what we mean by defining characteristics.

In getting at the meaning of terms, we can give several types of definitions. One of the ways we clarify meaning is by listing the defining characteristic in the term. As was explained earlier, a defining characteristic is a characteristic in the absence of which the word would not be applicable to the thing. Having three (3) sides would be a defining characteristic of a triangle, whereas being large would be merely an accompanying characteristic.

In defining words in this manner, we must avoid making definitions so broad that they include things that we do not intend to include. On the other hand, we must not make the definition so narrow that it excludes things which we wish to have included. Further, our definitions must cover possible as well as actual cases. And we must distinguish between defining characteristics and universally accompanying characteristics. To avoid this latter problem, we still raise the same question. If this characteristic were removed, would we still call it an X, even though this characteristic always accompanies X? If the answer is yes, then we have an accompanying characteristic.

Now, disputes will arise over whether X "really" is whatever we claim, or about the nature of, or essence of X. Quarrels will arise over whether this thing is really an X. All such disputes, it should be remembered, are merely, verbal disputes. All that is ever established when one establishes "the nature of," or "the essence of," X is a decision about the way we wish to use the term "X."

It might also be wise to remember that when the defining characteristics of X have been given, this does not exhaust all possible statements about X. X still has accompanying characteristics, and these must be kept in mind if we're to understand X. Another significant distinction between defining and accompanying characteristics is that when we are dealing with defining characteristics, we are dealing with words, whereas, when we use the accompanying characteristics, we are referring to things.

"Pencils are cylindrical objects with graphite centers whose purpose is writing," is listing the defining characteristics of the term "pencil" and tells simply how I plan to use the word. "Some pencils are large and some pencils are small" is referring to the accompanying characteristics of pencils, and gives me information about the *things* called "pencils."

Other ways of defining terms include *denotation*. Occasionally when called upon to define a term, you may not have clearly in mind the defining characteristics, or what combination and number of characteristics it takes in order to define the term. However, there is a way out of this problem of knowing but not being able to say. You simply point out examples of the things which the word names. One of the problems of denotative definitions is that we may agree on what things we use a word to denote, but may disagree on why, (i.e., we disagree on the conditions of applicability, or on what constitutes the defining characteristics.)

Agreeing on definitions, however, proves nothing. When we have resolved our dispute about what "education" *really* is, we have simply agreed on how we plan to use the term. In distinguishing between the characteristics that define education and training, we simply settle on the different ways in which we will use these terms. Also, we have not brought anything into existence simply by defining it, nor have we proved anything about whether a thing "really" exists, by this method.

As words are symbols for things, so sentences are symbols for states of affairs. Many of the things that have been said about words could also be applied to sentences. For example, meaning does not inhere in sentences, sentences have whatever meaning we assign to them. When we wish to check this meaning, we may question the person using the sentence. He may reply by simply uttering a different, but equivalent sentence. This is similar to giving a word-word definition.

Another and more useful way of getting at the meaning of a sentence is to check to see what would verify whatever is asserted in the sentence. When we know how a sentence is verified, we know its meaning. This does not mean that the sentence must be actually verified, but simply that it is capable, at least in principle, of being verified. For example, if someone asserts that "The physical world is a world of illusion only," we can find meaning in this only if we know how to go about verifying it. Now, in the case of the assertion listed, there are no possible experiences that anyone could engage in that would either confirm or refute what the sentence asserts. We cannot conceive any possible state of affairs that would either confirm or refute the statement. Therefore, the statement must be regarded as being meaningless.

Since sentences are about, or represent, or stand for states of affairs, we must know what state of affairs a sentence is about or grant that it is meaningless for us. It is not enough simply that every word in the sentence have a meaning. *All* must have meaning in the context in which they occur, and together they must be about some possible state of affairs. This does not rule out the use of language in a poetic or metaphoric fashion. Such sentences may appear, initially, to be meaningless, but examination will reveal that they are translatable into the ordinary idiom. An example from the work of a German writer Heidegger will illustrate some of what has been said.

> What is the nothing? Does the nothing exist only because the not, i.e., negation, exists? Or do negation and the not exist only because the nothing exists? We maintain: The nothing is more primitive than the not and negation. We know the nothing. The nothing is the simple negation of the totality of being. Anxiety reveals the nothing. The nothing itself nots.[2]

2. Quoted in Paul Marhenke, "The Criterion of Significance," in Leonard Linsky (ed.), *Semantics and the Philosophy of Language* (Urbana, U. of Ill. Press, 1952), p. 148.

The sentences in the above quotation are not themselves about any states of affairs, nor can they be translated into the ordinary idiom. No conceivable state of affairs could confirm or refute anything in them. Therefore, they must be regarded as meaningless. This is the problem of those assertions that turn out, on examinations to be metaphysical utterances. It is not, as some writers have asserted, that they are beyond the comprehension of the human mind. Rather, they are, on one basis or another, simply devoid of meaning.

Frequently, in the past, traditional philosophers have puzzled themselves over such sentences as Hegel's "Being and nothing are one and the same." In fact, there are many sentences in which the word "Being" occurs that have attracted the attention and taken the time and effort of philosophers who have pondered over them. All of the words in sentences such as Hegel's can have meaning. But they do not have meaning in such sentences, and therefore the sentences are meaningless. Inevitably, in such sentences, terms like "Being" and "Nothing" are treated like substantive entities, and this creates confusion.

Imagine, for example, a room filled with chairs that had nothing except "Being." That is their sole characteristic. They have no other characteristics at all. No shape. No size. No color. No texture, etc. They have only "Being." What would be the difference between those chairs and no chairs at all? No difference? Then to talk about "Being" in such fashion is to talk about nothing at all. Yet, Hegel denied that this was what he meant.

Occasionally, words will be added to sentences that purport to change the meaning of the sentence. Examination may reveal however that nothing has been added. Let us compare, for example, two sentences such as "It is raining," and "It is true that is is raining." How would one go about verifying the first sentence? Obviously, by going outside and checking to see if we experienced those sensory experiences that would confirm or refute, i.e., verify the statement. Now, how would we go about verifying the second sentence? In precisely the same way. What is the meaning of the two sentences? It is the same, since the verification is the same.

The point of all of this is that many of the problems that have consistently plagued traditional philosophers have been problems of meaning and nothing more. Consequently, analysis, and criticism and clarification can frequently clear up the problem by showing what sentences mean, or by showing that statements are meaningless.

IV

It may also be instructive to examine questions in some detail, since the traditional problems of philosophy are put in the form of questions. Further, philosophers have been purported to be able to answer questions about "the whole of reality," yet have consistently been unable to provide reliable answers. Some examination of questions, and particularly of some of the specific questions which philosophers have attempted to deal with may account for their phenomenal lack of success. Some questions may even be "answered" though not in the fashion which we have been led to expect.

We might note, initially, that questions have an interrogative function if they are genuine. This may seem a truism, but truisms are sometimes true and occasionally, worth repeating. The point of raising questions is to seek some answer, and once the answer has been obtained, the question loses its interrogative function. Having been laid to rest, a question need not be dealt with further. Generally, the only point of dealing with questions after they have been laid to rest is to sanctify and consecrate. This is not to suggest that there is anything wrong with sanctification and consecration. But such activities should not be confused with answering questions.

One other point might be made clear. In education, we use questions frequently when their purpose is not to obtain information in the same sense in which we obtain information in other areas. For example, when we raise such a question of a child as, "In which New England state is Falmouth located?" we do so not to obtain any information about Falmouth or New England, but simply to check the child's knowledge. Such questions have an interrogative function, but it is not the same as when classical philosophers have raised some of the questions which they have raised.

In raising questions, we must have some idea in mind about what would constitute an appropriate answer, if the question is to be a genuine one. Questions, if they are to be meaningful must point toward the answer. If I raise a very simple question: Which of these answers is right, Answer 1 or Answer 2, I know where to look for the answer. I know that one of the two alternatives will be the right answer.

If I raise the question: Which of these answers is right, A1, A2, A3, ... A10, I have farther to look for the answer, but I still know where to look for it. I know that one of the ten possible answers will provide an appropriate response. In a question such as: which of these answers is the correct answer, A1, A2, A3, ... An, the larger the *n*, i.e., the larger the number of possible answers, the more general the question is. Now, when a question becomes so general that it suggests no possible answers, then the question has lost its interrogative function. It is no longer a genuine question. That is to say, if we not only don't know whether an answer is right or wrong, but we don't even know how to tell whether an answer is related to the question, then the question is meaningless.

When answers are provided for questions, we want to be able to know whether the answers are true or false. If we do not know how to check whether an answer is true or false, or beyond this, we are not even sure of its relevance, then the apparent question is a pseudo-question. Such questions may be relatively meaningless, or generally meaningless. Relatively meaningless questions are those which are meaningless only if we, personally, do not have the knowledge which would enable us to recognize an appropriate answer to the question. They may be said to be generally meaningless if they are related to no body of knowledge at all.

For example, someone raises the question: What do you do about fuel mixture control when you're on the downwind leg of the traffic pattern in a Cherokee 180? Let us provide a possible answer to the question. Let us say: Make sure the carburetor heat is full off. Now, unless you happen to be familiar with flying an airplane, you not only do not know whether that answer is true or false. You do not even know whether it's relevant. Not being able to judge whether or not an answer even makes sense, in relation to the question, you must grant that, for you, the question is a pseudo-question, i.e., it is relatively meaningless.

Questions have been raised in the past about which no one is able to determine relevance. Such questions suggest no possible answers, and are related to no existing field of knowledge. Such questions, for example, would be: Are essence and existence identical in God? Or, when did time begin? In the case of the first question, no observations are relevant to confirming or refuting whatever answer might be offered. There is no method of establishing whatever response might be made to it. The reason that no satisfactory answer has ever been provided is that no answer is possible. We do not know what, even in principle, would establish an answer. In the case of the second question, the sense of the question is: what time was it before there was time? Clearly, this question is also unanswerable. The only possible answer that we can give to such questions is, after analysis, to point out that they are meaningless questions.

Now, to respond to such questions with the response that they are meaningless, or are pseudo-questions, is clearly not the sort of answer that the questioners may have been expecting. But when, "That question is nonsense," is the only possible answer to a question, it must be accepted. Clearly, when questions have been seen to be meaningless, they have lost their interrogative function; they have been effectively laid to rest. There is no more that can be done with them. Therefore, they have in that sense been answered, and it is inaccurate to suggest that they are unanswered, or that they continue to puzzle philosophers.

Similarly, when answers to meaningless questions are provided, the responses are equally nonsense. There is no question but that the form of a statement may be changed. The words: Are there flotasogs? may be changed to: There are flotasogs. But there is no more meaning to the group of words than when they were in interrogative form. Before this was established by philosophers, whole books were filled with questions and their corresponding statements that were empty of content. It is interesting to note that even with the change in the nature of function of philosophy from apparently providing answers of a positive sort to an activity of analysis, criticism and clarification, there are still many who continue to indulge in this pasttime of engaging in nonsense. And there are still many, outside the field of philosophy, who take this effort seriously.

When traditional philosophers did engage in their classic enterprise, analysis reveals, what they were engaged in was simply tracing logical connections among statements. By tracing such connections, philosophers often came up with new arrangements of the language. Such new arrangements often led them to believe that they had made exciting new discoveries about the world. No observations ever served to establish their statements, however, and the systems thus developed never satisfied more than a few followers. Their problem was that they were giving no account of anything verifiable.

Some of the problems that were raised and filled philosophers with puzzlement can be dispatched simply with analysis. In the case of questions about reality that differentiate between idealists and realists, philosophers were engaged in searching for answers to questions that can now be laid to rest. For example, if we are engaged in a dispute as to whether a particular airplane is a Cherokee or a Musketeer, we have methods of resolving such disputes. We can examine the airplane under question and on the basis of the shape of the wing, fuselage and tail, the type of engine, etc. If on the other hand, we try to respond to the question of whether the airplane which we perceive is really just a perception, or is objectively real, we have no way to proceed. There is simply no way of establishing one claim over the other, because there is no way to go about verifying either question. Our only possible solution to this "problem" is the recognition that if there is no verification there is no meaning. The only answer to questions about the "reality" of the airplane is that such questions are meaningless.

Now traditional philosophers, and others, will object to their questions being answered in such fashion. Obviously, the answer is not the one expected. But no other answer is possible. The answer effectively lays the question to rest. The question has lost its interrogative function. This is all that we mean by "answering a question." Therefore, the question has been answered. To engage in further responses to it, or reworkings of it, will simply be to engage in sanctification and consecration.

Some will also object to the claim that in their ponderings, philosophers have merely been engaged in tracing logical connections among statements. Generally, such objections will be followed by counter claims that what the philosophers have done is engage in thinking and then clothe their thoughts in words and sentences. Any problems pointed out above are simply problems of language being inadequate to their thought.

Such claims are based on mistaken notion that thought is somehow prior to and independent of language. To check the possibilities of this, one need simply to try thinking without using language, and he will find himself limited to a very primitive level of simply conjuring up "images." Claims about such efforts of philosophers also involve an assumption that meaning somehow inheres in words, that we can simply examine words and statements and have revealed to us truths about the world. This, also, is linguistic naivete.

V

On the basis of what has been considered regarding language, it is reasonable to point out that the questions and statements of metaphysics do not need to concern us. The altered nature and function of philosophy indicates that it is not necessary to engage in doing metaphysics as a first step in doing philosophy of education. Indeed, since metaphysical statements are literally meaningless, there seems little point in concerning ourselves with them on any other basis than analysis, criticism and clarification.

There are those who will object to this, who will claim that we need to get our metaphysics in order before we can proceed to talk about how education should take place. Such claims, however, may be discounted. There is no question but that we proceed on the basis of certain assumptions. At times it may be useful, or important, to examine the assumptions on which we operate, in order to see whether or not they warrant the claims we make. But, this examination of assumptions is an entirely different matter than attempting to establish a system of metaphysics and from this to deduce educational directives.

The other reason for the rejection of metaphysics is that which has been referred to before, *viz.*; that it cannot be claimed to be a reliable body of knowledge. Even were it granted that such statements as those found in metaphysical systems did have cognitive significance, there would still be grounds for rejecting them. These grounds, as has been pointed out earlier, are provided by philosophers themselves. No sooner has each system been offered than it is promptly refuted by another system builder who offers his own set of metaphysical statements. No system offered has ever proved to be publicly testable by experts who are equally knowledgeable in the same field, nor has any system proved to be consistent with everything else that we know. The systems, in fact, have no practical consequences. On these bases, then, we need not take seriously the claims of metaphysicians. The service that has been rendered by the newer approach to philosophy does warrant regarding that with some seriousness.

The foregoing consideration will indicate the further basis for some of the assertions offered in the last section of chapter 3. There, it may be recalled, an alternative position to the traditional one was offered. Connections between metaphysics and education were denied. Indeed the whole notion of establishing something regarded as "philosophical knowledge" from which educational directives would be derived was rejected. With the bases for that position established, we may now further clarify the points of contact between philosophy and education.

As was pointed out in chapter 3, there are no sciences for handling questions of values in education. Many of the problems in education revolve around values. Therefore, this is a fruitful place for philosophy to operate. What philosophy will have to do with such questions as will arise may be seen in what has been established so far. If one expects philosophers to provide answers of a positive kind, he will be disappointed. What philosophy can offer, is what we have seen it offer so far, *viz.*, analysis, criticism, and clarification.

Chapter 6

Axiology: Problems in the Justification of Value Judgements

I

In the realm of values, as in the other traditional areas of philosophy, *viz.*, reality and truth and/or knowledge, philosophers have, since antiquity, promised to give us truths that are certain. Such claims generally are no longer entertained in matters of reality or knowledge. At any rate, when knowledge established by the sciences comes into conflict with what is offered as knowledge by philosophers, it is inevitably and invariably the philosopher who surrenders. What is surprising is that men still entertain the notion that philosophy may provide us with indubitable knowledge in matters of goodness and beauty.

The strange part of this is that, using the empirical sciences as a model, we have come to regard as superstition any tendency to hold beliefs more strongly than evidence warrants. On this basis we have come to dismiss metaphysics as knowledge and do not consider doing philosophy a fruitful endeavor for the establishment of knowledge about reality. All the evidence that we have, *viz.*, centuries of fruitless effort to establish reliable moral knowledge, points to the conclusion that philosophers cannot give us knowledge of the type which has been sought. Yet, despite all the evidence to the contrary, many still cling fondly to the belief that it is only a matter of diligence and perseverence until we are led through philosophy to moral knowledge that is certain.

The fact that philosophers have not succeeded in giving us knowledge of the sort that was expected of them, and there is good reason for believing that they never will, does not rule out any role at all for philosophers. If we do not expect the wrong things of him, the philosopher may have something of great value to offer. Certainly the sciences cannot be of service here, for the methods of science are not appropriate for answering questions about the good life, or settling apparent disputes in matters of taste. What the philosopher will have to offer will come through his role of analyst, critic, and clarifier. He can subject questions and answers to analysis and show, if not the answers we sought, the answers that can be found, or at least where such answers may be found.

What has been suggested is not novel, nor startling. Philosophers have, in fact, been engaged in this sort of pursuit for some time, and have established much in the area of values. The fact that many problems still appear to remain is largely the result of inadequate analysis. It is not that analysis and criticism, and clarification are not appropriate; it is, rather, that they have not been carried far enough. What they have yielded, however, has been most helpful in eliminating false hopes and pointing up where efforts are likely to be fruitless.

It takes little analysis to indicate that we are dealing with different kinds of statements here; i.e., that moral judgements are distinctly different from descriptive statements or statements of fact. If we say, "More engineers and scientists are currently being produced by our schools than ever before in the past, "we know what facts will confirm or refute such statements. Even with such a statement as, "In Pitman, New Jersey there were 432 wooden desks in all the classrooms in 1932," we might not be able to actually gather the facts that would confirm or refute such a statement, but we know what facts would verify it if they were available. But with a statement like, "Even in periods of crisis our schools should not be steered away from humanistic disciplines," it is not clear what sort of facts would establish the truth or falsehood of this statement.

At times, the distinction may become a little blurred because of the form of the statements. If one suggests that, "The diagramming of sentences is a good way of teaching English," his use of the term "good" in one sense, may be verified, and has one sort of meaning. The meaning of "good" in that sense will differ from that in the assertion: "The study of one's language is not simply instrumentally valuable, it is good in its own right." The sort of data that would establish the truth or falsity of the first statement would not even be relevant to the second. Whereas disagreements about the claims made in sentences like the first sentence are resolvable by the amassing of appropriate facts, we have a different sort of problem when disputes arise about sentences of the second type.

One distinction that is often made between such statements is that, it is asserted, statements like the first type give us information about what is. At least as often as not, value judgements, or statements of the second type, do not even purport to give us such information. They are claimed not to be about what is, but about what ought to be. This is not held to be true of all value judgements, however. There are those who would claim that statements like "Ms. A is beautiful" does give information and can indeed be proved to be true or false. What has not been made clear, however, is what sort of evidence is relevant. We are not sure of how we can tell when such a statement is true, or indeed, if it is even appropriate to say of it that it is true or false.

There is a level at which there appears to be agreement. There is no question about the fact that I not only "know" certain things, but I also have feelings about them. Not only do we have feelings, but we seem to believe that it is perfectly "reasonable" to express such feelings. In the process of such expressions, we often render judgements. There is no quarrel about this. People seem to agree that it is appropriate to use such terms as "good," "bad," "beautiful," "ugly," "moral," "immoral," "should," "ought," and the like. When disagreements arise, they do not appear to arise, at this level.

Rather than give us a final and absolute answer to questions about the Good Life or about the *Summum Bonum*, philosophy serves in its analytic role to indicate to us wherein disputes about values do arise. Analysis indicates that disagreements arise over either or both of two points. The first is what we have said of something when we have said of it that it is good, right, or moral. The second point over which we may disagree is about what things we ought to call by those names. In other words, disagreements about values will arise over meaning or over the application of terms, or both.

In instances of the first sort, we may disagree in the following manner. I may suggest that a particular action is good, and by that term mean that whatever action is under consideration is generally valued in our society, or by most of mankind. Another may use the same term and mean by "good" that the action which we are assigning is good in that it is consistent with revealed divine will. Or, by "good," I might mean simply an accepted tradition or more, while someone else means by "good" that an act is legal. Or, outside of all of these, we may mean simply that the act has consequences which we desire. Even this list does not exhaust the possible meanings of the term.

It is possible for us, however, to come to agreement over how we are using the term, i.e., over what meaning we are giving to it, yet we may disagree over what actions we wish to apply the term to. We may agree that when we use the term "evil" or "immoral," we mean "whatever contravenes divine will." Despite this agreement, you may wish to apply this term to such an act as divorce, while I may insist that such an act is not inconsistent with divine will, i.e., is not evil or immoral.

Perhaps some consideration should also be given to the senses in which people may be said to disagree. Suppose one teacher says, "An eclectic approach to the teaching of basic reading is most effective." A second teacher responds, "No, the method of phonetic analysis will produce more and better readers." Now, both cannot be correct, because, they are making competing, and exclusive, assertions; both could be wrong, however. This type of disagreement is regarded by contemporary philosophers as a *disagreement in belief*, since the two parties to the discussion have attached their loyalty to incompatible statements.

To see a different kind of disagreement, let us look at the following. Teacher A says, "I like the new basic reading instructional materials." Teacher B responds, "I don't because I have never liked having the teacher's manual in a separate volume." There is nothing incompatible about these statements. The first does not deny or contradict the second. Yet there is a sense in which the first teacher is entertaining feelings that are not consistent with those feelings held by Teacher B. Some contemporary philosophers have been calling this a *disagreement in attitude*. What the connections are between disagreements in belief and disagreements in attitude can constitute a lengthy study in itself. It might be noted briefly, however, that the latter can be a "result" of the former.

It might also be instructive to spend a moment on the settlement or resolution of a dispute. Clearly, there are several ways in which this might occur. If you and I disagree over a value, one way of terminating our disagreement is for me to remove you from the scene permanently. This is not being offered with any intention of recommending it as a way of ending disputes, but it does illustrate one method of termination which has on occasion been used. In fact, war represents the institutionalization of this method. Disagreements may also be terminated by one party's persuading another to one point of view, or by correcting the mistaken beliefs on which another has based his belief. This list is not exhaustive, but is merely illustrative. All of these ways may lead to the termination of moral disagreements.

What some will wish to maintain is that such *termination* does not represent *settlement* or *resolution*. They will claim that although one party may be *convinced*, the other party has not *proved* his point. What is not clear is what such a claim asserts. If, in fact, a question has been laid to rest, if it has completely lost its interrogative function, there seems little point in entertaining it further. Indeed, one may wonder what we *could* do further with a question, once it has been answered. What usually happens is that when we continue to entertain questions after they have been effectively dealt with, they become the center of sanctification and consecration. This is not to suggest that sanctification and consecration are to be condemned. We mean only to point out that it is an error to confuse activites of sanctification and consecration with providing appropriate answers to questions.

What has been pointed out is that moral disagreements of various sorts may arise concerning either the meaning of terms or the application of these terms. This is less likely to happen in other areas than values, although it can occur. When it does, there are ways of dealing with it. With some terms, however, it is impossible to separate meaning and application. The meaning of a term like "blue" for example cannot be separated from its application. I can define "blue" meaningfully only by indicating its application. The same is true of proper names. When I am talking about Ms. A, for example, the term has no meaning outside its application.

Value terms are not like these terms, however. It does appear to be possible to separate meaning from application, giving rise to one basis for disagreements. This is not a unique characteristic of value terms, however. Disagreements will arise over meaning and application in areas other than values. Where these disagreements arise in other areas, we have worked out methods of handling the disagreements. If the dispute arises over meaning for example, we can work on establishing a list of defining characteristics. This may not always be easily settled, but at least we can come to be understood. What should also be clear is that this disagreement over meaning is a purely verbal issue.

There are also other ways of handling such disputes. One is simply to consult a dictionary to see meaning in terms of a word-word definition. Another method is to refer to standard usage, what we have called appealing to the standard example. The problem that we face with such an issue, however, is that value terms seem to be more vague than other words. If I say "desk," or "pupil," etc., you have only a vague idea of what I mean. For example, you do not know in the one instance if I mean a metal or wooden desk, a pupil's or teacher's desk, a single or double pedestal desk, etc. Similarly, in the case of the second word, you do not know whether I mean a college or kindergarten pupil, male or female, etc. But despite the vagueness of such words, you have a clearer notion of what I mean when I say "desk" or "pupil," than when I say "good," "moral," etc. This increased vagueness of value terms appears to add to our difficulty, because we're not always clear on what is being asserted.

Not only are such words vague, but the use of value terms itself seems hedged about with values. We have feelings about how such words get used. When a dispute arises over the meaning of a word, we may use a dictionary, or rely on an appeal to the standard example; even point out that the word has never before been given the meaning which our opponent is giving it. Yet, he still may insist that his use is the proper one, and all other meanings represent misguided uses of the term. What is being asserted in this instance has seemed to be even more difficult to assess.

Beyond showing us where disputes over values arise, philosophic analysis also reveals that when we use terms like "good," "best," etc., we sometimes are referring to *instrumental* goods, and at other times are referring to *intrinsic* goods. *Instrumental* goods are those goods whose value lies in the fact that they are good for something. Intrinsic goods are those goods which are valuable in and of themselves. For example, college seniors interested in obtaining teaching positions value the contracts which they receive. Are the contracts valuable? Of course, Why, or in what sense? Why, because they enable one to work. Is work valuable? Naturally, because working enables one to earn money. What value does money have? Obviously money allows one to purchase goods and services which he has need of and desires. What is good about these goods and services? Well, they lead to one's happiness.

Now in each of the instances above, except the last, we were talking about instrumental goods. The thing under question each time was good in that it led to something else which was valued. In each instance, we could check whether or not the item was good, (had value), by checking to see if it did indeed lead to the thing we claimed. We could empirically check to see if it produced the desired result. But what of the final result in our chain? What would we say to justify calling happiness "good or "valuable"? Here, we appear to have a different sort of problem.

On the basis of the analysis, the justification of instrumental goods appears to be an empirical matter. In education, for example, we might agree that teaching English through the use of linguistics instruction is a good teaching method. By "good" here, is meant effective; i.e., it leads to certain results which are themselves held to be valuable. We can empirically verify such an assertion. Of course, it is not up to the philosopher of education to determine whether or not such a method is in fact a good method. He does not, as a philosopher, have the body of knowledge that would equip him to settle such an issue. It would make sense to call on someone who does have such knowledge, e.g., an educator, psychologist, educational researcher, or other appropriate behavioral scientist. But, such questions can be settled empirically.

The question of whether or not pupils ought to be instructed in English is another matter, however. This issue is not resolvable by the accumulation of the same sort of evidence. There are those who do, in fact, insist that the "real" value in such instruction is its intrinsic value; i.e., they assert that knowledge about one's language is valuable in itself. What is not clear, is how one goes about "proving" such a statement, or resolving the dispute when a disagreement about such a matter arises. Factual evidence does not seem to help. Neither does reference to consequences, since we're talking about intrinsic worth. Logic cannot be used either, unless we're starting with a value judgement, which leaves us still with a justification problem. (This will be explained fully later in the chapter.) One response to this has been the suggestion that such problems cannot be resolved because we have not yet found a method for settling such disputes. Philosophers who suggest this generally urge continuing our search for a solution. A number of efforts at solution have been made, but none has yet won general assent.

II

One effort at solving problems regarding the justification of moral judgements has been referred to as the objectivist approach. It has already been suggested that one of the problems with moral statements is that we're not always sure what is being asserted, since value terms appear to be even more vague than descriptive words. Another of the difficulties with moral statements is the fact that they resemble descriptive statements. It is asserted by some that if we are adequately to account for moral statements, we must include these resemblances in our consideration.

One of the ways in which value statements resemble statements of fact is in linguistic form. The statement "She has blue eyes," looks in form exactly like the statement. "She has beautiful eyes." Or a statement like "Walter Benton has written a book of poems in free verse entitled *This is My Beloved*," clearly resembles the statement that, "Walter Benton has written a book of tender and beautiful love poems entitled *This is My Beloved*," The fact that such statements resemble each other so strongly in form may lead us to the conclusion that all these statements may be treated alike. We may be led to believe that since the first statement is giving objective data about someones eyes, the second sentence performs the same functions. Similarly both the third and fourth sentences may come to be regarded as purporting to give factual information about Benton's book.

We may, in other words, tend to treat all such statements as *objective* statements. "Objective," in this sense, does not *mean* that the statement is a necessarily true statement, nor does it mean that it's a statement for which I have unusually strong evidence. It also, in philosophic use, does not mean that it is being uttered without bias. What is being claimed, when a statement is said to be objective, is that information is being given about something other than my state of mind, or feelings. Objective data would be data that is independent of anyone's feelings about it, or data that is capable of being confirmed, at least in principle, by anyone's observation. Objective statements, in other words, are descriptive statements about a subject rather than expressions of personal private feelings.

Although the similarity in the forms of descriptive statements and value judgements may lead us to treat them all as objective statements, the moral objectivist has other bases than the linguistic form of his moral statements for claiming that such statements can be treated objectively, i.e., proved true or false. In fact, they will frequently argue from the opposite point of view, saying that we do not conclude from the form of moral statements that they are objective, but that we put them in this fact-stating form precisely because we recognize that what such sentences assert is independent of anyone's preference.

The claims of objective theories of values have been put forward on a number of bases. One of these is that we can verify such statements *deductively*, i.e., we can deduce moral prescriptions from statements of fact, or statements that purport to be factual. In other words, from sentences which state what we "know" about man, nature, God, the universe, we can *deduce* values. On this basis, we can confirm or refute value claims, in fact, arrive at knowledge of values that is certain.[1]

Another basis for the claim that moral statements are objective is the claim that we can know values intuitively. People will claim that we *see* values in the same sense in which we *see* other things, i.e., that we can have *perceptions* of values. I certainly need no one to tell me when I am seeing blue. (I am not talking here about using the word "blue"; I mean having a visual experience with an extended patch of color) I know when I am seeing blue. Similarly, I do not need to be told, or have explained to me, when I am seeing good. I can know good by direct intuition. A variation of this claim for intuition is G.E. Moore's argument that moral terms are indefinable, a position which we will shortly take a brief look at.

One piece of evidence sometimes offered for the objectivity of moral terms is that once having learned the meaning of a term like "good," we do not need to be instructed in each new use of it. If we learn to talk about "good" food, a "good" picture, a "good" method of teaching mathematics, we do not need to be instructed in the use of "good" for each new class of words. We are able to use the term for each new class of words for which we have never used it before. "Good" therefore is recognized as having a constant meaning which can be understood regardless of what class of objects is being considered. The meaning of "good" therefore is independent of our feelings. We are talking about an attribute of the object under consideration when we use the word "good" to describe it, the objectivists claim.

In establishing the truth of value statements, we may rely on either or both of two approaches. In the first place, it is claimed, there are necessary connections between some sequences of events. For example, it is not possible to think of a thief without feeling disrespect for him in that aspect. One cannot think of a wife-beater

---

1. One fascinating piece of deduction whereby we arrive at a moral prescription is the following piece of reasoning found in a well-known philosophical treatise. After describing systems of ethics as falling into four classes, definition, descriptions of moral experiences, exhortations to virtue, and actual ethical judgments, these are assigned to particular fields such as philosophy, psychology, sociology, etc. No determination has been offered of the classification of the last class. Clearly, they are not definitions, so they do not belong to ethical philosophy. From the foregoing, we may logically conclude: "A strictly philosophical treatise on ethics should therefore make no ethical pronouncements." This ethical rule, obviously, "objective" and arrived at on the basis of deduction is included in a chapter devoted to refuting claims about the objectivity of moral judgments. The book we are referring to is: A.J. Ayer, *Language, Truth, and Logic* (New York: Dover Publications, 1946), p. 103.

without feeling disapproval. Such moral attitudes are something over which we do not have control. The problem with this account is to determine what the nature of the connection is. As Hume has pointed out about such connections between events, the most that one can ever observe is, not some sort of link, or *nexus*, but simply that whenever one event occurs, the other is present. This is called *constant conjunction*. To claim that events and feelings are constantly conjoined is very difficult to confirm. In the absence of the appropriate feelings, one could hardly claim "Goodness" or "badness" about anything. In fact, the independence of moral qualities from feelings, seems to become lost in this effort to establish the necessity of ethical truths.

It is also claimed that, aside from the necessity of certain sequences, certain moral attitudes may be justified by the fact that statements may be necessitated by other statements. For example, the statement. "A is greater than B," and "B is greater than C" necessitites the statement that "A is greater than C." Now, statements which are not themselves necessarily true may be necessitated by other facts. Therefore, moral statements which are not themselves necessarily true may be necessitated by facts about man, the nature of human nature.

Now, we know in advance of hearing any such arguments that they are doomed to defeat. It is not even necessary to wait for the specific claim to be put forth, we can be assured of its refutation. This was made clear by David Hume more than 130 years ago in his famous *Treatise on Human Nature:*

> In every system of morality, which I have hitherto met with, I have always remarked that the author proceeds for some time in the ordinary way of reasoning, and establishes the being of a God, or makes observations concerning human affairs; when all of a sudden I am surprised to find that, instead of the usual copulations of propositions, *is not*, I meet with no proposition that is not connected with an *ought* or an *ought not*. This change is imperceptible; but is, however, of the last consequence. For as this *ought* or *ought not*, expresses some new relation or affirmation, it is necessary that it should be observed and explained; and at the same time that a reason should be given for what seems altogether inconceivable, how this new relation can be a deduction from others that are entirely different from it.[2]

2. David Hume, *Treatise on Human Nature* (Book III, Part I. Section i).

Hume's point is that we cannot get out of statements what is not in them. For example, if we consider the syllogism that is used to introduce every new student to inference, we can see his point. Consider the following:

All men are mortal: (major premise)
Socrates is a man: (minor premise)

Now from these two premises the conclusion fairly leaps out at us that:

Therefore, Socrates is a mortal.

The reason we can draw this conclusion is because, when we have stated the premise, we have already, as a matter of fact, uttered the conclusion. That is, we can validly draw the conclusion because it was contained in the premises. We could *not* however, validly deduce:

Socrates was good and just; or
We ought to honor Socrates.

The reason we cannot validly deduce such conclusions is because they are not contained in the premises. Similarly, Hume instructs us, we cannot validly deduce *ought* statements from *is* statements. Since there is no *ought* contained in the premises, we know, without seeing any such conclusion, that it cannot be validly drawn.

Occasionally, someone will claim to have drawn such a conclusion. Inevitably and invariably, however, analysis will reveal either that there is some flaw in the logic and the conclusion has not been properly drawn, or that if it is validly drawn, then the premises contain value judgements. The latter simply compounds the problem, for we now have at least two value judgements to justify. Either way, the moral objectivists must surrender their claim. Therefore, Hume's analysis, criticism, and clarification refute all moral theories that claim to derive statements about duty and obligation from statements about God, or the nature of human nature.

In response to this, moral objectivists have sought to maintain their position on other grounds. They claim to have perceptions of values, as was pointed out earlier. The arguments that are usually offered in support of this position generally attempt to establish the reliability of intuition through demonstrating our use of this method. What such arguments point out is that (1) noted authorities in many fields have testified that they have arrived at significant and meaningful ideas through intuition; (2) that in any ethical arguments we must ultimately come to rely on intuition. In fact, all reason comes to rely on intuition. In establishing connections such as A entails B and B entails C, this must either be seen immediately (without mediation) or further argument is required. But further argument can only impose an intervening connection, e.g., A entails X and X entails B, etc., which must then be seen immediately, i.e., grasped intuitively.

What such arguments overlook is the difference between recognizing that intuition does indeed take place,[3] and relying on intuition as a certification of knowledge. To grant that intuition occurs, even that it is a valuable experience, is not to grant that we can rely on it to establish or certify knowledge. The problem with intuition is that people very frequently intuit conflicting values. If you intuit that extramarital sex is to be condemned, and I intuit that it is acceptable, which statement about extramarital sex is to be regarded as "true"? We are left with no method of resolution.

If we compare this to other perceptions, the problem may be seen more clearly. If I insist that the walls of this room are green, and you insist that they are grey, we have methods of resolving such a dispute. Through the use of a color chart, or spectroscopic analysis, the issue can be decided. But there are no such checks for "good," and "moral," etc. Therefore, this claim of the moral objectivist, like the preceding claim, must be rejected.

G.E. Moore, in a variation of this position, has claimed that our problem lies in the indefinability of good. This does not mean that the term is meaningless, but simply that like "green," is not definable in other terms. Such terms represent the simplest kind of quality and cannot be analyzed into anything simpler. Good is a quality which belongs to a thing, and unless one knows what good is, there is no way of telling him. Similarly, we cannot "explain" what green is. If Moore is really talking about good as an attribute of something, then he overlooks a very important distinction between good and green. If a dispute arises over whether or not an object has the latter characteristic, there are ways of confirming or refuting the assertion. There are no such tests for verifying the claimed attribute of goodness. If by "green" he means the visual sensation which someone experiences, and it is to this that he compares good, then he can no longer regard good as an attribute of the thing.

One other method of establishing values requires consideration. In this view, objectivity has a dual aspect. Not only are terms like

---

3. Intuition in the sense in which it is generally used simply means a sort of inexplicable insight. We move from a premise immediately to a conclusion without going through normally intervening steps.

"good," "moral," "immoral," attributes of things and situations, rather than simply being expressions of anyone's preferences; the meaning of the terms are independently established by the will of God and we come to know through revelation. The goodness of any acts or situations can be judged, not in terms of preferences, or even of consequences. Goodness is established through consistency with objective moral codes, such as the Decalogue. The problem with such a position is that God appears to reveal himself in conflicting ways. Not only do we find differences between such religious groups as Christians and Moslems, but Catholic and Protestant Christians will disagree, and Protestant groups quarrel among themselves over values, each claiming to have the divine route to truth.

III

There are philosophers who agree with Moore that "good" is indefinable. Their agreement is only apparent, however, for what they insist is that good is meaningless. It designates nothing at all in the thing it is purported to be about. Statements about "right" and "good" assert nothing true nor false, since they are merely exclamations that express feelings. Certainly, if there are similarities between moral judgements and descriptive statements, there are also resemblances between value statements and subjective statements of preference. The most telling resemblance, subjectivists claim is that with value statements, as with subjective statements of preference, we cannot adduce evidence to "prove" our statements.

If we take three statements:

    (1) War is inconsistent with international law;
    (2) War is hell;
    (3) War is immoral;

it is clear that the first statement is one which can be verified. Whether it is true or not, is not the point; the point is that we can check the truth of the statement, present evidence and conclude that despite our feelings about it, the statement is either true or false. In the case of the second statement, it is obviously meaningless to call for evidence to "prove" it true or false. It merely represents the expression of someone's emotional state. (Actually, two subjective accounts are available, as we shall shortly see.) But what of the third statement? It is certainly not like the first, in that evidence that would be accepted generally cannot be produced. Does this not simply place the third statement in the same category as the second?

Moral subjectivists assert that it does; that there is no increment of meaning in the third statement beyond whatever is in the second.

Perhaps, some consideration of the various uses of language will help to make the position of the moral subjectivist clear, and will further distinguish his position. One use of the language of course is to communicate facts; to convey information. This is the *descriptive* or *informative* use of the language. Such statements are sometimes called "is" statements to indicate that they purport to say what a situation is. Such statements are generally about observable facts of experience. This is also called the "fact-stating" use of the language.

A more primitive level of language usage is to express or evince our feelings. This is called the *expressive* or *emotive* use of the language. Such usage does not include those statements in which we state what our feeling is; i.e., this does not include descriptions of our feelings. The expressive use of language is on the order of the dog wagging his tail or the cat purring. It is exemplified by utterances like, "ah" or "ouch." Not all expressive statements are that simple, but they are distinguished from those sentences in which we purport to describe our feelings. When I claim "I've got nothing against that damned jerk!" in an emotionally charged tone, the expressive content of the statement is clearly distinguishable from the description of my feeling that is being offered. We can also express or evince our emotional state with scowls, blushes, cheers, boo's, etc. While some will call such statements meaningless, others will insist that they are informative to the extent that they give information about the speaker's emotional state. These represent the two subjectivist accounts mentioned earlier.

A third use of the language is its *persuasive* or *imperative* use. It's very difficult at times to separate out this sort of statement from the expressive use of the language. Indeed, it may be noted, expressive or emotive, statements do seem to have some persuasive impact. The most direct and obvious characteristic of persuasive statements that is not claimed for emotive or expressive statements is that whereas the latter only express or evince the speaker's feelings, the former is intended to arouse an emotion, or stimulate the activity of the listener. Such statements are not always obviously persuasive, since we can sometimes more effectively sway another by disguising our intent and offering our emotive or our persuasive statement as though it were descriptive.

Now, the point of the foregoing is simply to make clear the position of the moral subjectivist, who asserts that the only content of moral statements is their emotive and persuasive content. Actually, to be more precise, since some statements contain elements of all three (i.e., description, expression, and persuasion), it might be better to say that the moral content of statements adds nothing to the cognitive content of statements. The cognitive content of "You acted immorally in stealing that book" is no different from the cognitive content of the sentence, "You stole that book," uttered in a tone that evinced disapproval.

Bertrand Russell points out that no amount of evidence can resolve questions of good, and that all that disputants ever offer are appeals to emotions. He insists that questions of values lie not only outside the realm of the sciences, but also wholly outside the domain of knowledge. Assertions of value are not assertions about facts which would still be true if our feelings were different. In fact, Russell insists that ethics is related to politics; that ethics simply represents our attempt to give universal significance rather than merely personal meaning to our desires.[4]

What objectivists claim, and what subjectivists deny, is that normative ethical statements are reducible to empirical statements that can be verified. The moral subjectivist denies that moral (or esthetic) statements are genuine synthetic statements. Such statements are indeed, they claim, unanalyzable, but not because they contain terms which are simple, but because value concepts are pseudo concepts. This accounts for the fact that ethical symbols add nothing to the factual content of statements.

Similarly, if someone utters a statement like, "Adultery is immoral," this is a sentence which, in one sense of the subjectivist view, contains no factual content. It is as though I had simply uttered the word "Adultery!" with a particular tone of disdain in my voice. It is not appropriate, then to describe such sentences as either true or false, since they assert nothing. There is no descriptive content to be verified. If someone responds with what appears to be disagreement, i.e., makes a remark of moral approval, there is no contradiction. The two speakers may quarrel, but there is no genuine dispute, and their quarrel is simply over moral sentiments. It would not make sense to claim that either is right. When a third party to such a situation does declare one or the other of the two persons to be "right," he is using "right" in its ethical sense and adds nothing to the argument except his own moral sentiments.

In this view, there is no criterion for determining the validity of moral statements. Since the sentences make no assertions, actually

4. Bertrand Russell, *Religion and Science* (Cambridge: Oxford University Press, 1935).

state nothing at all, it makes no sense to look for truth or falsehood. Since they do not say anything, these sentences are expressions purely of feeling and are no more verifiable than expressions like "ah" or "ouch." There is no distinction, cognitively, between the statements "X is disapproved," "X is wrong," and "X is immoral." Whatever difference there is lies solely in the varying power of these statements to elicit feelings or stimulate action in others. In other words, the only difference is that some statements are more persuasive than others.

Some philosophers raise objections to such a view of value judgements on the grounds that we could then not argue about or dispute matters of morals. Moore, and others suggest that we do in fact argue, and not merely disagree, about matters of morals, whereas we disagree but do not argue about matters of taste. Therefore, it is argued moral statements do differ from expressions of preference. The philosophers who put forth this argument, however, never get beyond the mere *assertion* of the point. They never demonstrate it. In such an assertion, they appear to be assuming the point to be proved.

When arguments are offered, they are generally in the following vein. It is pointed out that when two statements are identical, any facts that disprove one will disprove the other. For example, take the two statements: "San Francisco is larger than New York," and "New York is smaller than San Francisco." Whatever facts are adequate to prove that the first statement is false will also prove that the second statement is false. The two sentences, "New York is an interior city," and "New York is the capital city of New York state," do not mean the same thing. The set of facts that disproves one is not relevant to refuting the other. What moral objectivists want to assert is that there is a similar distinction between the sentences "X is disapproved," and "X is immoral." It is easy to see, they claim, that the facts that establish the first statement are not the facts that would establish the other. But this clarity is present only in the person making the claim that there is a difference. The argument assumes precisely what needs to be proved. The moral subjectivist's very point is that whatever is offered to establish the first statement is all that can and will be offered to support the second. It is only when we are convinced that there is a difference between the two statements that it will be "clear" to us that different facts establish the "different" statements.

As for the notion that we disagree, and do not merely argue about matters of value, (i.e., that our disagreements are disagreements in belief not disagreements in attitude), this similarly assumes the point to be proved. Analysis of the arguments will indicate that wherever the dispute moves beyond disagreement in attitude, it involves us in questions other than questions of values. We will be found either to be arguing empirical points or matters of logic.

When we do seem to engage in disputes over values, we will find, in the first instance that our arguments, if they are not merely verbal, (i.e., solely about meaning) will be about matters of fact. When we engage in argument and attempt to persuade our adversary to join our position, we do so by trying to demonstrate that he is wrong about the facts. We do not hold values in a vacuum. Our beliefs in the realm of values are based on the holding of certain other beliefs. It is about the latter beliefs, the "facts" of the case, that we will argue. Or, in another instance rather than arguments arising relating to the source or bases of our values, they will arise over what is anticipated as outcomes, i.e., over consequences.

On the other hand, we also engage in arguments about the logic of our value judgements. This occurs, however, only where there is some basic agreement on matters of value, or where certain values are assumed. In such instances what is presupposed is that both parties will agree that a particular system of values is indeed established. The argument will then be about whether some act, A, is indeed an instance of a particular type, T, the latter being an assumed system.

Outside of such arguments about values, the only kinds of disagreements we engage in, the subjectivists assert, are claims about the superiority of our moral system over that of another. But such arguments, consist merely of laudatory statements about one's own value system, and derogatory statements about our opponent's. But, such statements are themselves matters of preference only and incapable of establishment by any arguments.

One type of meaning is asserted by certain moral subjectivists for their value judgements. This is the claim, mentioned in a number of places and now simply made explicit, that the meaning of moral statements is their descriptive content concerning the emotional state of the person making the statement. In this sense, it is *conceivable* that moral statements might indeed be proved true or false. The type of evidence that would be adduced to verify such statements, however, would be in the realm of psychology rather than philosophy. This is in no sense a way of "hedging" on this issue, for indeed, the only answer that the philosopher can give to certain questions after he has analyzed them, is that they lie outside the realm of philosophy. If this is the answer to which philosophic analysis leads, then it must be the answer that is given.

IV

It was suggested earlier that the problems in ethics that have perennially plagued philosophers were the result, for the most part, of inadequate analysis. This is not to suggest that, pushed far enough, analysis will yield indubitable information about the good life. But analysis can indicate the nature of the problems we face and what sort of answers are available, or where we may look for certain answers. Critical analysis has been of some value, as the preceeding pages illustrate. What is of the most enduring value has not been this or that moral code, or any particular system of ethics. The most permanent feature of ethics has been its method, *viz.*, critically analyzing moral problems and looking for ways of resolving moral disputes.

A search of the views and concerns expressed in ethical discussion reveals that in all the talk about justifying value judgements, one term has remained unanalyzed. It appears to have been assumed that the meaning of "justification" inheres in the term itself. Consequently, traditional philosophers have engaged in a search without ever clarifying what the object of the search is. Moral objectivists claim to have solved the problem by "proving" their value claims by logic or intuition. Yet, as has been demonstrated, there are flaws in both attempts. Moral subjectivists, on the other hand, have tended to "solve" the problem by dismissing it. Their claim that value judgements are subjective expressions of preference, or at most statements describing one's emotional state, "solve" problems of moral disagreement by attempting to show that there really are not disputes at all.

While the position of the moral objectivist seems clearly to have been refuted, the view of the subjectivist has not been dealt the same blow. Those who argue against moral subjectivism will assert that equating statements like "X is disapproved" and "X is immoral" does not adequately account for the meaning of the latter, but this is never demonstrated. No one has ever yet indicated what increment of meaning the second statement adds to the first. The moral subjectivist seems to come out of the fray battered but not destroyed. Still, there is some basis for indicating that while there is a certain truth to the position of the moral subjectivist, the view does not give the whole truth. If the holding of beliefs on insufficient evidence constitutes superstition, then moral behavior is unavoidably superstitious and irrational, if such beliefs can have no meaning.

It must be granted that if I make a statement like "You have blue eyes," this has a content, contains an assertion for which evidence can be adduced to prove it true or false. If we disagree, the dispute can be resolved through the introduction of empirical data. Clearly, the statement, "You have *beautiful* eyes," while resembling the preceding statement in structure, is a different sort of statement. The evidence required to support it may differ from that required for the other statement. Yet, to dismiss the statement regarding beautiful eyes as meaningless is to miss a very significant point.

If there is doubt that the statement "You have beautiful eyes" has meaning, try the following experiment. Find a particularly attractive person of the opposite sex, fix your gaze on them, gaze deep into the eyes and say "You have beautiful eyes." Whatever ensues will lend support to the notion that such statements are, in some way, interpersonal. Yet, one must grant that there is not the same objectivity in that statement as there is in the other. It does not seem to work either to claim objectivity or to dismiss as meaningless.

If such problems revolve in part about the lack of clarity of the term "justification," then it would seem to be fruitful to clarify that term. We would seem to know what we're talking about if in one instance of a remark about beautiful eyes we declared it to be justified and in another we felt it were not justified. What most philosophers appear to have been looking for, those who were not completely mystified by the term, is some type of "blessing" or assurance, or confirmation that would for all time, with absolute certainty, justify all value judgements. What they appear to have been searching for, in other words, is some meta-ethical principle that would warrant all principles. Or, they have been searching, if not for a principle, then for a meta-ethical system that would authorize or sanction any moral utterance that might be encountered.

It might be pointed out that traditional philosophers engaged in the same search in the physical realm until it became evident that not only was there no hope of finding a metaphysical system or principle that everyone would accept, there was also no need of such a system or principle. Whatever questions of a sensible nature arose in the physical realm were answerable by observation of one type or another without any need for some overriding, all-encompassing principle or system. Science, for example, operates in a spectacularly successful way without any warrant or grounds from metaphysics. Whatever would warrant dismissing metaphysics as being meaningless, or insignificant, and unnecessary would seem adequate grounds for sending meta-ethics down the same route. The most interesting feature of suggestions that value judgements ought to be justified is that no one ever attempts to justify this moral *dictum* to end all moral *dicta*.

If the model is followed that is set in the domain of empirical knowledge, it will be seen that all that is required is to deal success- fully with questions that really arise. In ethics, the only questions that need to be dealt with are those represented by the general question: What ought I to do in this situation? We are never faced with questions of a type of ultimate justification outside of certain philosophy courses.

The only sensible meaning that would be assigned to the term "justification," then, would be: that which satisfactorily resolves value disputes that actually arise, or that which satisfactorily answers questions which actually arise. The only such questions are those variants of what is good, or right? or put another way, what ought to be done in this situation? These are only questions that need to be dealt with.

In the empirical realm, if I raise the question of an astronomer: What is the distance from earth to Antares? he merely replies in light years. If he were to, instead, engage in a lecture as to whether or not there really were an earth and an Antares, or whether distance "really existed," we should think him a strange fellow indeed. In- stead, he gives us the answer in light years and once the response has been given, no further answer is required. He does not need to give any metaphysical "justification" for his answer. The same thing may obtain in the realm of values. Once a question has been answered, there is no need to entertain it further, nor to bring in answers to questions that are not, in fact, raised.

The reason that both moral objectivism and moral subjectivism, as these have been handled traditionally, appear to leave problems unsatisfactorily resolved is because the authors of such views have not adequately analyzed the term "justification." Yet, the solution to this apparent problem cannot stop simply with clarification of the term "justification." Once this term has been properly analyzed, it will be seen that what we are dealing with are contextual problems. What also needs to be determined then is what is meant by "X is good." Since this meaning is contextual, one must continually look to see precisely what is being asserted. As with "justification," so with terms like "good," "right," and "moral," etc. The meaning does not inhere in the term, and since we are dealing with contexts, we cannot assume that once a meaning has been found for one of these terms, it will hold good for all cases.

Analysis will indicate that sometimes moral statements do suggest objectivity in a very limited sense. Such moral statements may have a meaning that is independent of what you or I think. There is no reason to believe, however, that they are independent of what everyone thinks. Whereas, the basic meaning of "X is good" is "X is approved," this does not limit the meaning to "I personally approve of X." We may also mean, in asserting "X is generally approved," that most people in our society (used variously) approve of X, or that X is a custom or tradition, or that X is legal. Before we can know whether or not "X is good" is justified, we must know what, of these various possibilities, is being asserted.

On the basis of this analysis, several methods of justification may then be seen. If in uttering "X is good," I mean to say that "*I* approve of X," and we disagree over meaning, our disagreement can be worked out merely by clarifying terms. On the one hand, if I make clear that I am simply offering my own private preference, any dispute we have had will disolve. On the other hand, if our dispute is over meaning, then this, too, can be worked out by our clarifying our use of the term good. When we reach a point where you say, "Oh, now I see how you're using the term "good," our dispute dissolves. This does not require that you *adopt* my point of view. Only that you *see* it. Once you reach the point of saying, "Now I see . . ."; our dispute is ended. No further justification is required, nor is any possible.

Of course, if I am not satisfied that you merely *see* my point, I may go on with my statements. I may either point to the facts which support my case, or to the logic which leads to my conclusion. Or, I may engage in a strongly emotional appeal. All of these, of course, are engaged in not simply to have you see my position. I am now attempting to stimulate you to join me. I am not simply *evincing* emotion; I am trying to *evoke* a similar emotion in you. Once I have persuaded you join me, our dispute again dissolves. Since the dispute had arisen over a particular value, and involved you and me, when *we* lay the question to rest, it is, in this context laid to rest. There is no further justification problem.

If we go on to the broader meaning of "X is approved," *viz.* "X is generally approved." There are a number of possible justifications depending on which of the meanings of general approval is being used. If by general approval is meant that X is a tradition or custom in our society, there are several ways of justifying such a claim. We can check with historians, or anthropologists, or sociologists.

On the other hand, if the claim "X is good," meaning "X is generally approved" is claiming current approval, there are several ways to justify this claim. One of the ways to get at public approval and disapproval is through polls and surveys. Objections may be raised that this is a poor way to justify a value, simply to conduct a poll. But again, we must remember precisely what is being asserted, and it is to that which we must respond and not to some call for meta-ethical principles. Another bit of machinery for resolving such questions in our society are referenda and elections. These also are indications of where people stand on issues.

Yet another meaning for "X is good," is "X is legal," or the converse, "X is bad," is "X is illegal." Questions, or disputes of this nature may be resolved by checking the constitution or appropriate statutes. In some cases, this becomes extremely complex, or accutely meaningful. If you sell me some shoddy merchandise, I may claim, "It was wrong for you to sell me such merchandise under the conditions which you conveyed it to me." If you dispute this, I may at first merely try to persuade you of the "wrongness" of your act. If this does not work, or the issues are too complex for us to figure out, or I feel strongly enough about the matter, I may seek support for my position. I might in fact, call on the machinery we have for handling such disputes. I might, in other words, sue you. We then call on the courts to resolve our value disputes, and ultimately your value judgement or mine will be justified.

"Wait a minute," some may protest, "The courts may be wrong." Again, before we can proceed here, we must have clarified exactly what is being claimed. If someone is simply saying, "I personally do not approve of the courts decision," there is little to be done but allow him his opinion or sway him to ours. If he is asserting something beyond this, then his meaning must be made clear before we can proceed in one of the ways being suggested here.

Some moral judgements may be checked by examining them for their consistency with some other code than constitutions or statutes. If the claim "X is good" means "X is consistent with some code (such as the Decalogue)," then this consistency is what must be checked. Now, no claim is being made beyond consistency with the code; but if the question is, "Is this act consistent with the code?" then that is the question to be answered. Again, the objection may be raised that the value in question is not "justified" unless the code from which it is drawn is justified. But again, this assumes some meaning for "justification" beyond that which we reasonably expect to find.

Still another method of justification would be the examination of the beliefs on which values are held. Values are not held in isolation. The evidence of this is that we generally do not regard it as an unreasonable question, if one asks why a certain value is held. Occasionally, disputes will arise as a result of mistaken beliefs. When we examine the facts on which values are held, we may find that we have been misled. Clearing this up may resolve the question of whether or not "X is good." Such questions may revolve about either the sources of values, or the consequences that we associate with the values held. In similar vein, it is also helpful at times to examine the logic of our beliefs.

In none of the foregoing has any claim been made that any method of justifications offered will justify all values or any values for all times. No new knowledge in the realm of values has been offered nor have any absolute certainties been established. Analysis has simply indicated to us all what we can reasonably expect in dealing with questions of values. What has been insisted throughout is that such solutions as we have are contextual. All that has been engaged in is analysis, criticism and clarification. Yet, several troublesome problems of philosophy have been resolved.

One other consideration remains. At times, clarification, persuasion, empirical checking, referring questions to appropriate agencies, all have failed to resolve the dispute over values. One other solution remains. When disputants have argued the point from every aspect open to them without reaching agreement, when it becomes obvious that further argument will be fruitless, one course remains open. The parties who cannot find agreement may simply agree to disagree. We simply agree to go our own ways respecting the position of the other. At that point, our dispute again dissolves.

There will be those who will insist that in all of the foregoing we have not dealt with what is really *right*. They want to insist that there are *right principles* independent of expediency, or agreement, or persuasions, or desireable consequences. What such persons are asserting is not really clear. The notion that there exists some meta-ethical justification principle is probably manufactured. It is like the notion of connection that we feel compelled to assert between cause and effect, when all we can observe is constant conjunction. It may be no more than the remnant or residual effect of having learned morals as objective codes when we were young. But this is speculation for the behavioral scientist. Suffice it for philosophy to point out that we have no good reason to expect any more than has been offered.

V

The significance of all of this for philosophy of education will be made explicit in chapters 8 and 9. For the time being, let it suffice simply to point out that questions of values must be handled differently from questions of fact. What should be clear is that, analytic skills, i.e., philosophic skills, are required first of all to see what sort of questions are being raised. Having once sorted out the questions which deal with values, the next chore is to see precisely what questions are being asked in order that those questions, and not some others, may be answered.

What is important to realize is that not all issues, and concerns, and questions in education are technical matters. Clearly, some of the most important questions (if we may be permitted a value judgement) are, or involve, matters of values. Perhaps no more important service could be rendered by philosophy of education than to make this clear and to clarify the ways we have of dealing with such issues.

Chapter 7

Epistemology: A Critical Examination
of Theories and Explanations

I

The notion that the task of the school involves, at least in part, the transmission of knowledge would probably win general assent among educators. But the question of what one transmits when he transmits knowledge would not bring such general assent. Instead, it might bring suspicious glances, (one might be suspected of being an educational philosopher), and it surely would result in disagreement. The task of clarifying what such transmission is about falls to the philosopher of education who will use his tools of analysis, criticism and clarification on this and such terms also as "believing," "learning," and "teaching."

Another dimension of the role of the philosopher of education would concern itself with the body of knowledge which is called "education." This is not to suggest that philosophers of education are going to make pronouncements about the truth or falsehood of educational directives. If the role that has been suggested for philosophy is maintained here, it will be seen that the philosopher of education will assess educational statements on the basis of determining their content, their logical worth, connections among them, etc.

Since one task of philosophy of education is the analysis of knowledge, an initial view would indicate that the common, everyday concept of what knowing is covers a wide range of matters. As Scheffler points out,[1] included is familiarity with things, persons, places, a variety of competencies, ways of controlling and understanding nature, intellectual arts and experiences, and our standards, ideals, tastes, conceptions of truth and evidence, etc. Thus, the task of education is not only to transmit what we claim to know, but also all that is associated with our ways of knowing.

1. Israel Scheffler, *The Conditions of Knowledge* (Glenview, Ill.: Scott Foresman and Company, 1965), p. 2.

A cursory consideration of terms such as "knowing," "believing," "learning," and "teaching" seems to indicate a rather easy and obvious connection among the terms. We see "teaching" and "learning" as simply opposite sides of the same coin, and "knowing" and "believing" as products of this operation. Yet, the connections among these terms are not as simple as the first glance may make them seem.

If we take relatively simple examples like "John has learned that water is composed of hydrogen and oxygen in a particular combination," we would generally be willing to grant that he knows this. Hence, there appears to be some definite connection between "learning" and "knowing." On the other hand, if we were to take an example like, "Mary has learned from her astrologer that those born under the sign of Leo have an affinity for those born under Gemini," in this instance, we may not be willing to grant that Mary *knows*. This is explained by the fact that in the former item, we ourselves are committed to the truth of the statement, which is not the case with the latter statement. "Knowing" appears to have a force that "learning" does not. Hence, we cannot make any easy equation between the two. It would seem, however, that to suggest that someone has learned something does suggest that, while the learner may not necessarily be thought of as knowing what he has learned, he will be regarded as at least believing it. In both instances, however, we would generally be willing to grant that teaching had gone on. Therefore, we do not reserve "teaching" for the act that results in what we regard as knowing, but would associate it with causing someone to come to believe as well.

Other problems revolve around what we mean when we attribute knowing to someone, i.e., what it means to "know." For some, this means simply that the knower simply has a belief that is true.[2] Some, however, would not regard the learner as knowing unless he were in a position to offer evidence to back up what he truly believes. In this latter view if a pupil has learned something in school, he must move beyond truly believing to the point of being able to supply supporting reasons. It is not enough simply to be committed to $2 + 2 = 4$; he must know why $2 + 2 = 4$ to be said to know. This distinction is more apt to be made for complex subjects, however, than for relatively simple, isolated "pieces" of knowledge.

There is also a distinction offered occasionally in the way the student has acquired his "knowledge." This distinction goes back at

---

2. Knowing will be analyzed more fully later in this chapter.

least to St. Thomas, who affirms that the learner must appropriate his own piece of knowledge if he is to be regarded as knowing. It is not enough to have been presented with the item, even when the item is true. The student in this view must find out for himself. This tells us that the discovery sense of learning, and knowing, is not new to education. On this basis, there are those who offer as justification for the discovery approach, or problems approach, as a teaching (learning) method this notion that one does not *know* unless he finds out for himself. It should be noted, however, that this "truth" begins with an assumption that is no more than a definition. Yet, when we are looking for the "best" method, we may be looking for something that can be justified empirically rather than logically.

Analysis will indicate, too, that "teaching" and "learning" are not *merely* two sides of the same coin. It is rather obvious that learning may go on whether actual teaching is involved or not. Also, learning may go on whether we intend it or not. Teaching, on the other hand, suggests that someone is engaged in an intentional activity. What teaching intends is that some pupil(s) will learn the matter to be taught i.e., will at least come to believe that such and such is the case. This is at least true of "learning that." There are those who will suggest that teaching may also go on whether or not we intend it, i.e., that we may teach without intending to. For example, I may be engaged in an activity that has no educative goal, yet someone may learn from what I am doing. Or, in the activity of teaching, I may *intend* certain outcomes, yet other consequences than I intend occur. However, such use of teaching generally would be qualified with some such adjective as "unintentional." At any rate, intention seems implied even in such uses, in the sense that if learning were not associated we would not come to call the activity "teaching." Such use seems to recognize the intentional nature of teaching.

Now, there are other ways for us to get the student to come to believe that such-and-such is the case. In recognition of this, we use such terms as "instruct," "indoctrinate," "condition," and "train." All of these are associated with, but not identified with education and teaching. For example, most educators will insist on distinguishing between "education" and "training." The distinction, analysis reveals, is based largely on "education" having a broader scope than "training." An educated man, for example, is seen to have a fairly wide range of attainment. Training, on the other hand, while not indicating any distinction in level of attainment, appears to be reserved for a narrower range. Someone, for example, will be spoken of as being trained as a philosopher rather than educated as a philosopher. While "training" usually denotes a recognized level of attainment, we generally associate the term with a rather narrowly defined set of skills, i.e., with *knowing how to* rather than *knowing that.*

"Instruction" seems to imply less than "training." Like "training," the term "instruction" is usually used to represent a relatively narrow field of effort. The term differs from "training" however, in that there is no sense of attainment associated with the term. Also, it might be pointed out that historically, "instruction" has been associated with the presentation of material, i.e., with telling, rather than with demonstration that involves pupil activity. Both "instruction" and "training" are generally included within the concept of "teaching."

Also related to "training" is the term "conditioning." Although the terms are not identical, there appears to be a point at which "training" merges with "conditioning." There are types of changes in behavior intentionally wrought, that appear to be largely automatic responses, which we will regard as training because something has been learned. In its classic sense, conditioning is not usually associated with learning. For example, where "conditioning" labels uncontrollable reflexes, such as a dog's salivating whenever a bell is rung, the term "learning" has not generally been associated with that outcome.

On the other hand, it has become the habit of some persons to regard "learning" and "conditioning" as identical terms. In the case of programmed instruction, for example, the term "learning" is seen by behaviorists as having no increment of meaning over the term "conditioning." Opponents of this view suggest that if the subjects are merely making responses that are not related to the subject's judgement and control, then we may regard them as being conditioned. If, however, the subject recognizes that, and recognizes how, his response is instrumental in obtaining a reward or avoiding punishment, then there is more involved than simply conditioning. In this view, there is a distinction between "learning" and "conditioning" with the forms involving not merely altered behavior, but also judgement and control. "Learning" will be associated with "coming to believe that," whereas "conditioning" does not carry this connotation. Classic conditioning has not usually been regarded as being within the concept of "teaching," but this has changed in recent years with certain types of conditioning being regarded as teaching.

"Indoctrination," on the other hand, is inevitably and invariably associated with believing that. The term is not identical with "learning," however. "Learning" would appear to be the broader term since one would recognize that in all successful cases of indoctrination, learning of some sort has gone on. Yet, there are many instances of learning that move beyond indoctrination. Also, instances of indoctrination would not fall outside the concept of "teaching." This is to say that when one is speaking of "teaching" and/or of "learning" that there are times that this would refer to or include instances of indoctrination.

"Indoctrination," however, does include within its concept certain notions of "mindlessness." In this regard, it would more closely resemble "conditioning" than "knowing." Also, "knowing" would include concerns for "truth" that would not necessarily be involved with indoctrination. Indoctrination is carried on with the intent of the subject coming to believe that what is being presented is "truth," but outsiders judging the results of indoctrination might be loathe to regard the subject as knowing that. It is more likely that he would regard him as simply believing that. Unlike "conditioning," the term indoctrination is aimed at altering *belief that*, rather than altering behavior.

So far, what distinguishes indoctrination from teaching has not been made explicit. The chief distinction seems to be that the goal or intent of teaching is broader. Both activities, teaching and indoctrination, aim at bringing about belief. The intent of indoctrination does not go beyond this. The goal of teaching, however, includes a willingness on the part of the teacher to include rational explanation and critical scrutiny. Also, whereas "teaching" would include dealing with isolated items of belief, "indoctrination" refers to bodies of belief, i.e., the passing along of doctrines. What makes indoctrination difficult to distinguish at times is that a degree of explanation and criticism may be allowed, even encouraged. But at some point, we will be required to accept some basic premise without question or reason. Often, too, such premises are not publically demonstrable. At times, "teaching" may seem to come very close to indoctrination. This is the case where students are encouraged to assume a particular point of view. However, the degree to which the pupil is encouraged also to question the assumptions of that position, and to recognize it as a position is the degree to which he has been taught rather than indoctrinated.

The point of all of this is not to urge particular notions of "teaching," "learning," "believing," "knowing," etc. Rather, the intention was to indicate that such terms are not always immediately clear. The term "teaching," for example, covers such a wide range of activities that educational directives containing the term require analysis. For example, in the interest of clarity, it might be well to refer to teaching machines as conditioning machines, but this is not done. Further, even those programs which are fairly obviously indoctrination programs will be called "educational" because the latter term carries friendlier connotations. These examples point up the need for analytic skills on the part of those who will be reading literature on the topic of education, or those who will be offering, or attempting to implement, or simply to understand, educational directives.

II

Although initially there might not be much question but that the task of education is the transmission of knowledge, a little analysis indicates that some clarification is needed if we are to understand what this means. The term "knowledge" itself is not perfectly clear. And, as was also shown, whether one is said to *know* what is transmitted to him, or simply comes to hold new beliefs is not always clear. The problems involved in knowing and believing will be dealt with in the following section.

Whether we know or believe things about the process and activity of education may be clarified later. But, without raising that set of questions, it might be pointed out that what we regard as the body of knowledge called "education" is largely or at least partially, in the form of the theories. Some of the specific "theories" that people hold will be considered in the final chapter. For the present we will examine what a theory is and what a theory does, in order to, later on, assess the logical worth of what are offered as "theories of education."

In order to get at the meaning of the term "theory" we might simply stipulate a definition. This would serve to indicate how *we* plan to use the term, but it would not get us very far along the route of determining how the term is generally used. Nor would stipulation help us to get at the meaning of "theory" as it is used in various contexts. This is simply a way of saying that the dictum, "Define your terms," is not a good starting point for philosophic analysis. We want to *end* with terms defined, but we do not want to *begin* there.

In the first place, the term "theory" may be used with a qualifying term to label simply a set of related problems. For example, all chapter 6, dealing with many of the problems related to values and their justification might be called a chapter on value theory. Or, the content of the present chapter might be referred to as epistemological theory. Another illustration of this use of the term may be seen in the title of a journal which deals with many of the problems of education, and the analysis of those problems. Although most of the articles are philosophical, the journal is titled *Educational Theory*.[3]

In another sense, the term "theory" has been used to refer to a conceptual framework, or a highly organized and systematized "picture," or a set of conventions. Such conceptualization need not have a bearing on a practical activity. An example of such use of the term would be number "theory," or set "theory" in mathematics. In psychology, there have been efforts to give systematic "pictures" of what is meant by the term "personality," such conceptualizations are called theories of personality.

Often, the term "theory" will be used to mean a system of precepts which guide or which underlie actions of various kinds. If I were, for example, to collect all the rules for flying including the appropriate·methods of manipulating the controls, the reasons for such manipulation, the rules of safety and of courtesy in the air, etc., and publish all of this material in a book, my book might be said to be on the theory of flying. Similarly, learning theories, are often sets of rules that either guide, or in some cases are offered as underlying, what goes in the classroom. Like the previously mentioned use of the term theory as a conceptual framework, this use is also a conceptualization, but it is a conceptual background for practical activities. It is an effort to unify and systematize what we see ourselves as doing in a particular activity.

Finally, there is a fourth use of the term "theory." This is the way the term is used in such sciences as chemistry and physics. In this use, the term refers to a confirmed hypothesis, or to a logically connected set of such hypotheses. In the first instance we might refer to some scientist's explanation of a single phenomenon as his "theory." More generally, however, theory has been used to refer to a whole set of hypotheses that explain a wide range of phenomena.

Considering what a hypothesis is will help to clarify what a theory is, and lead to what a theory does. Actually, a hypothesis is a guess. However, it is possible to distinguish between what is generally meant by guess, and the way "hypothesis" is used. A guess usually

---

3. It may be noteworthy to point out that *Educational Theory* is the organ of the Philosophy of Education Society, along with the John Dewey Society.

denotes simply idle or random conjecture. It is usually related to efforts to account for something unusual in the course of everyday activities. It is what is offered as an effort to remove puzzlement or uncertainty, or to fill in where we feel that some gap exists, in our experience. Despite the fact that it is intended to remove an uncertainty, "guess" usually implies that a degree of uncertainty remains with one's conjecture.

It would have to be granted that "hypothesis" is also generally used in reference to more technical, or complicated, or sophisticated material. If I dial a telephone number and no one answers, it would be appropriate to guess that no one is home. To call such conjecture "hypothesizing" would be regarded as a rather stilted use of the language. Or, if I turn the key past "Both" on my Cherokee airplane, and the engine does not turn over at all, I might "guess" that someone who had flown the plane previously had left the master switch and some electrical gear on. If I suggested that this piece of conjecture was a hypothesis, I would be thought strange.

Aside from the technicality, or sophistication, of the conjecture, other characteristics generally distinguish the use of hypotheses. It was noted that a degree of uncertainty seems to accompany the use of "guess" that is not found with the use of "hypothesis." It is the randomness of a guess that accounts for this. To be regarded seriously as a hypothesis, a piece of conjecture would have to be regarded as what is popularly called an "educated guess." An "educated guess" in this sense would be one that was not random. The randomness would be reduced, in the first place, by the guess coming out of what was already known. The hypothesis, then, has some genuine basis on which it is offered. In the second place, the randomness of the conjecture would be diminished by the hypothesis being directive in a sense. That is, it would point to certain answers, indicate what would be appropriate and what would be simply irrelevant.

In addition, to be regarded seriously, as a hypothesis, it must be in such terms that, if true, it will have observable consequences. If, for example, I am looking for a hypothesis that was to answer a question about why a child behaved as he did, it might be a genuine hypothesis to point to traits in his character that would enable us to make predictions which we could then observe. It would not be a genuine hypothesis to suggest that his behavior was caused by original sin. This is not to say that hypotheses must be *true*, in order to be regarded as hypotheses; only that they must be such that *if* true, they have observable consequences. If, of course, the predicted consequences are not observed, then the hypothesis is false. There is no logical problem in speaking of a false hypothesis. The use of the term "hypothesis" does, however, indicate that our answer is capable, at least in principle, of confirmation or refutation.

If the hypothesis is a *valid* hypothesis, the consequences which were foreseen will occur. However, the establishment of the consequences, (i.e., the fact that we actually observe the consequences which we deduced from our hypothesis) does not establish our hypothesis positively, or with absolute certainty. It merely indicates the *probability* that our hypothesis is correct. On the other hand, if the consequences which we predicted are not observed, then our hypothesis is conclusively refuted. The reason for this may be seen in an illustration.

If in the case of my Cherokee, I note that although, when I turn the key, the engine turns over, it still will not start, I might suggest that the reason is that the plugs are fouled. If I remove the plugs, clean and replace them, and the engine still does not start, this conclusively refutes my "hypothesis" that the reason the engine would not start was because the plugs were fouled.

On the other hand, if I clean and replace the plugs and the engine starts, I am entitled to say only that it was *probably* because of fouled plugs that the engine would not run. In the first place, my action has not positively removed all other possibilities. Perhaps the engine was flooded, and the time I spent removing, cleaning and replacing plugs allowed this situation to correct itself.

In the second place, there is, in my hypothesis, an implied prediction that *whenever* plugs are fouled the engine will not start. The fact that this places the confirmation forever in the future and that there is always the *possibility* that at some time in the future my hypothesis may be refuted rather than confirmed, means that I have established only probability. In other words, on this basis, as well as on the earlier basis, all of the evidence that would confirm or refute my hypothesis is never in. This is part of the basis for our saying, earlier in this section, that what we regard as knowledge in education is in the form of theories.

From what has been said so far, it should be clear that hypotheses do not arise spontaneously. The sort of conjecture that the term hypothesis refers to is the result of an unexpected happening. On the basis of what we already have established, we move about in the world with certain expectations. Occasionally, those expectations are not met. We have a *disjoint experience*. For example, suppose we had made careful observations and noted that whenever we heated water, it consistently began to bubble and steam after a fairly regular amount of time. We checked this phenomenon carefully and finally associated the tendency of the water to commence its bubbling with a particular temperature. Further observation established that temperature at 212° on the Fahrenheit scale. Repeated efforts confirm this figure.

Proud of our new knowledge, we decide to parade it before our friend, who happens incidentally, to live on top of the mountain nearby. We carefully carry out our demonstration and—lo and behold—the water boils, not at 212° F. but at 200°! This is a disjoint experience. It raises the irritation of a doubt, and we wish to have the irritation removed. We cast about for some way to account for this disjoint experience.

After much conjecture, we finally arrive at the conclusion that there must be some new factor that has not been considered. It occurs to us, because of other things we know, that the air pressure is lower on top of the mountain than it is down on our plain. So, we establish that there is some connection between pressure and temperature and the way water behaves. We propose an answer to our question as to why the water behaved unexpectedly. We check this proposal out by observing certain facts that we have deduced from our proposal, and establish some regularity among these factors. There, we have it; a new hypothesis.

Although the experience which we have described is at a relatively low level of sophistication, it illustrates the way new knowledge is established. At a different level, scientific thinking goes on in essentially the same way. The description in chapter 1 of the discovery of the planet Neptune follows this same pattern. The only differences are in the level of the sophistication of the questions raised and the quality of the observations that must be carried out to verify (confirm or refute) the proposed hypothesis.

Our illustration also indicates further what a hypothesis is. It is a proposal to account for a disjoint experience. This proposal, if it is confirmed, is regarded as a valid hypothesis. These hypotheses, if they are general enough, and reliable enough may come to be thought of as laws of nature. The word "theory" is used to refer either to such a law, or to a logically connected set of such laws.

III

We have, in dealing with what a theory is, also given some indication of what it is that a theory does. In accounting for what we take to be a disjoint experience, a theory explains to us the phenomenon under question. This explanation is a description of the way some part of the world "really" is behaving. In the process of explaining, however, our hypothesis, or theory, also implies a prediction. In every explanatory description of the way the world, or some part of it, behaves, we are giving a direct account of what we have in fact experienced. But, our description is also saying to us, ". . . and this is the way it will behave in the future." Since explanation, description, and prediction are inseparable, we will not consider them separately, but will, for our purposes here, consider that the word "explain" will sufficiently cover the case. What a theory *does*, then, is explain its subject matter.

There are at least two aspects of "explain" that require some further elucidation. One of these is to consider what it *means* to explain. The other is how we go about doing this. If we look at what happens when we receive an explanation, we might get some idea of what it means to explain. When we receive an explanation, one consequence is that, assuming the explanation to be appropriate, whatever question we have loses its interrogative function. It is laid to rest, so to speak. There are at least two accounts of how this occurs.

One account of what it means for a theory to explain is simply that it removes puzzlement. It eliminates what Charles Sanders Peirce calls the irritation of doubt. As some have pointed out, on the other side of the issue, it affords some degree of satisfaction, or some feeling of certainty. In satisfying the demands required by our disjoint experience, the explanation joins up the *explicandum*, (the thing to be explained), with our presupposition. Whatever is causing our puzzlement is brought into harmony with our beliefs.

This explanation is clearly a psychological one. The explanation that is most satisfactory would appear to be the one that satisfies a psychological craving. This "feeling" of satisfaction is the sole criterion for judging the worth of an explanation. The chief criticism leveled at this view of an explanation is that it would admit as a theory whatever explanation suited one's fancy. On this basis, the witch doctor's view that headaches are caused by devils inside the scalp is to be accepted as a legitimate "theory," since it connects up with what is held as a belief. It matters not whether the explanation is "true" or not.

Those who criticize this psychological account of what an explanation is, offer what they regard as a more reliable basis for regarding an explanation as satisfactory. The criterion for judging the worth of an explanation in this view is not the degree of satisfaction that it affords. What counts here is truth. This is the sole criterion.

What a theory must do in order to remove puzzlement is link up the explicandum to what we *know*, not to what we merely believe. If an explanation is satisfactory, it is not enough simply to be satisfying; it must be true. If our beliefs are faulty, then no satisfactory explanation can be given. This means that where ignorance of a topic is present, legitimate or genuine theories are not possible.

The way we go about providing an explanation may follow any one of several patterns. There are some relatively distinct ways in which explanations are given, but the line of demarcation that divides them is not perfectly distinct nor absolute. The ways that we shall consider fade into one another imperceptibly. But it is helpful to an understanding of how explanations take place to classify these ways.

In the first place, when we encounter a disjoint experience, one of the ways of explaining it is to demonstrate that, rather than being disjoint, the phenomenon under question is, in fact, simply an instance of a general law. For example, we may be puzzled by the fact that the small glider, when we pitch it, soars through the air instead of simply falling to the ground. Since most objects when pitched forward would simply drop to the ground, the fact that our glider soars is a disjoint experience.

Now, what we might point out is that when we supply thrust to a plane surface with an air foil, the air will move faster over the upper curved portion of the wing creating a lower pressure across the upper surface and thereby providing "lift." To one to whom such an explanation has meaning, this will be regarded as a "theory" of flight. If we have given a true explanation, we may regard our explanation as a genuine theory. What originally was taken to be puzzling is now seen to be an instance of a regularity of nature. Such an explanation will satisfy the uninitiated, but it may not last for long. As we ponder over such an answer, we may begin to wonder about why this particular regularity in nature exists. That is to say, we may begin to look for an explanation of the general law itself.

Normally, such a concern will not occur to the novice, the uninitiated, or unsophisticated. But, to the learned scientist, such a question might well arise. How is the regularity that explained the soaring of our glider to be explained itself? Such an abstraction is hardly within the province of a philosopher. However, while the philosopher may not be equipped to provide the specific answer, he can note how the scientist, even in an advanced science, goes about providing such an answer. What we see is that the general law will be explained by demonstrating that it is itself an instance of a still more general law.

Such an explanation serves its purpose, but it cannot be carried too far. If we carry such a *unifying theory* too far, it may end by explaining nothing. (We call such a theory a unifying theory because it brings together what we previously regarded as unrelated phenomena. In some instances, whole fields of science have been brought together by devising theories that made two sciences special cases of the general explanation.) In the past, and occasionally in the present, we find theories offered that are so general that they "explain" everything. In this case they end by explaining nothing.

Suppose that I am holding an object in my hands. On releasing it, I find that the object rises instead of falling. This is a disjoint experience. I look for an explanation that will account for this unusual experience. Someone says to me, "The reason the object rises instead of falling is because it is the will of God." Now, I apparently know why the object rose. The next time I am holding the same object in my hands, I release it again. This time it *falls* instead of rising. I seek an explanation. Again I am offered the explanation, "The reason the object *fell* instead of rising is because it is the will of God."

Such an explanation turns out to be no explanation at all. If any, and every, event regarding the object is explained as "the will of God," then I have no information at all. I do not have any idea what to expect when I release the object. Every experience, then, is a disjoint experience, i.e., since I never know what to expect, whatever the object does leaves me puzzled. The "explanation" has not really accounted for the unexpected behavior of the object.

We might take a similar problem in the behavioral sciences. Imagine, if you will, a boy seated before a piano. He is pounding the keys furiously. What he produces is not music; it is discordant and simply loud and noisy. This is not what I expect of someone seated at a piano, so I seek an explanation. "The reason the boy sits and bangs at the piano is obvious. He is simply filled with aggressive hostility." Now, I apparently "know." The information can be useful. I can predict how a boy filled with aggressive hostility will act when he's seated before a piano. Similarly, whenever I see someone behaving this way, I will know that he's filled with aggressive hostility.

Now imagine another situation. A boy is seated before a piano. He is sitting quietly with his hands folded before him. He is so different from the former case that we are again puzzled. We seek an explanation of his behavior.

"Why it's very clear," we are told, "that boy is filled with aggressive hostility."

"But you said that the last one, who was banging furiously, was filled with aggressive hostility."

"Of course, but this one is too. Only this one is compensating."

In other words, being filled with aggressive hostility is the explanation for all types of behavior. It explains so much, however, that it explains nothing. Whereas we thought we knew what behavior to expect from anyone filled with aggressive hostility, we see now that we do not. The "explanation" is consistent with any type of behavior at all. We do not know what to expect and can make no predictions at all concerning someone "filled with aggressive hostility." The point of all this is simply to demonstrate that while we may explain a law of nature by offering a unifying theory, we cannot make the theory too general, or it loses its function as a theory. It cannot then be regarded as a genuine theory.

A third way of removing puzzlement, or offering explanation, is by using a model. Some models are *physical models*. For example, scientific apparatus jobbers offer a device known as a wave machine. On this device, it is possible to set the spring-like affair in motion and produce waves that will move from one end of the machine to the other. The waves which it reproduces resemble ocean waves. In fact, it helps us to understand things we did not know before about ocean waves. It also "explains" things about sound, or about anything, in fact, that moves in such waves.

Another example of physical models would be the pigeons and monkeys that are used to study behavior. We can, for example, engage the animals in behavior that is called learning. By observing the behavior patterns of the animals, we can develop new insights into what goes on in learning. On the basis of what we observe with these physical models in the laboratory, we may come to understand certain things that go on in classrooms.

The chief problem with using models, however, is that people sometimes forget that they are using models. The models become confused in some minds with the things the models are supposed to explain. The wave machine is not an ocean, nor are pigeons and monkeys pupils in a classroom. There are similarities between the models and the things models are used to explain. This is what enables us to use models. But there are differences, too. This is why models, by themselves, *prove* nothing. They can merely generate hypotheses. Occasionally, when this is overlooked, the use of models then gets in the way of generating hypotheses and models lose their value as models.

Models serve essentially the same function in theorizing that analogies serve in argumentation. They provide new ways of viewing the phenomenon under question. They can suggest fresh approaches. But, by themselves, they prove nothing.

In some sciences, we move beyond using physical models and rely instead on *mathematical models*. Einstein's famous formula, $E=MC^2$ was a mathematical model which helped scientists to come to understand the relationship between matter and energy. Mathematical models are not limited to the physical sciences, however. They have even been proposed for use in the behavioral sciences. One such model is Raymond B. Cattell's famous representation of personality.

$$P_{ij} = S_{1j}T_{1i} + S_{2j}T_{2i} + \bullet\bullet\bullet + S_{nj}T_{ni}S_jT_i$$

In this model, the capital letters represent factor endowments, or traits, and the subscripts represent factor loadings. What the model suggests is that if we combine appropriately weighted factors, then we can predict behavior in a given situation.

We may, by noting the resemblances between models and the things which models represent, be led to notice new things that we have not recognized before. But it will require experimentation to confirm or refute what the model suggests. In educational research, we sometimes move from using pigeons and monkeys as models, to using people. For example, classes will be used as control or experimental groups. This does not avoid the problems involved in using models, however. Such groups still serve merely as models for whatever group we may wish to apply theories to. For example, a particular class or group of classes may be used as a model to represent all classes in all situations. Because the class or group is not all classes, we must be cautious about generalizing from the group to the class. Used reasonably, however, models can serve as a valuable stimulus to thought.

The final type of explanation is that which is used to connect spatially or temporally separated phenomena. For example, a child may ask why pushing a switch on the wall causes the lights on the ceiling to go on. It may be pointed out to him that there are wires in the walls and ceilings that connect the lights to the switch; that electricity moves in a sort of closed circle; that pushing the switch closes the circle, etc.

There are those who regard this gap-filling explanation as the most primitive, or lowest level, explanation. This may be true. It is a relatively simply explanation, and would be of little use in highly sophisticated sciences. This does not detract from its value, however. When what is called for is a gap-filling explanation, then this is obviously the most appropriate one, and the only one that will answer the question being raised.

IV KNOWING VS. BELIEVING

In the foregoing sections, we have made an assumption that now itself bears examination. This is the assumption that we can distinguish between knowing and believing. This is a very common assumption. As was suggested in chapter 2, if there are items about which you say "I believe," but would not be willing to say "I know," and on the other hand, if there are items about which you are willing to say not merely "I believe," but you would be willing to say "I know," then you are among those who make this type of distinction. When it was suggested that genuine theories are those which connect an explicandum (thing to be explained) with what we know, rather than what we believe, it was implied that such a distinction could be made.

The type of knowing we shall be dealing with is the type which engages most of our attention in formal education, *viz.*, *knowing that*, rather than *knowing how* to. This is called *propositional knowledge*. Most recent accounts of such knowledge is represented in some fashion similar to the following:

> X knows that Q
> if and only if
> (i) X believes that Q,
> (ii) X has adequate evidence that Q,
> and (iii) Q.

The first of these is called the *belief condition* and means that the person who is claiming to know would not use the term "know" to describe anything that he did not believe. Believing, then, is a *necessary condition* for knowing. It is not *sufficient* however, since we would require more than merely a belief to regard as an item of knowledge whatever item is held.

The second condition is called the *evidence condition*. Like belief, this is a necessary but not a sufficient condition. That is to say, we would not describe anyone as knowing if he did not have adequate evidence to support what he was claiming to know. Yet, if one simply believed, and had evidence for his belief we still would not necessarily regard him as knowing.

So far, what we have described would as readily describe believing as knowing. The evidence for this is that in the first place, the belief condition obviously describes believing. In the second place, beliefs are not held in a vacuum. We have reasons for our beliefs. When someone cites an item that is held as a belief only, he does not regard it as an unusual or unreasonable question if we ask him why he believes as he does. Asked such a question, the believer will inevitably respond with the reasons for his belief.

To make something distinctive of knowing, most current philosophers add the third condition called the *truth condition*. This condition, though it is simply cited as Q, is sometimes said to mean Q is true. Another way of stating it would be to say that we cannot be said to *know* a proposition unless, in addition to meeting the other conditions, the proposition is a true proposition.

In order to be clear about the distinction that most philosophers make between knowing and believing, it will be helpful to examine the conditions of knowledge in some detail. In the case of the first condition, the belief condition, most contemporary philosophers who make the distinction described here would not regard belief as a performance or activity. The basis for deciding whether or not believing fits the category of activity or performance is as follows. If one asks the question "What are you doing?" the reply "Believing that he will be there as he promised" is not an appropriate response.[4]

Since belief is regarded as more than an activity or a performance, it becomes necessary to account for what a belief is. One effort is called the verbal theory of belief. In this view, what is meant by "belief" is that one is disposed to respond affirmatively to sentences which contain the item about which we say "I believe." The problem with this theory is that often we will regard believing as more than the alteration of verbal behavior. In fact, we often appeal to evidence beyond a verbal response in order to determine what a person's beliefs "really" are. A person's claim to hold a certain belief may be disputed by citing other behavior patterns than verbal behaviors.

The basis for rejecting the verbal theory of belief is that belief leads us to act in certain ways rather than merely talk in certain

4. Conventionally, it is awkward; that much must be granted. But what is one doing when he says, "I believe . . . "?

ways. This account is called the general dispositional theory of believing. This view involves not merely a way of talking but a whole cluster of dispositions to do various things in various ways. Objections may be raised, even to this account, since the tendency to behave in certain ways does not seem to exhaust all that we mean by believing.

It seems that in addition to a disposition to act, and speak in a certain way, there is also something of the person's objectives involved. What is left undecided in most accounts is *in what ways* one has a tendency to act when he is said to believe, and *under what circumstances* a person is said to act. Beyond overt actions, there also seems to be a psychological set, or feeling, that characterizes, or at least accompanies, a belief. Something of what is generally meant by the term "orientation" seems also involved in what is meant by believing.

The second of the conditions set for one to say that he knows is the evidence condition. There are at least two parts to this, one being what it means to have evidence; the other being what constitutes adequate evidence. In the case of evidential adequacy, there is clearly a need for recognizing relative standards. We would not set the same requirement for a young child first being introduced to a subject as we would hold for the sophisticated knower or scholar. We also seem to make a distinction between more and less sophisticated adults. It might be pointed out that it is necessary to regard the adequacy of evidence as relative, not only because of differences in age and background, but also because of the constantly changing standards and sophistication of the various sciences.

Scheffler has suggested that "X has the right to be sure of Q," would be a better formulation than "X has adequate evidence that Q."[5] This substitution is suggested because certain statements, he claims, do not require that the evidence condition be met to be regarded as knowledge. This would include such statements as, "I know I feel a pain." In such a case as this, it would not be appropriate to request of the person making the statement that he provide evidence. He simply *knows* that he is in pain.

A more appropriate analysis, however, might be to point out that when the person utters the statement "I feel" or some similar statement, he is already citing all that need be regarded as evidence. The addition of the words "I know" to the statement "I feel a pain"

5. Israel Scheffler, *The Conditions of Knowledge* (Glenview, Ill.: Scott Foresman and Company, 1965), pp. 58 ff.

adds no meaning at all. There appears to be no difference in meaning between my being in pain and my knowing I am in pain. Since Scheffler has changed the form of the evidence condition to admit such statements, but since such statements do not require such alteration of the evidence condition, there appears to be little point in making such an alteration.

It seems more to the point to clarify what it means to have adequate evidence. Here, Scheffler is instructive.[6] He suggests that having evidence means more than having the clues, or having the rules and items needed to support a proof. It also involves, aside from having such clues, recognizing them as clues. This means that one is able to pick out relevant data from the entire field of the environment, i.e., recognize what is relevant.

Aside from *having* the proof, in order to be regarded as knowing, one must understand the proof, i.e., see the point of it. Seeing the point of it means that one has the ability to recognize the force of the argument not only in the instance under question, but also in analogous situations. To have adequate evidence then means that one has the ability to deal with new cases beyond the one of immediate concern. This involves not simply having the argument that supports the item being considered, but also appreciating the force of the argument. This appears to be like saying that we not only have evidence, but also have evidence for the evidence, so to speak.

If the preceding points seem difficult, it will soon be seen that the third condition, the truth condition, is the most stubborn to struggle with. What makes it difficult is the problem involved in determining what is being asserted by the third condition, "And (iii) Q," or the assertion that "Q is true," or that the proposition in question is a true proposition.

There are particular kinds of truth that are demonstrably and indubitably true. For example, as Hume pointed out, propositions like "The square of the hypothenuse is equal to the squares of the two sides," or "Three times five is equal to the half of thirty" are certainly true. We do not need to go out and check squares, nor to count objects to conclude that such statements as these are true. We can discover the truth of such statements merely by the operation of thought, i.e., starting with certain, basic axioms, postulates, and definitions, we can check the "truth" of such statements by checking their logic. "Truth" in this sense refers to the statements' consistency with their premises. On the basis of analysis alone we can check the truth of such statements.

6. Scheffler, *op. cit.*, pp. 66 ff.

Empirical "truth" is quite another matter, however. Here, it is not quite so clear what is being asserted when we claim that propositions are true. One thing is clear, however. Such statements (e.g., The sun will rise tomorrow.) are neither certain nor verifiable on the basis of thought alone. Some appeal to other types of experience (e.g., sensory experience) is required to demonstrate its truth or falsehood. Having once validated such a statement, it still has not been made clear what it means to call the proposition "true."

Most philosophers will insist that there is more to the assertion of the truth of a proposition than simply talk about the psychological state of the person claiming to *know* the *truth*. What most philosophers will insist is that in attributing truth to a proposition, one is making a claim about the world. To say that "Q is true" is to say not only that someone holds Q to be true, but that Q is independently true. If truth is what is distinctive about knowing, then knowing requires not only the proper state of the knower's mind, but also the proper state of the world, some will insist. "Knowing," on this basis is not simply a mental or psychological affair, for it makes reference to an appropriate state of the world.

What such arguments inevitably include is insistence that truth is independent of our beliefs concerning it, and is likewise independent of the evidence that we have for it. Truth, supporters of this position argue, is absolute. One effort to support this view is based on the notion that there are undiscovered truths. The evidence for this will usually be some argument such as, that there is such-and-such an object lying undiscovered on the side of the moon which we cannot see. If there is such an object, then we can discover it and the claim of its being there will be a true statement. Even if we discover the falsehood of the statement, it is asserted, we will have discovered a truth that was not known before. Therefore, it is clear that there are undiscovered truths. The problem with this view is that it assumes the thing to be proved, i.e., that truths are "out there" waiting to be discovered. There is a more appropriate analysis of such statements, as we shall shortly see.

Another argument is based on the so-called *laws-of-thought*. One of these laws is called the *law of the excluded middle*, (*p* is either true or false, or Either A or not A, or either Caesar did or did not have breakfast on the morning he crossed the Rubicon). Another of these laws which is called on to demonstrate the independence and absoluteness of truth is the *law of noncontradiction*. (Not both *p* is true and *p* is false, or, not both A and not A, or I cannot both have and not have a toothache.) Those who offer such arguments will agrue that it is *true* that Caesar did have breakfast on the day he crossed the Rubicon, or it is true that he did not. We cannot confirm which of these statements is true, but one of them is absolutely true whether we can confirm it or not, and regardless of whether we establish it as true.

What needs to be understood about such claims is that the so-called *Laws of Thought* on which they are based are merely conventions for the use of language. We simply agree to use "not" in such a way in sentences that it would be inconsistent to use both *is* and *is not* about the same object in the same sentence. Actually, rather than claiming that one of the statements must be true, it would be more accurate to say that neither is true. We can establish the truth of only one because of their construction, but neither can be regarded as true until we have gathered some evidence to establish the truth of one or the other. However, this makes truth contingent upon the evidence that is gathered, and this is precisely what those who argue for the absoluteness of truth want to deny.

What must be noted, however, is that such claims as these about the absoluteness and independence of truth are metaphysical. Either that, or the third condition is meaningless. It may be observed that if anyone is asked how he knows that a proposition is true, he will inevitably and invariably begin to cite evidence. What is more, the person who is raising such a question will always be satisfied by this type of answer. He will regard the citation of the evidence on which a belief is based as an appropriate response to his question about the truth of the proposition in question. What this signifies is that the third condition of knowledge, the so-called truth condition, adds nothing at all to the conditions for knowing. At the most, it is merely a short-handed repetition of the first two.

Other arguments along this vein will concern truths in the past. For example, we once held it to be true that Columbus was the first European to set foot in the new world. We no longer hold this to be true. "It cannot be," proponents of absolute and independent truth argue, "that it was once true that Columbus was the first European to set foot in the new world, but now it is no longer true." Again, this argument assumes the very thing to be proved, *viz.*, that truth is somehow independent and absolute. Yet, as we have seen, "truth" has no meaning outside of our belief, and evidence for it. Truth is what we verify and is nothing more than this.

Another effort at establishing some meaning for the truth condition is Tarski's semantic criterion of truth. This is a schema as follows: " '_____' is true if, and only if,_____." In this schema, the first blank, surrounded by quotation marks is the statement or proposition purported to be true. The second blank represents a factual condition, or state of affairs. We might say, for example, " 'Snow is white,' is true if, and only if, snow is white." One might verbalize the schema by saying a statement is true if, and only if, it corresponds with reality.

There are at least two problems with this approach. One of these has been dealt with earlier. That is concerning what it means to claim "correspondence" between statements and "reality." What constitutes "correspondence" is never made clear, and talk about reality will involve us in either metaphysical statements, or discussions of evidence. The other problem concerns what has been added to a proposition when one adds the words "is true." Is there any real difference between the statements "Snow is white" and "Snow is white is true"? The way to check this is to see how we would verify the two statements. It is plain that both statements would be verified in precisely the same way, whatever would establish the first sentence would also establish the second. Therefore, the meaning is the same. Hence, the addition of the words "is true," gives no increment of meaning. The only force that is added is that the second sentence may be more persuasive than the first, but this is saying only that some psychological force is added by the addition of the words "is true."

One other effort to save the absoluteness and independence of truth may be examined. This is Carnap's argument that a statement may be true but not believed by X, or vice versa. On this basis, the claim goes, it may be seen that truth is one thing and being believed, accepted or confirmed as true is quite another thing. But this does not follow unless we accept the thing to be proved. If we hold that truth means nothing beyond belief and evidence for belief, (which is what we have established about truth), then it becomes nonsense to talk about truth being one thing, and belief, confirmation, etc., being another. To say that a statement may be true, but not believed by X is to say no more than that a statement that is believed by others who have evidence for their belief is not believed by X. To move from saying that a statement is independent of what X believes to saying that the truth of a statement is independent of what everyone believes is a poor piece of reasoning.

What have we established at this point, about the conditions of knowledge? We have established that typical efforts to distinguish between knowing and believing on the basis of a truth condition are not successful. It seems reasonable to conclude that we cannot distinguish knowing from believing *on this basis*. Since one cannot distinguish between knowing and believing on this basis, it might be more fruitful to look elsewhere. Some further examination of the belief and evidence conditions might indicate a way of making this very useful distinction. The truth condition is not useful because it is meaningless.

The problem with the conditions that have been generally established is that they seem to admit as an item of knowledge, any item that is grammatically sound. For example, the statement that "Reality is the Absolute expressing Itself," has the same force as the statement that "The world is round." In the first place, there are people who claim to believe both. Secondly, those who hold these beliefs are able to offer evidence for their beliefs. In the case of the first statement, the evidence cited would probably resemble St. Thomas's five proofs for the existence of God. The second would be supported by empirical evidence. Both would have met the first two conditions of knowledge, the belief and the evidence conditions. As for the third condition, the truth condition, how does one proceed here? There seems to be no way to check to see if this condition has been met outside of repeating the evidence condition statements.

Yet, the two statements do appear to be two different kinds of statements. Most people would probably label the first statement as a belief statement while the second would generally be regarded as an item of knowledge. The clearest difference between the two is in the method used for collecting evidence. This is not to suggest that there is something magical about empirical evidence. The only claim that would be made would be that distinguishing between different statements on the basis of how evidence is gathered could lead to a useful distinction and would probably reflect the distinction that most people make. Even this distinction however would have to include exceptions that would admit analytical statements as statements of knowledge. Therefore, the distinction suggested here would be for distinguishing knowing from believing among statements that were purported to be synthetic statements.

If the rule were followed, then, that genuine theories were those hypotheses that connect the explicandum to what we know, rather than what we merely believe, "theory" would take on a slightly different meaning than that suggested earlier. This, of course, would be applicable only to that use of "theory" in which the term refers to hypotheses or logically connected sets of hypotheses. As was demonstrated, there are different uses for the term "theory" i.e., a theory is anyone of a number of things. If what a theory does is connect up what we wish to have explained with what we know, rather than what we believe, then this will affect what comes to be taken seriously as an educational theory.

Chapter 8

Educational Theories

In the simplest terms, an educational theory may be thought of as that which explains why we do what we do in education. The fact that there are in the field of education statements and logically connected sets of statements whose function is to explain their subject matter ought not to lead us to expect to find theories serving identical purposes which theories serve in other areas. For example, we also find the word "theory" used in such bodies of knowledge as physics and chemistry. Yet, while the use of the term "theory" in these sciences may serve as a useful model for elucidating the worth of educational theories to some extent, it must be remembered that the use of models has limitations.

The extent of these limitations in regard to the comparison of educational theories with theories in other fields may be seen if we view education on the one hand, and physics on the other, as representing in their classical sense an art and a science. Since education is an art, in the classical sense of the term, and physics is a science, there are bound to be limits on the similarities which we find between the two.[1]

Analysis of these fields will show us that education is not, like physics or chemistry, a science. In that education aims at other results than adding new knowledge to that which is already held by the race of man, it is more like such endeavors as medicine and engineering than it is like physics or chemistry. Further, explanations frequently differ. What we have usually meant by scientific explanation is that an event is covered by a general law and is explained as an

1. There is no intention here of establishing some sort of dualism which sees education as purely "doing" and physics as purely "knowing." Such distinction may be useful for our purposes of discussion here, but it does not reflect an ontological separation. To suggest that it did would do an injustice to an adequate conception of both education and physics, rendering the one mindless and the other purely abstract.

instance of that general law. In education, however, we frequently have different explanations. When, for example, we explain why we include music or art in the curriculum, or why we use democratic models of organization, we do not use the "covering" explanation used in the sciences. Instead, we explain in terms of purposes, or use any of a number of forms of explanation. Therefore, although theories may serve the same general function in all these activities of man, there are some differences to be found.

Like medicine and engineering, education aims at a different and what would popularly be regarded as a more practical result than the creation of new knowledge. However, in all three of these areas, what is done is based, at least in part, on what is known in certain fields. On this basis, it seems reasonable to speak of the *practices* of medicine, and engineering, and education rather than the *sciences* of these fields. While education, like medicine and engineering, is not itself a science, it is based to a large extent on sciences.

Some will claim, however, that the undertaking or activity which we call education does not rest upon a *discipline* of education. That is, they will deny that there is a body of knowledge that underlies the practice of education. One such claim is based on tradition. The fields of knowledge in antiquity did not include education; therefore, education is not now to be admitted as a discipline. It is not always necessary to look back that far, however, since the medieval universities did not include chairs of education. On such bases, education is denied status as a discipline.

Others will deny that education is a discipline on other grounds. In the first place there is no specific or particular realm of things that relates uniquely to education. There is no autonomous branch of knowledge that is unique to education. Also, there is no unique class of phenomena that is related to education. And, though educators are occasionally accused of indulging in pedagese, whenever they attempt to make their use of language precise and specific, there are no uniquely educational terms. For these reasons, education is considered by some not to be a discipline, though, admittedly, those who have argued the point this far are few in number. Generally, tradition alone is deemed sufficient.

Many of the arguments about whether or not education is "really" a discipline turn out to be verbal arguments about how far we wish to extend the definition of the term "discipline." Hence, there is little to be learned about either education or discipline from such arguments. Further, most of the arguments that deny that education is a discipline would similarly rule out activities like medicine and engineering, artistic pursuits like poetry and painting, and even such scholarly pursuits as history.

Among the consequences of failing to regard education as a discipline is the tendency to dismiss educational theory rather easily. The ready discharge of educational theory then leaves the practice of education adrift on a sea of choice with neither anchor nor flag. What will be relied on then will be rules of thumb or folk levels of knowledge about education.

Yet, it must be granted that there are some ways of teaching that are preferred, and preferable, to other ways, i.e., there must be some rules for good teaching that would help us to avoid the worst practices. Also, such skills as are required in the practice of education must be learned, i.e., they are the result of training, and experience and astute observation. Such skills are not acquired genetically. Taken together, these rules, training and experience, which are acquired, serve to guide the educator. Further there are realms of objects (schools, pupils, curricula), phenomena, terms and principles that have particular significance for education. On these bases, there is some point to regarding education as a discipline.

On the other hand medicine and engineering do not rely on specific, or unique or distinctive branches of science. Nor does literature, painting nor history. All of these may be governed by specific rules, yet the rules do not constitute specific sciences. All may draw upon a host of intellectual disciplines rather than a distinctive intellectual inquiry, yet they are regarded as practical, or in the case of history, scholarly, disciplines.

Another basis for taking educational theories less seriously than those on which other activities are based is the fact that education draws on the behavioral sciences, and such activities as medicine and engineering are based on the natural sciences. The natural sciences, for a number of reasons are regarded by some as being more reliable and valid than the behavioral sciences.

One of the differences frequently cited is that the principles which the behavioral sciences give us are more obvious to the intelligent observer than the laws of the natural sciences. What is generally claimed is that simply by virtue of being human and having thereby had such experiences as living in social groups, being educated, etc., we know the content of the fields of the behavioral sciences in rough outline. Consequently, it is claimed, the only role which the behavioral scientist serves is that of making our knowledge more precise, citing or ordering the evidence on which our commonly held knowledge is based, and systematizing what would otherwise be regarded as belief or opinion.

If our folk knowledge were reliable and valid, the knowledge that comes to be established by behavioral scientists ought not to be surprising. Yet, at least as often as not, we find that, rather than supporting tenets commonly held, the behavioral sciences frequently refute or dismiss folk knowledge. For example, some years ago Alfred Kinsey brought out his first volume on *Sexual Behavior in the Human Male.*[2] Great furor was created, although the book became a best seller. There were undoubtedly a number of reasons for the response to Kinsey's book, but the chief objection seemed to be that it shocked people. Rather than support popular notions about male behavior in this area, this scientific work dismissed much folk knowledge. Of course, there was also the problem of the work's points violating some of our cherished values, which also led to some tendency to reject it. But, the point is, that, as frequently occurs, the findings of a behavioral scientist did not bear out popularly held folk-knowledge.

A more recent example has been Dr. Reuben's volume on *Everything You Always Wanted to Know About Sex.*[3] This, too, created something of a sensation. Some of the sexual practices that Dr. Reuben finds to be perfectly normal have long been regarded at the folk-level of knowledge as indecent and lewd. In fact, in some states, certain of these practices are actually outlawed on the basis of common "knowledge." This is another example of the findings of the behavioral scientist coming into conflict with folk-knowledge.

Teachers encounter such problems frequently. In their courses in psychology they come into contact with laws of learning that are novel to them. They also learn about new and different techniques in their methods courses. Armed with such knowledge, they enter their classrooms to teach on the basis of what they have learned. But these new methods, rather than being merely folk-level knowledge made more precise are novel and startling to the public. Consequently, the new teacher occasionally finds himself the center of a controversy over the introduction of newer approaches. If folk-level knowledge were really reliable and valid, none of these surprises should take place. That it does, indicates that we do not after all have a good idea of what the behavioral sciences come to know.

One reason of course is that, rather than the subject matter of the behavioral sciences being simpler and more obvious, there is good reason to believe that it is infinitely more complex. We are able to

2. Alfred C. Kinsey *et al.*, *Sexual Behavior in the Human Male* (Philadelphia: W.B. Saunders, 1948).
3. David Reuben, *Everything You Always Wanted to Know About Sex* (New York, David McKay, 1969).

predict the movements of a heavenly body, or the reaction of a chemical combination much more readily than the behavior or reaction of human beings. There seems to be a much larger number of variables to take into account in the case of human behaviors. This would seem to call for greater rather than less study, and to require increased sophistication. The point of all this is simply to indicate that it may be more reasonable to rely on educational theories in making educational decisions than to draw simply on folk lore.

There is another basis on which theories in the behavioral sciences, which are largely the theories on which education draws, are regarded as less reliable and valid. By comparing theories in the behavioral sciences with those in the natural sciences, we may be led to the conclusion that the former are in an earlier stage of development than the latter. Sciences, it is pointed out go through stages of development. In the most primitive stage, we have the casual understanding that ordinary intelligent observation leads to. The next stage is when such understanding begins to be ordered through careful observation, recording of facts, classification and clarification. Finally, it is suggested, the science reaches the stage where the whole complex system of interacting causes and effects are understood.

The natural sciences, it is claimed are at the third level of development. The sciences of man, however, are barely beyond the first level. Being barely into the second stage of development, they are neither reliable nor valid. There can be no doubt that there is a certain truth to this. There is enough truth in fact, for us to be misled. But it is not the whole truth. In the first place, it says too much for the natural sciences, and too readily discounts the sciences of man.

What such a view overlooks is that in all of their stages, the natural sciences have appeared to be in the final stages. Newtonian physics, for example, was thought to be the final stage of physics with absolute and immutable laws of cause and effect being rather thoroughly understood. Yet, Newtonian physics has been replaced rather than supported by later physics. The other assumption that the view expressed above holds is that all sciences will have a history precisely like that of physics, and there is already some indication that this may not be the case at all. Therefore, to judge theories to be less than trustworthy on the basis of their not conforming perfectly to the model of physics may cause us to misjudge educational theories.

One basis for supposing that the behavioral sciences may follow a different course than that of sciences like physics and chemistry lies in one of the differences between these sciences. The type and extent of experimentation that takes place in the sciences of human nature differs from that in the natural sciences. In the first place, there are practical difficulties in the way of conducting laboratory type experiments. For example, if we wished to study human genetics on a laboratory basis, it would take a great deal of time to conduct breeding, produce offspring, then breed the offspring, etc., through several generations. Aside from this, it would be regarded, in most quarters, as highly immoral to have humans engage in sexual intercourse under laboratory conditions. Where this has been done on a very limited scale to gather information about sexual behavior, for example, it has created some furor.

This need not seriously limit the pursuit of knowledge in the sciences on which education is based. It does however, point up the need for some other approach to experimentation and hypothesis checking than that used in physics and chemistry laboratories. But this need not make educational theories less useful.

What must be kept in mind is the point that was suggested early in the chapter, *viz.*, that activities like education, medicine, and engineering aim at different outcomes than sciences like chemistry or physics. Whereas the latter represent efforts to account for the behavior of objects and to explain phenomena, the behavioral sciences aim at explaining man. Consequently, some of the explanations that are called for in areas like education and medicine, and to a lesser extent engineering, may involve us in customs, traditions, and values.

Very often in the empirical sciences, once the object or phenomena, has been subjected to laboratory tests and we have reached the point where puzzlement ceases, that is the end, in that context, of scientific investigation. It is the end in the sense of whatever *answer* we arrive at being the thing that we aimed for, and it is the end in being, contextually at least, some sort of termination.

In the realm of the sciences which support education, however, such is not the case. The establishment of an item of knowledge in educational theory serves the purpose of guiding activity in a public, value laden, and "practical" activity. This is not to say that the item of knowledge arrived at in physics is an inert piece of information. It, too, serves to guide activity. Yet there is some distinction to be made here. What we are suggesting is that, for example, medical theory is not composed simply of a collection of physiological, and chemical, and other such technical knowledge. Included in the principles that guide the activity of medicine are extra-technical considerations.

The same thing is true of educational theory. Since education is not simply and solely a matter of techniques, the theories that guide the activity of education are not simply and solely those parts of psychology that have to do with learning, motivation, conceptualization, etc. Occasionally what requires explanation in education can be met only by reference to history, or sociology, or anthropology, or some such endeavor. Consequently all of these areas constitute the grounds of educational practices. Having considered to some extent what the role of educational theories may be, it remains to see what kinds of statements are offered as educational directives.

II

Although it is possible to identify three distinctive kinds of statements, this is not to suggest that statements inevitably or absolutely fall into one of the three classes suggested. What is being offered is not any kind of positive science, but merely a useful operational guide. As will become clear, not all statements are obviously or purely of a single type. Some sentences will be fairly clearly or obviously of a particular type. Others will contain elements of more than one class. Frequently it will be necessary not merely to study the sentence itself, but also to take the context into account. But with all these problems, it will be useful to see what type of statement is being offered in order to know how to treat it. The different classes of statements function differently and require different types of support.

One class of statement offered as an educational theory is metaphysical. Metaphysical statements are statements that purport to be factual or descriptive, but are not empirically verifiable. In at least two ways, they resemble empirical statements. In the first place, they resemble empirical statements in form. A statement like "You have an immortal soul," has the same form as the statement "You have blue eyes." On the basis of form alone, then there is generally no way to distinguish metaphysical statements from any empirical statements. Secondly, like empirical statements, metaphysical statements purport to be informative, or descriptive, or factual.

One difference between the two types is that metaphysical statements purport to prove the existence of facts or entities that lie outside the range of normal human experience. If such statements do not purport to give proofs, then they generally claim to be giving information about such facts or entities. Occasionally, such sentences are recognizable by the fact that their subject matter is about gods, or souls, or supernatural things, as are usually regarded and immediately recognizable as lying outside the range of ordinary human observations. But, occasionally, the statements also deal with minds, and selves, facts that do not appear to be supernatural. It will be noted about such statements, however, that like all other metaphysical facts or entities, they are not empirically verifiable. That is, we cannot confirm their existence or truth through the usual methods of observation and human experience.

This is not to say that all statements that are not, in fact, verified are to be considered metaphysical. But they must be capable, at least in principle, of empirical verification. For example, a statement like, "The side of the moon that consistently faces away from the earth also contains craters, mountains, rays and rills," could not at some time in the past be verified because we had not developed the tools and techniques for such verification. It was not possible *in fact*, to verify the statement. It was known, however, how *in principle* to verify the statement. That is, we knew what sort of observations and data would confirm or refute the statement, even though such matters were at that time actually beyond us. Therefore, since the statement could at least in principle be checked, it would not be considered metaphysical.

A statement like "Human destiny is in the hands of God," is also impossible to verify empirically. Unlike the preceding statement, however, it is not even possible in principle to verify this latter statement. We have no idea what sort of observation or experience would confirm or refute whatever is asserted by it. Some will quickly respond that if God should appear and make such an announcement, then we would have the evidence we need. They reject the notion, however, that the contrary condition refutes whatever claim is being made. On the basis of their own refusal to admit such evidence then, we must point out that we do not know what would verify such a statement. If we do not know what would refute it, then we also do not know what would confirm it. Since such a statement is, even in principle, beyond verification, it must be regarded as metaphysical.

In attempting to arrive at an educational program, Aristotle considers the nature of the recipient of education. He finds that the soul of man is divided into two parts, one of which has reason in itself, the other, though not having reason, is able to obey reason. From this "information," we are able to arrive at all sorts of conclusions about how education should take place. The problem with such a view is that, in the first place, what Aristotle asserts has never been demonstrated, nor established by any generally recognized argument. In fact, it has never been made clear how one can go about establishing it.

One of the problems with such a statement is that it serves no real purpose in education. Although it may be offered as part of an educational theory, an effort to explain why we do what we do in education, it fails in this function. No one knows for sure what sort of activity is connected with souls, however they be divided. Further, even if it were possible to establish some connection, it is not clear how one would verify the effects of the activity on the soul, since no one has ever been able to observe a soul.

Metaphysical statements are not limited to sentences about souls, however. Some look like ordinary statements of fact, and in fact come to us from behavioral scientists, or from those who are purporting to do science. When the psychoanalyst tells us that "The personality is most clearly revealed when the intellect is exercising least control,"[4] he is engaging, not in science, but in metaphysics. To see that this is so, try to imagine what observation would refute such a claim. At first glance, it may seem that we would need only to find personalities that revealed themselves most clearly when the intellect is in control. But, this is not possible; what is revealed then, the analyst replies, is not the *real* personality. There is, as a matter of fact, no observation that could, even in principle, refute the claim. Since the principle is consistent with any observation that could conceivably be made, there is no observation that would clearly confirm it then. No evidence can be collected that will confirm or refute the statement.

There is a current trend in education to base educational directives on notions of "selves." There are many who would attach feelings of loyalty to and claim to be able to derive educational principles from such statements as, "Self-actualization is the creative trend of human nature. It is the organic principle by which the organism becomes more fully developed and complete."[5] A number of personalities associated with psychoanalysis, education, and existentialism have developed a fair-sized cult of the "self," and "self-realization" in recent years. However, no amount of evidence nor any publicly recognized methods are capable or sufficient for establishing such a claim as that made above. Indeed, not being provable, it is not at all clear what statements such as those above are asserting.

Aside from the problem of the lack of clarity of such statements, there are at least two other difficulties with metaphysical

4. J.A.C. Brown, *Freud and the Past-Freudians* (Baltimore, Md.: Penguin Books, 1961), p. 4.

5. Calvin S. Hall and Gardner Lindgey, *Theory of Personality* (New York: John A. Wiley and Sons, Inc., 1957), p. 304.

"theories." One problem is that, since they are not demonstrable, metaphysical truths seem to be evident only to their authors. Yet, their authors will generally claim the statements to be indubitably true. The apologists for a particular view, in fact, see opposition or challenges to their views as heresy, or treason, or at least obstinancy, if not ignorance. Yet, on the same grounds used to support their position, any other view would be as defensible.

Beyond this, there is the question of how useful such principles are for education. There is, first of all, a problem of how one moves logically from metaphysical statements to educational directives. And, it is inevitably on the basis of logic that the metaphysician will defend his stand. In fact, this is often a clue to the fact that we have been offered a metaphysical statement. Since the metaphysical statement may be consistent with any situation, or at any rate not inconsistent, then we are not able on the basis of metaphysical offerings, to select from among alternatives. This will be made more obvious when purported theories that are largely metaphysical are offered in the last chapter. Let it suffice at this point to question whether such a "theory" actually performs the function of an educational theory, if it has neither an empirical nor a logical connection with what it purports to explain.

III

Value judgements resemble metaphysical statements in some ways. In the first place, the form of such statements is similar to metaphysical statements. Also, value judgements are generally not proved by the introduction of empirical data. At any rate, they are not "proved" in the same fashion, and, if the chapter on value judgements is recalled, what is proved, at times, may not be precisely what was expected initially. At any rate, value judgements, like metaphysical statements, are not proved in exactly the same fashion as empirical statements. In fact, it may be helpful to speak of "justification" rather than proof in order to maintain the distinction between value judgements and other types of statements.

Obviously, value judgements differ from metaphysical statements, too. The chief difference lies in what is being asserted. Whereas metaphysical statements purport to be factual, or informative, or descriptive, value judgements are emotive or expressive. A short-cut way of referring to this difference is to say that metaphysical statements are "is" statements, while value judgements are "ought" statements.

There are clues that are sometimes helpful in identifying value statements. If the sentence contains words like "should," or "ought," or "good," "best," "preferred," etc., one may suspect that a value judgement is being offered. Such words are helpful, but they do not make identification absolutely positive. Words like "good" and "best" are sometimes used in their instrumental sense, in which case we treat them empirically.

Even "should" sometimes has another meaning than simple, pure preference. For example, if we are in a hospital room and view a sign that says, "Oxygen being used in this room—Caution!", I am doing more than expressing simply preference if I say, "You should not light a cigarette in here." Such statements would not be taken as simply a value judgement. Similarly, in education, if I have found a technique that is a particularly effective method for teaching a particular principle, I may be offering more than a simple value judgement if I say, "You should try this technique." Consequently, even though certain terms are frequently clues which may help identify the type of statement being offered, it is often still necessary to get at the sense of the statement and, perhaps, see it in context.

On the other hand, statements that are not obviously value judgements may turn out to be so on examination. One way to be persuasive is to make statements extremely emotive. But that is only one way. At other times, it is effective to appear to be offering factual, informative statements. Consequently, at times value judgements will be disguised as "is" statements. Only by placing them in context and examining them carefully does it become clear that what is being offered is a value judgement.

The statement that "Since growth is the characteristic of life, education is all one with growing, it has no end beyond itself,"[6] appears to be giving us information about connections between education and life. It would appear that we need not be concerned about the selection of ends for education. We simply look at "life" itself. But life contains many aspects which Dewey would not regard as educative. Of all those experiences which may be "educative," only some will be appropriate for the formal education that takes place in schools. It is when "life," and "growth" and "ends" begin to be specified that such a statement will be seen to be a disguised value judgement.

6. John Dewey, *Democracy and Education* (New York: The Macmillan Co., 1916), p. 53.

Some value judgements will be more obvious, as the following statement illustrates.

> We want no teachers who say there are two sides to every question including even our system of government; who care more for their "academic freedom of speech" and opinion (so-called) than for their country. Academic freedom of speech has no place in school, where the youth of our country are taught and their unformed minds developed. There are no two sides to loyalty to this country and its flag. There is nothing debatable about allegiance to that flag and the Republic for which it stands.[7]

Such statements, concerned as they are with what schools ought to do, are rather clearly in the realm of values. It is safe to assume that any proposal relating to aims or objectives involves the author in values. Consequently when disagreements arise over such statements, the resolution of such statements can take place only in the ways in which value judgements are resolved. Generally, what must first be made clear is what value is being expressed in the statement. If the author is simply offering his own personal preference, then there is little to be argued. If the content of his statement is essentially "I prefer, or approve of X," then we may either allow his preference or, if we wish to sway him, use persuasion to bring him to our side. Occasionally, it will also be fruitful to examine the beliefs on which he bases his values, or to look to his logic to see if his position is "justified."

If on the other hand, the author of the aim or objective is claiming it not merely as his own preference, but is asserting that it is the wish, or has the approval, of our community, or society, then this may be checked through polls, or surveys, or elections, or some such device. If he is claiming that his stated aim is the outgrowth of some general value, then we may check to see if it is, in fact, a part of custom or tradition, or, in another respect, required by law. In short, when disputes arise over aims or objectives, there are a number of ways of resolving such disputes, but the nature of the claim or dispute must first be made clear.

Very often, popular slogans which serve as rallying cries for educational directives turn out on examination to be disguised value judgements. The suggestions of the romantic naturalist that we

7. Address by the President General in the *Magazine of the Daughters of the American Revolution*, 57 (May, 1923), p. 70. Quoted in John T. Childs, *Education and Morals* (New York: Appleton-Century Crofts, Inc., 1950), p. 184.

"educate according to nature," is a disguised effort to persuade us to adopt his educational program. When he begins to specify what "nature" dictates, it will be seen that by a happy coincidence what nature requires are precisely those aims and methods and content that the romantic naturalist cherishes. The same thing is true of such statements as "Education and democracy imply each other; hence schools should be run democratically." Or, urging that education should prepare for citizenship will be seen to be a disguised way of urging the adoption of values and programs held dear by the author of the statement.

This is not to suggest that value judgements are to be eschewed. Nor, would it be appropriate to suggest that they have no important place in educational theory. Those who pretend that the only issues in education are technical problems, are generally either consciously attempting to hide their own value system, or are unconsciously overlooking the kinds of questions that are held to be most important by those concerned with education. To suggest that value questions should, or even can, be ignored in educational theory would be to grossly mislead those who are concerned. Values cannot be ignored, and to pass over such questions in favor of purely technical questions, (which is itself a choice based on values), would be to ignore what, in most quarters, would be regarded as questions of prior concern.

What is needed, rather than the ignoring of such questions, is the recognition of them. One of the reasons why certain issues in education have not been laid to rest may be that they have not been appropriately dealt with. Undiagnosed value judgements have been treated like factual statements, resulting in an issue's outliving the introduction of all the empirical data that is available to us.

One such issue that has plagued educators for many years has been the question of the "best" method of grouping children for instruction. Studies have been introduced that claim to prove that heterogeneous grouping is superior. These have been matched by similarly documented studies purporting to prove that homogeneous grouping is better. The issue continues to outlive all the studies and "proofs." What has not been recognized is that there are prior questions involving values, (specifically questions about aims) that will need to be resolved before the issue can be laid to rest. Yet, there are those on both sides of the questions who continue to treat it as a purely technical issue. Recognizing that there are questions of values involved might lead to less dogmatism and diminished feelings of certainty on the part of all parties to the controversy.

IV

Finally, educational theories may be in the form of empirical statements. Like metaphysical statements, empirical statements are "is" statements. They purport to be factual, or descriptive, or informative. They take the same form as metaphysical statements. Even value judgements will sometimes be put in the same form as empirical statements. Consequently, it often becomes necessary to see the statement in context in order to determine what type of theory is being offered. What distinguishes empirical statements from the other types considered is that such statements can be verified (confirmed or refuted) by observable evidence.

The sources of such educational directives may be either the common experiences of educators, or what we have learned about human behavior and learning from the behavioral sciences. In short, when such a statement is offered as an explanation for why we do what we do in education, it will be in terms that can be empirically checked. The test of whether or not a statement is empirical is to see whether one can conceive of an empirical check on whatever is being asserted.

As a practical suggestion, it is usually helpful to see if one can conceive of what type of evidence would *refute* what is being offered. Try to imagine being able to set up control and experimental groups that would try out the suggestion and whether or not the failure to observe predicted consequences would be regarded as refuting the claim. If the statement meets this test, then it is an empirical statement. The importance of being able to recognize empirical statements is that when disputes arise, we know, at least in principle, how to go about resolving such disputes. Consequently, it also can be made clear what is being asserted.

When the supervisor of student teaching suggests to the student teacher that while motivation is important to learning, performance is at its best when activation or arousal is at a moderate level, he is making an empirical statement. This is the type of directive that can be checked by ordinary human observation. If one knows the source of such a statement, he has another clue that the statement is empirical. In this instance, the statement comes from what we have learned in the behavioral sciences.[8]

8. R.B. Molino, "Activation: A neuropsychological dimension" *Psychological Review* 1959, 66, 367-386, reported in John M. Stephens, *The Psychology of Classroom Learning* (New York: Holt, Rinehart and Winston Inc., 1965), pp. 92 f.

Ideally, such theories should result in some practical advantages when we apply them in the classroom. We may learn, for example, that interference with learning may occur when two tasks that have similar stimuli call for different responses. Interference is especially likely when the different responses are incompatible, or easily confused. One way of reducing such interference is to embed the different responses in different structures. For example, when the student must on one occasion learn to think "friend," *amicus*, and on another occasion to think "friend" *amigo*, there may be less interference if the student has a clear feeling for Latin and Spanish as separate structures.[9]

Now, such a theory as the preceding is capable of being supported by observable evidence. Also, it makes useful recommendations for educational practices. It is clearly empirical. If some question arises as to which of a set of practices should be adopted, that which is recommended in the preceding paragraph or some competing recommendation, there is some basis for making a choice between the alternatives.

What must be remembered, however, is that all that is being established by empirical theories are probabilities that certain consequences will occur. Because of the complex nature of the behaviors we are trying to predict, the probabilities are sometimes less reliable than those in sciences like chemistry or physics. Because of this, some educators are ready to dismiss educational theories as genuine or genuinely helpful. Admittedly, the connections between what are offered as educational theories and what occurs in classroom situations are sometimes weak and tenuous. But the alternative to this is to operate on no bases at all, or to rely on simply rules of thumb or impulse. If some empirical theories are rejected on the basis of their weakness in probability, impulse and rules of thumb seem poor substitutes. Consequently, empirical theories may be most helpful if they are viewed as being the better from among genuine alternatives. To reject them because they do not fit some model of perfection leaves the educator little to operate on.

Occasionally, what may in the beginning be offered as an empirical statement may, on examination turn out to be simply value judgements. As such they cannot operate in the same way as genuinely empirical statements. For example, suppose we are offered the following statement.

---

9. Stephens, *op. cit.*, pp. 204 ff.

The special value which the study of Latin has is increasing the English speaking student's understanding of his own language. The study of Latin has proved to be the best introduction to the inflectious in our own language and to the understanding of those other devices which we use in place of the inflections.

Now, this appears on the surface, to be an empirical statement. It is the sort of recommendation which could be checked out by experimentation, and, if established, result in practical advantages when applied in the classroom.

Imagine that we have in fact checked this statement out. We have conducted numerous studies using control and experimental groups and can clearly demonstrate that the study of Latin, in fact, has no significant influence on student's understanding of English. What kind of a statement do we have now? It is still an empirical statement. The fact that it has been proved false does not alter it. Empirical statements are not necessarily true; they simply must be capable at least in principle, of empirical verification.

If the statement is empirical, or being presented with the evidence described, the author of the statement should respond. "Well, I guess I was mistaken. My theory is not valid." Suppose, however, that on being presented with such empirical data, the author of the statement responds, "I don't care what your studies show, I still say that teaching Latin is the best way to teach English." Now it is clear that the statement is not an empirical statement after all. Note that the statement has not changed. Only the context has changed. The author himself is rejecting empirical data. If he will not admit empirical data as refuting (or confirming) his "hypothesis," then the content of his statement really is simply, "*I like* the teaching of Latin."

Terms like "value," "best," etc., can be used in an instrumental sense. When they are, they can be checked empirically. But, if the context reveals that empirical checking is not possible, on one account or another, then the terms are being used in their intrinsic rather than their instrumental sense. They must then be treated as any other value judgement. When the authors of educational directives themselves reject the relevance of empirical data, then it is safe to assume that we are being offered disguised value judgements.

Since it is not always clear initially what sort of statement is being offered, a useful principle to follow is to treat statements as empirical when in doubt. Then check the context. If the author is simply making a disguised value judgement, this will become evident soon enough.

V

To review the three types of theories briefly, some comparing and contrasting may be helpful. In the first place, one may first examine a statement to see what is being asserted. If the statement claims to be about what "is" rather than what ought to be, then it probably is not a value judgement. One need check only to see whether or not the statement is capable of verification by observation to distinguish the empirical statement from a metaphysical statement.

To proceed on a slightly different basis, one might look first to see whether or not empirical data are relevant to confirming or refuting the statement. If such data are relevant, then we may call for, or expect, empirical data. If such data is not applicable, then we need to see whether such statements purport to be factual or simply express the way the author wishes things to be. Another clue to look for is that metaphysical statements are often supported by the use of logic alone. This is not to suggest that other theories lack a logical basis. However, as will be noted in the following chapter, since there is no other basis for supporting metaphysical theories, except such personal bases as intuition or introspection, metaphysicians will rely almost solely on the use of logic.

Empirical theories have the advantages of being verifiable by publicly acceptable methods, and having some practical import for the practice of education. On the other hand, the "truths" that are established by these methods are at best tenuous and probable rather than certain. For those who seek absolute certainty, such theories may be regarded as falling in the realm of opinion. Empirical theories must be regarded at best as merely tentative hypothesis. We must be ready to alter them the moment that evidence goes against them.

Metaphysical theories, on the other hand, do offer absolute certainties. Such theories begin with self-evident first principles, truths that are indubitable, and proceed on the basis of deduction to arrive at other truths. Since they lie beyond mere human experience, they are not contingent. The problem with such theories, however, is that the nature of their connection with educational practices is not clear. They appear to be merely rationalizations for practices, rather than explanations as to why we do what we do in education. Also, such theories leave no room for learning from experience. Experience being contingent, it is regarded as capable of developing mere opinion.

One fact should be noted about the positions presented in chapter 9. None of them can be characterized as being devoid of value judgements. All will have some basis in values. This is not characteristic simply of the theories presented here. Although they are sometimes disguised, values will in part underly every educational theory. One use of philosophy in relation to educational theory is to sort out such statements and make clear what they are.

Chapter 9

Contemporary Educational Theories

I

Unlike theories in the natural sciences, educational theories have not been resolved to a single theory that finds general support among its practitioners. As was suggested earlier, a part of this may be explained by the state of the sciences on which education is based. But it is probable that, even could the various schools of psychology, or various efforts at sociology, anthropology, and other behavioral fields come to agree on a single theory, there would still be varied and conflicting educational theories. This is because the problems that arise in education are not all technical problems. An explanation, therefore, that gave a purely technical account of why we do what we do in education would not answer all the problems nor exhaust all that can be said about educational practices.

Since the connection between philosophy and education is largely one of critical analysis, the philosopher may contribute to educational theory, not on the basis of pronouncing certain theories to be true and others to be false, but rather by examining theories on the basis of their meaning and logical worth. This is only one possible direction for philosophy of education. Another aspect of it would have us analyzing concepts like "mind," "self," "intellect," "aim," "teach," "learn," etc., in some detail. The preceding chapter gave one basis for assessing contemporary educational theories. While it can serve as a useful tool for analysis, this is not to suggest that this is the only role of philosophy of education, nor the only basis for examining various theories.

The theories will be examined on a roughly chronological basis. This approach has no particular significance, it is simply a matter of arbitrary choice. The order in which the theories are presented is no clue to their importance, nor any measure of their general acceptance. If the theories were judged on this basis there would be good reason to list essentialism first since that has probably had the broadest acceptance in the United States. Perennialism would most likely be ranked second on this basis. If the extent to which it were practiced were the basis for ranking theories, progressivism would come in a poor third, never having achieved very wide support and enjoying only a brief life.

The other two theories that will be considered have never enjoyed wide trial, but they are included because both show some indication of having some import for education. Reconstructionism shows signs of resuscitation after a brief flicker in the 30's. Affective humanism, a name coined by this author of this book, is included because it is being associated with other contemporary social movements and on this account may come to have some import on educational practices.

A word of caution is in order. For the sake of convenience, the views of various educational theorists have been combined in the five classifications presented in this chapter. Like any attempt at classification, it can present only general views. One should not imagine that theorists set out to present this or that position. They simply endeavor to answer certain questions and deal with particular problems. On the basis of the answers provided, theorists are classified. The classifications are only approximate, and there is variation within each theoretical position.

II PERENNIALISM

In terms of age, perennialism far outclasses all the other theories, since it traces its origins back through St. Thomas Aquinas to Aristotle and Plato. The term "perennial" meaning "everlasting" gives some clue to the position which its advocates take regarding their views. Since truth is changeless, so are the basic principles of education. So claim the protagonists of perennialism, Robert M. Hutchins, Mortimer Adler, Jacques Maritain, Etienne Gilson, Stringfellow Barr, Mark Van Doren, John U. Nef, William J. McGucken, and a number of others.

Among the points on which perennialists will agree would be the view that the comtemporary world is in a crisis of its own making. Furthermore, the crisis is deepening, rather than being cured largely because of the nature of contemporary society. It is not any particular ideas in science or philosophy that the perennialist really objects to, although these are among his targets for criticism. Nor is it simply the educational theories that he is protesting, despite the fact that he attacks these. What the perennialist sees as the real basis for the failings of the contemporary world is the whole pattern of western culture with its emphasis on science and technology, on empiricism, and on our almost completely secularized institutions.

The problem goes back a long way. In the first place, Plato had established that there were existing universals (forms) which were independent of particulars. These universals (forms) in fact were what constituted ultimate reality. But a problem persisted in that though Plato posited that particulars owed their natures to "participation" in universals, the nature of this connection was not clear. If universals in fact existed prior to and independent of particulars, then any connections appear to have been severed absolutely.

Aristotle put back together what Plato had divided. He introduced his form-matter hypothesis, which we know as hylomorphism (hylo-matter, morphism-form). This principle suggests that matter stands at the base of all things. Matter, however, cannot exist alone. To become anything it must contain form. Matter represents *potentiality*. To actualize this potentiality, matter must assume some form. Form, then, represents *actuality*. Matter and form may be considered separately, logically, but they are always found associated in things in the universe.

Furthermore, there is an order of increasing perfection. As was pointed out above, matter stands at the base of things. But as we rise in the order of things, we find increasing form until there emerges at the apex, pure form. We can only know pure form by logical extension. But if we consider that as we rise in the order of things we find increasing evidence of immaterial things, it becomes plain that at the peak of perfection we find pure mind, or absolute reason.

St. Thomas carried this union of potential and actual a further step, when he took Aristotle's position another step. Aristotle had seen the combination of form and matter determining the *essence* of a thing. Aristotle has suggested that what all things held in common was that they had an essence, a "what-ness." St. Thomas suggested that what everything shared in common was more basic, namely their very existence. Essence, to St. Thomas, constituted potentiality, while existence represented the principle of actuality.

Though their positions may seem to differ, they really represent continuing elaborations on questions of universals. What really challenged all these positions was the notion of *nominalism*, particularly as it was put forth by William of Occam in the fourteenth century. This position said essentially that there were only particulars and that what was regarded as universals actually was merely a *name* used to refer to particulars. For example, there is no such universal as a rose; *rose* is merely the name that we use to refer to certain particulars.

One may justly wonder how such questions, argued so long ago, have any meaning for us today. But it was precisely the triumph of nominalism that accounts for our orientation today. The consequence of nominalism has been to turn us away from the reality established by the mind alone and to move us through materialism into the empiricism of the contemporary world. It will not be until we have corrected this monumental error and returned to truly objective ways of knowing that we can come to know true reality. What we must return to are axiomatic truths about reality, knowledge, and value that are permanent and immutable.

Such a course will help us correct that error that infects all our institutions including education. What we must begin with, in education, is a true perception of man. Only then can we know what education is about. The true conception of man comes not from psychology, or sociology, or anatomy, or biology, but from metaphysics.

What can we learn about man? In the first place, we know that man shares certain characteristics with other material things. At the very lowest level, he is composed of matter, like any rock. However, it is obvious that he has qualities which rocks do not have, viz., he is living. This he shares with all other living things. But, being higher in the order of things he also has other characteristics, e.g., he is mobile. Again, this is a characteristic which he shares with other animals. But, beyond this, being still higher in the order than other animals, he has something that makes him different from all other animals. This is his ability to reason. This ability to reason, this *rationality*, then, is man's essence. Aristotle tells us, in fact, that man is a rational animal.

This is not to say that all men are the same. The perennialist recognizes that there are differences. These differences are what are called *accidental* qualities. Some people are dark; some are light. Some are large, some are small. Some have one set of talents; others will have differing talents. But by virtue of being human, they all have a quality that is intrinsically human, that characterizes their humanity. This is their ability to deliberate, meditate, speculate; in short, to reason. This is what man can do that no other animal can do. Therefore, we can say, it is the nature of human nature to be rational.

This has serious and meaningful consequences for us. In the first place, it reminds us that man is basically the same everywhere. His language, his color, his culture are all matters of accidence. Essentially (i.e., in essence) he is everywhere and for all time, the same. Man's essential nature tells us something about the education that should take place.

Obviously, education exists to develop man, not as mere matter, not as mobile matter, but as *man*. We bring schools into existence to do the job of educating. Now, if the role of the school is to develop man as man, and if it is the nature of man to be rational, then it follows that it is the role of the school to develop man's rationality. That is what schools are uniquely equipped to do; they are the sole institution in society with that charge. Whatever other needs man has will be met through his other institutions. Schools will develop man's ability to reason and through reason, he will come to know.

Knowing of course means coming to grasp the basic meaning of reality. The way we come to know begins in self-evidence. Intuitively, or through introspection, we come to know certain indubitable propositions. An obvious example is that I exist and I know this. And I know that I know it. I cannot deny this without denying the existence of my denial. Such self-evident principles are known as *first principles*. I cannot know them all, nor can anyone. But the necessity for establishing and studying such principles gives us not only a method for education, but one of its subjects. That subject is metaphysics whose task is such study.

Accompanying the need for knowing first principles is the need for logic. We proceed in knowing by establishing new knowledge on the basis of deduction from first principles. This does not mean that intuition and deduction are the sole ways of knowing. We may use induction, too. In fact, we may be led to some of our premises by induction. But it is only through deduction that we can come to know with certainty.

The model for knowing, to the perennialist, is represented by geometry. This not only serves as a model for knowing, but it also constitutes an important subject in the curriculum of the learner. How is learning to proceed, then? There is no secret, here, the perennialist insists. We have known this for two thousand years.

Since human nature is everywhere the same, education will everywhere be the same. The mind of the learner will be developed by immersion in those ordered subjects that represent true knowledge. The ordered subjects are those which represent (literally represent) the orderliness in the universe. Such immersion will develop the natural powers that are potential in human nature.

What subjects do this? In addition to metaphysics and geometry, they are the subjects that follow these models. The study of languages (grammar), mathematics, history (here the logic is chrono-logical), and whatever has been conceived to constitute the *liberal arts.*

This has varied, although the strictest of the perennialists will still insist that it means the *trivium* (grammar, rhetoric, logic), and the quadrivium (arithmetic, geometry, astronomy, and music, the latter really being the mathematical study of harmony). On this basis, whatever did not fit the bill of developing reason had no business being retained in the curriculum. The more extreme perennialist would eliminate other subjects such as physical education, home economics, driver education, current events, even music and art.

The content of the liberal arts could best be studied in the "Great Books" which represents the spiritual and physical permanencies of the world. The "Great Books" originally started out as the "One hundred great books" which purportedly contained all the knowledge that was worthwhile in the world, or at least all the knowledge that anyone needed. That number has now been increased, therefore, the list is too long to be included here. A late listing shows 144 titles, although some titles list more than one work, and certain works comprise two titles.

Suffice it to say that most of the titles represent ancient classical or medieval works. A very few titles are from the present century, and those are just beyond the turn of the century. There is no volume from a recent decade of the twentieth century. But it is almost misleading to focus attention on these few volumes, because the bulk of the works are from the remote past.

The "Great Books" program has not remained merely an ideal. The program of studies at St. Johns College in Annapolis, Maryland, represents the application of the perennialist doctrine. Education there was to consist essentially of reading and analyzing through lecture and discussion the "Great Books." This constitutes liberal education in its purest form in American education.

The point of this liberal education is not to teach man to make a living, but rather to teach him to live. Learning to live means developing man's actuality; leading him from potentiality to what he is to become. In order to do this the school must create the type of environment which will develop his intellect. The intellect is developed by acquaintance with true knowledge. Since this is provided for through the great classics, perennialists eschew contemporary or "real-life" situations. Education, in this sense, is seen to be preparation for the adult life to come.

The role of the teacher is exemplified by the role which Socrates played. This makes the role of the teacher central in importance. This does not mean that the teacher is a mere conveyor of data and facts. But, through his questioning, and also through his lectures, the teacher helps children to come to adjust to eternal truths. Learning is by instruction but it leads to self-learning as the mind is developed. But there is no place in the perennialist scheme for pupil-teacher planning. Indeed, such a suggestion would be preposterous.

At the elementary level, instruction will be in the basics that underlie the liberal arts. The child will learn to read, write, and figure. There is little need for bothering unexperienced children with other subjects. Later on, however, such subjects will be introduced as history, geography, and foreign languages. Equally important is character training. The moral virtues as well as the intellectual virtues will be developed. The use of appropriate didactic material can do much to accomplish this. Of course, it will be necessary to impose discipline externally. The aim is to develop self-discipline. But, children are potential, not actual. Therefore, external controls must be imposed until discipline has been developed.

If we may summarize the position of the perennialist, certain principles may be abstracted from what has been said above. The first of these is that it is the nature of human nature to be rational, and that human nature is everywhere the same. No empirical checking can verify this. Indeed, the perennialist would regard empirical proof as irrelevant. This is a truth that we know intuitively, a first principle. In this sense, then, this aspect of perennialist theory is metaphysical.

A second principle of perennialism is that since human nature is everywhere the same, then education also is everywhere the same. As Adler instructs us:

> If man is a rational animal, constant in nature throughout history, then there must be certain constant features in every sound educational program, regardless of culture or epoch.[1]

1. Mortimer J. Adler, "The Crisis in Contemporary Education," *The Social Frontier*, V. (February, 1939), 141-144.

Again this is a "truth" that purports to be factual, but is not capable of empirical support. Indeed, empirical checking would seem to reveal to us that education is not everywhere the same. The perennialist retort would be that what did not follow his prescription is not education. Since the statement is offered as an "is" statement, but is not capable of empirical verification, it must be regarded as metaphysical.

Related to this is the perennialist principle that truth is universal and immutable. This constitutes yet another basis for the requirement that education be everywhere the same. As we learn from Hutchin's famous "syllogism,"

> Education implies teaching. Teaching implies knowledge. Knowledge is truth. The truth is everywhere the same. Hence education should be everywhere the same.[2]

Since truth is universal and immutable, it is truth that is the focus of education. Not vocational training, not concern for contemporary issues, but the pure pursuit of truth for its own sake constitutes the aim and purpose of education everywhere. There is still a strong movement in certain quarters to eliminate all significant differences in educational patterns, to turn all institutions of higher education into temples of liberal learning. There have been educators urging a return to the days of yore by eliminating all "majors" and having all students acquire essentially the same "liberal" education or universal Truths.

Purporting to give us information about the world, yet not susceptible to empirical checking, the statement, about the universality of truth is metaphysical.

Another principle of the perennialist is that what is required to be learned is best learned through the liberal arts, either interpreted literally as the seven liberal arts or regarded more loosely as represented by the three R's initially and culminating in the reading of the ancient and medieval classics. There is no empirical evidence at all to support the perennialist's claims for what his program does. Indeed, what evidence we have would seem to refute such claims. The perennialist, however, firmly rejects all such data. When he suggests that his program is "best," then, he is using best in its intrinsic sense. He is merely expressing a preference for such a program. This principle then must be seen as a value judgment and must be handled as such.

2. Robert M. Hutchins, *The Higher Learning in America* (New Haven, Conn: Yale University Press, 1936), p. 66.

In a sense, the position of the perennialist may be seen as even more value-based than our brief survey indicates. For example, the claim that man is characterized by his rationality is, at the bottom, a matter of choosing. We might as readily have chosen any of man's other "unique" characteristics, his use of tools, his artistic ability, certain aspects of his irrationality, to represent his "humanness." But, for all that, perennialism is largely a metaphysical theory and is so avowedly.

Being metaphysical, the principles that support the perennialist theory are of little use when we are called on to make decisions, or to explain why we do what we do in education. As a case in point, we are faced in education with deciding what will constitute the educational program. Since children cannot be taught everything that is known to man, some selection must be made. On the basis of the metaphysical arguments of the perennialist, we receive no guidance at all. His premises are no more defensible than any other set of premises. There is no way of knowing whether our choices are appropriate or not because, not being empirical, there is no basis for checking them. Hence, we either simply accept the perennialist's word for what is best, or we are left with indefensible choices in which one set of choices is no more valid than any other. Despite the heavy emphasis on "rationality," the perennialist finds himself required in several places to make irrational leaps, from the choosing of his premises to the claimed connections between rationality and the subjects which he cherishes.

III ESSENTIALISM

Despite the fact that it has been as consistently attacked by perennialists, as has progressivism, essentialist patterns of belief tend to be "friendlier" to the perennialist position than to any other. Like perennialists, the essentialist leaders call for a return to the past. However, the past to which essentialist leaders would take us, is usually the relatively immediate past, rather than the remote past. In some few instances, the past to which the essentialist looks back fondly is the Middle Ages. For the most part, however, the past which serves as a model after which the present is to be patterned ranges from late 19th century to "When I went to school . . . ," (The precise date in the latter case varies with the speaker.)

Essentialism covers much under its umbrella, including both idealists and realists. Most philosophers regarded as critical analysts, or philosophic analysts, seem also to be essentialist in outlook. It is questionable whether this latter group should be considered an additional group or included as simply one of the branches of realism. Among those who are generally considered to be among the essentialists are William C. Bagley, Herman H. Horne, Ross L. Finney, Isaac L. Kandel, F.S. Breed, William Brickman, James B. Conant, Council for Basic Education leaders Arthur Bestor and Mortimer Smith, and such analysts as R.S. Peters, C.D. Hardie, and a number of other educational writers.

The views of essentialists range from polemicists like Smith and Bestor to more experienced and thoughtful educators like Brickman who is more inclined to call for data than to deliver broadsides. Also included are those analysts who, like Hardie and Peters, frequently slip from their analytic role to become prescriptive. Hardie, for example, finds that " . . . if Latin and mathematics are properly taught, then they are the ideal subjects for improving the intelligence."[3]

The compatibility of views held by idealists and realists is not strange if one recalls that both hold objective views of reality, truth or knowledge, and values. Both see reality and truth as existing prior to and independent of the individual. Although the idealist embraces a coherence theory of truth while the realist holds to a correspondence theory of truth, both presume truth in some manner reflecting what is "really" out there. An idea is true if it accurately and consistently represents (literally re-presents), an object or situation to the mind.

The educational significance of this view is that it places the student in the role of recipient spectator of the universe. Whether the universe is essentially physical or spiritual, whether what is brought to mind is recalled or implanted, knowledge, which is objective, must be present in the mind if we are to be said to know. Teaching is the art of presenting historical and contemporary facts, laws, values, traditions in an efficient and effective manner.

Not only are reality, and knowing, objective, but what is presented by the teacher is also not simply a matter of choice. Essentialists insist that there is a basic core of "essentials" that are to be taught to every human being if he is to be fully developed. These essentials are to be presented in some form at every level of education and no education can be called that unless it includes these essentials.

3. C.D. Hardie, *Truth & Fallacy in Educational Theory* (New York: Teachers College, Columbia University, 1962), p. 96.

Like the perennialist, the essentialist sees at least the institution of education, if not all of society, as being in the midst of a crisis. The basis for the problems which he sees is a departure from practices, habits, institutions, principles that once had our support, but which have been abandoned in favor of contemporary and transitory values. The essentialist does not advocate turning our back on the current crises. But what he maintains is that much of what we face is the result of the dilution of the intellectual and moral standards that were once held. Therefore, what is called for is a return to the intellectual standards and moral rigors of the past.

The program of education that the essentialist calls for is one that will give an ordered view of the physical world, which will itself train the intellect if rigorously handled. In addition, of course, character must also be developed, although the school's primary role is intellectual training.

The subjects which the essentialist would include would consist initially of the tool subjects which would train the intellect and make further learning possible. These would be the three subjects called for in the perennialist curriculum, reading, writing, and arithmetic. The essentialist is very specific about the content of these areas. The reading for example, is not to include any of the methods of recent reading programs. These are dismissed as ineffective "look-and-say" methods. Also dismissed are notions of "readiness," "child development," and "individual differences." These notions simply interfere with proper teaching and learning. Reading instruction will consist of instruction in phonics which will enable every normal child to learn to read easily and accurately in the first grade. Such instruction will not only give children one of their essential skills, but will also go far toward correcting juvenile delinquency.

In the area of mathematics, the chief recommendations are that topics and processes should be introduced earlier, that we should not be concerned with relating arithmetic to "real life experiences," and that textbooks should not be so pleasant to look at. More serious suggestions than some of these have generally been along the line of introducing topics to children at an earlier age.

English suffers from problems also. At some point in our past, we enjoyed a common bond of language governed by tradition, logic, and standards understood by all. This is no longer the case; English has become corrupted by a slip from standards and the abandonment of the teaching of the essentials. What is called for is a return to the rigorous study of grammar, and to the great literature of the past.

Pupils must also be saved from the scourge of social studies by a return to the separate subjects of history and geography. This will call for knowing the locations of states, counties, and cities. In history, what will be emphasized will be the facts of history as presented by respectable scholars, rather than dealing with debatable issues like the United Nations, or some of the current and complex social problems.

In addition to these subjects, pupils will also be exposed to biology, and a year of physical science. Everyone will be required also to take a foreign language. The study of a foreign language is called for, not only on grounds of its serving to train the intellect, but also because of our need to recapture our position of world leadership.

Physical education, music and art may also be included. The essentialist does not appear to be willing to make many concessions but these seem to constitute a compromise. Inevitably, when the essentialist allows physical education to enter the program, he does so with the caution that it be properly subordinated to the academic disciplines. Music and art, while admitted to the program, are not granted full-fledged subject matter status. They are to be approached simply on the basis of appreciation and may be granted only the status of being elective.

In addition to these subjects which will constitute the curriculum for everyone, pupils will also be required to commit to memory certain great classics. Some of the passages from Shakespeare and other great poets should be memorized, along with certain parts of the Bible. Also, the great documents of our political heritage would be included, the Preamble to the Constitution, the opening of the Declaration of Independence. Certain of the great speeches of our great leaders, e.g., Lincoln's Gettysburg Address, would be memorized. All of this, of course, would develop the memory as well as teach valuable lessons and inspire noble thoughts.

Not only would all children be required to engage in such a program, but teachers would be committed to teaching it. These essential subjects are the vehicles of the transmission of our heritage, and the teacher is the agent of the transmission. In this scheme, there is no place for teacher-pupil planning. Indeed, there is no need for it, since the whole curriculum is prescribed.

The child's progress through the program is also very carefully controlled. No child would be promoted, or graduated, from any phase of the program until he had demonstrated mastery of it. His mastery of the content will be determined by objective measures. If he is able to demonstrate the fullness and accuracy of his mind's agreement with reality, by giving back the physical and moral world to which he has been exposed, he is educated. If he is incapable of such presentation, he is not educated and therefore is not eligible for promotion, graduation, or any honors.

Much of what has been said about the curriculum proposed by the essentialist points toward the methods that would be employed by the teacher in process of transmission. The methods as well as the content are hinted at in the following quotation.

> When we were boys, boys had to do a little work in school. They were not coaxed; they were hammered. Spelling, writing, and arithmetic were not electives, and you had to learn.
>
> In these more fortunate times, elementary education has become in many places a sort of vaudeville show. The child must be amused and learns what he pleases. Many teachers scorn the old-fashioned rudiments; and it seems to be regarded as a misfortune to read and spell by the old methods. As a result of all the improvements, there is a race of gifted pupils more or less ignorant of the once prized elements of an ordinary education.[4]

With the essentialist emphasis on content, it is difficult to sort out what methods will be used. As the quotation above hints, intellectual training includes hard work and application. Many of the tasks are granted to be unpleasant, but it is up to the pupil to overcome any lack of interest and distaste. Teachers may help, of course, by stimulating interest wherever possible. But the essentialist's emphasis is on effort rather than interest. The important point is that the child learn how to read, write, and figure, and these basic purposes are not to be diluted with activities or concerns that merely divert.

Since the purpose of education is transmission, and the view of the pupil is largely as a receptor, there is great emphasis on memorization, the "exercise" of reason, drill and repetition, and such devices. In short, the methods that are generally embraced are the traditional methods of mental discipline.

---

4. The statement quoted above is an illustration of the fact that it is difficult at times to know precisely what period of the past the essentialist looks back to with fondness. The statement is typical of those of the 50's and 60's following Sputnik. As a matter of fact, however, the statement appeared in the *New York Sun* on October 5, 1902.

Such methods are based on a school of psychology that has not enjoyed intellectual respect for several decades, faculty psychology. In this view, the mind is viewed as, in some ways, like a muscle. It consists of parts, or faculties, like memory or reason. These faculties could be developed through exercise. Therefore, certain subjects, which exercised the faculties, or provided mental discipline were to be used to train the intellect. Subjects like mathematics, or grammar, or certain languages provided such discipline. The method most frequently used for learning was memorization of the content of such courses.

The most recent development along these lines has been the introduction of programmed learning. In programmed learning (or programmed instruction), the structure of knowledge, or of a particular subject, is broken down into brief, logically connected components, or steps. The pupil is expected by means of filling in blanks, or depressing a button or key, to respond to each step. If he responds correctly, he is moved along to the next step. If he fails to respond properly, he chooses another response and keeps trying until he makes a correct response which moves him along to the next step. By moving through this gradual and continuous sequence, the pupil comes to "know" the subject matter. Of course, he is also being continuously tested as he makes each response, so he constantly knows how much he has learned.

Since the essentialist view of learning sees the learner as the recipient of the essentials, and the teacher as the transmitter, this position allows for a teaching machine to be substituted for the teacher. By such means education, it is asserted, can be made very efficient and highly effective. The complicated questions that such techniques raise are too numerous to be considered here. Those interested in philosophy of education would find the literature of this field fertile grounds for sharpening, or practicing analytic skills. The literature is voluminous and teeming with concepts calling for analysis. Suffice it to point out here that such learning as is generally done through programs is largely verbal manipulation.

A summary of the position of the essentialist would reveal the following basic principles. In the first place, there is a basic view among both realists and idealists (and, there is good reason to believe, also among philosophic analysts), that there is an objective reality out there prior to and independent of the workings of the mind. Since it would only be through some "working of the mind," that such a view could ever be verified, this places the notion inevitably beyond verification. This much of the essentialist view then is clearly metaphysical. For reasons which have already been given, such statements have no import for, nor bearing on, educational practices. Therefore, as a theory, such a view can be dismissed.

A second principle of the essentialist is that the purpose of the school is to provide intellectual and moral training. There would be little quarrel with this principle were it to remain at this level, and if it were not held to exclude all other purposes. However, when the essentialist comes to define such concepts as intellectual training, he is inevitably and invariably involved in using the terms intellectual and moral training as a rationalization for what he wants in the schools, rather than as an explanation for what we do. On this basis, the principle must be seen as a value judgment. This is not unusual, since statements about purposes are usually value judgments.

Thirdly, the essentialist sees the curriculum of the school as a logically ordered series of essential subject matters. These are very similar to the subjects which would be found in the perennialist curriculum. The chief distinction would be one of emphasis; the perennialist would lean more heavily toward the humanities, whereas most essentialists, while not ruling out the traditional humanities, would play them down in favor of a heavier emphasis on the sciences and mathematics. The subject matter selected by the essentialist is claimed to be selected on the basis of what it does for the mind. Despite the certainty with which the essentialist makes his claim, there is no empirical data to support his claim. In fact, most of the research that has been done during the past half century refutes rather than supports this claim of the essentialist. The fact that the essentialist himself rejects such empirical data indicates that in the selection of subject matter, he is merely exercising his preferences. Consequently, this principle, too, must be regarded as a value judgment.

An additional principle in the essentialist's position is that the appropriate method of instruction is the traditional approach of mental discipline. There was a time when the claims of retention and transfer that were made by essentialists were regarded as empirical statements which were supportable. However, the data that has been collected indicates that such claims as were once made have no validity. Despite this, the essentialist still insists on maintaining his position on this point. Consequently, what appears to be an empirical offering must, on the same grounds as for the preceding statement, be dismissed as an empirical statement and regarded as a value judgment. When the essentialist, in the face of contrary evidence, clings to his claim that the best teaching methods are those of traditional mental discipline, he is using "best" in its intrinsic, rather than its instrumental, meaning. He simply *values* those methods which he offers.

Aside from certain metaphysical assumptions about the nature of reality and mind, or the individual, the theories of the essentialist must be regarded as simply value judgments and defended or dismissed on the same bases as any other value judgments. At one point in the past, around the turn of the century, the essentialist's position would have been regarded as largely empirical, since most of the principles were derived from what was then known about learning in the behavioral sciences. Since most of these notions have long since been dismissed, and the essentialist in the face of more recent empirical data, still insists on clinging to these outmoded principles, his position must be regarded as largely value-oriented, rather than either metaphysical or empirical.

IV PROGRESSIVISM

Progressivism has been attacked by both perennialists and essentialists. The attacks have been out of all proportion to the influence which the movement has had. Progressivism has generally been associated with John Dewey and pragmatism. The theory had its inception shortly before the turn of the twentieth century. It enjoyed expression in the Laboratory School of the University of Chicago, which was founded in 1896. A few other schools and some scattered classrooms over the next two or three decades made some efforts in the direction of Dewey's progressivism. But, contrary to popular belief, the movement was never widespread and by midcentury appeared to have pretty well died out as an organized movement.

During the period of Dewey's progressive movement, which was also known as experimentalism, or instrumentalism, another brand of progressivism enjoyed some brief attention, too. This was the romantic naturalistic approach which would most likely trace its origin back to Rousseau, rather than to Dewey. Frequently, this distinction is not made, and all progressivism is often regarded as a single movement. The fact that Dewey himself recognized the distinction is evidenced by his attack on the later progressivism, the romantic movement of the twenties and thirties, in his little volume, *Experience and Education*.[5] This book, along with Dewey's *Democracy and Education*, will give the reader a clear picture of one branch of

5. John Dewey, *Experience and Education* (New York: Collier Books, 1938).

progressivism. This is not to suggest that Dewey, alone, was responsible for the movement. But he was clearly its leader. Other noted members of the movement included Boyd Bode, William H. Kilpatrick, John L. Childs, V.T. Thayer, William O. Stanley, Harold Rugg and a number of others.

Another point might help to put progressivism in perspective. The movement in education was not an isolated phenomenon. A look at the intellectual, cultural, political history of the period will indicate that similar movements were going on in other areas of society. Several social reform movements such as that to improve the treatment of the mentally ill, prison reform, efforts to secure rights for women, humane treatment of the indigent, were going on. There were also progressive movements in the arts, in painting and literature. In politics, a political party was established called the Progressive Party. In this may be seen the fact that the progressive movement in education was part of a tide that was moving on the American scene.

Like other parts of that movement, progressivism in education emphasized an effort to reform institutions that were not felt to be serving human welfare. In calling for better education, the progressive movement was simply adding its voice to others calling for men to face the issues of the times and to build a better society and therefore a better life for all. To that extent, progressive education was part of a larger movement.

In another sense, the progressive education movement was an isolated phenomenon. Despite the fact that progressives were devoted to the same goals and shared the same hopes as members of other progressive movements, progressives in education won few supporters to their cause. Many leaders who were noted for their liberalism in politics, in matters of social reform, in the arts, did not carry these same sentiments over to education. In matters regarding education, many of the most liberal thinkers in other areas either turned their backs on educational progressives, or joined in conservative, even reactionary, opposition to the movement in education. Consequently, the two leading educational systems, essentialism, and to a lesser degree, perennialism, came through largely unscathed by the progressive protest. While a number of other areas of society were relatively radically altered, the schools remained largely traditional. What influence progressivism has had, has been limited and indirect.

One departure from the traditional position to be found in progressivism is the view that the pupil is active, rather than passive. Like essentialism originally, progressive educational theorists took their views of the learner and learning from the behavioral scientists. But whereas, the essentialist remained fixed on a school of thought that has long since been replaced, progressive thinkers embraced the newer concepts that have replaced the older faculty psychology.

One result of this has been the progressive emphasis on educating the whole child. Newer movements in psychology picture the child as an organism and reject notions of mind isolated from physical existence. Consequently, to the progressive, rather than "the" mind being an entity which can be trained in isolation, "mind" becomes simply a summation symbol for particular ways of behaving. Education then becomes the alteration of whole behavior patterns. This places education squarely in the center of experience, rather than isolating it as happens in other theories.

It is for his view of the whole child that the progressive has often been bitterly attacked. His reply has often been disarmingly simple. He emphasizes educating the whole child because that's the only kind who ever shows up in his school. Hence, the focus, for the progressive educator, is on the learner rather than solely on a particular body of content to be mastered.

Since the child is an active learner, his learning takes place the way any learning takes place. Consequently, he is actively involved in the learning process. This means that what is to be learned is not simply imposed from above, rather, the pupil is involved at the appropriate level in the selection of means and ends. He is an active participant in the learning process. Consequently, his interests, and needs are central. This does not mean that the educational program consists of following every immediate childish whim. The teacher does not abdicate. But the teacher helps to control the environment and guide the child rather than simply imposing sets of fixed notions.

This was one of the areas where the romantic branch of progressivism differed from that represented by Dewey and his followers. To the romantic naturalists the child was viewed sentimentally as being a naturally developing, or unfolding, individual whose every whim must be met. Hence, there was a laissez-faire attitude in which the teacher simply followed the lead of the child and the program moved from whim to whim. Relevance simply came to mean the child's taste. In reaction to the highly controlled atmosphere of the traditional classroom, all controls were eliminated.

The progressive also viewed knowledge as a dynamic process rather than something inert which one possessed. This also had its influence on what went on in the classroom. Rather than viewing knowledge as a completed body of facts or truths which man had discovered, the progressive, drawing on his pragmatic views, regarded knowledge as a way of ordering experience. Since knowledge is viewed this way, coming to know, or learning, is then regarded as, in Dewey's terms, the "reconstruction of experience."

The child does not come to school as an empty vessel to be filled and sent home again to his family. Nor is he a raw material which the school fashions and sends out as its finished product. Children come to school already a bundle of experiences, and habits. The school's role, and the teacher's function is to reorder this experience in light of new experiences which the child is having. For example, even kindergarten children may come to school with some vague and imprecise experiences with fractions. The teacher, rather than pouring in, (or wringing out) completed, predigested bodies of knowledge will start with the child where he is, in his present situation, and make his knowledge of fractions broader, and deeper, and more precise.

This reordering of experiences into new experiences is what constitutes the aim of education. This reconstruction that leads to further reconstruction as the child carries his new knowledge into still newer experiences is what education is all about. As progressives like to point out, the real aim of education is growth. And growth is simply that aspect of development which enables further development to take place. Growth is subordinate to nothing except further growth. Education, in this sense, is its own aim.

The road to growth is not the simple path of having already completed bodies of knowledge imposed on one's psyche. Growth comes through effort on the part of the learner. This effort is in the direction of developing intelligence. Intelligence, in turn, is not the mere amassing of inert ideas or bundles of "facts." Intelligence, to the progressive, is a way of behaving. It is not an immediate (i.e., unmediated) response to every situation as though every situation were a novel. Rather it is thinking through and reorganizing a disorganized situation, calling on past experience, judging what is relevant, calling on appropriate experiences to help us meet whatever situation we happen in this context to face. What is called for is delaying responses until all our resources can be brought to bear. This is what education develops, rather than the amassing of bodies of content.

This is not to suggest that the progressive wishes to throw out subject matter, however. It is certainly true that education is to be active, rather than passive receptivity, that the learner will learn in the way learning usually takes place. What this signifies is that pupils learn when they are faced with some sort of disjoint experience that calls for resolution. In the process of resolution the pupil "learns." In school, this has led to an emphasis, on the part of the progressive, on an "activity" curriculum, a problems approach, rather than merely absorbing certain subject matters.

Still this does not mean throwing subject matter as it is usually conceived, out of the educational program. But, the position does have certain effects on the way the progressive views subject matter. In the first place, the value of subject matter is instrumental, rather than intrinsic. And, in the second place, subject matter comes to occupy a different position in the progressive school.

As for the first point, there is not a single item of knowledge that is indispensible in the progressive view. Obviously, children cannot, in the short time they are in school, come to know everything that is known to man. Therefore, any educational system must necessarily omit much more than it includes. What is does include, the progressive insists, is chosen because it does the job, not because it has some intrinsic worth. "Doing the job," of course, means meeting the aims of education, *viz.*, encouraging growth, i.e., developing intelligence. Whatever does this may be included, and contrary to the view expressed earlier by Hardie, there are no particular items of knowledge which uniquely perform this function. All that we have learned in the behavioral sciences teaches us this.

Secondly, the role of subject matter, in light of this, and what we know about how children learn, give us direction rather than serving to magically instill intelligence. Since organized subject matter represents, in Dewey's terms, the ripe fruitage of the experience of the human race, we would be very foolish to ignore it. It would simply mean we'd have the whole job to do over again. As Dewey points out:

> When engaged in the direct act of teaching, the instructor needs to have subject matter at his fingers' ends; his attention should be upon the attitude and response of his pupils.[6]

This is certainly not a call to throw subject matter out. Neither is it a call for the imposition of inert matter on passive children. The role that organized subject matter plays is that it serves to give the teacher, who has command of it, direction. That is, it indicates in what direction the learner is moving. Ultimately, the learner will reach a point in developing intelligence where that organized subject matter

6. John Dewey, *Democracy and Education* (New York: Macmillan, 1916), p. 183.

will come to have meaning. But this does not happen at the beginning. Therefore, organized subject matter is where the learner ends up. But it is not where he begins.

In the matter of history, for example, the child does not learn history by memorizing, or coming to correspond with the content of a history book. To suppose that he does is to engage in folly. It is when history is presented in this fashion that it becomes, to pupils, merely a matter of memorizing largely meaningless names, and dates, and events. Instead, we need to begin with the pupil where he is.

In the primary grades, this might mean such a simple thing as having an older person in the community come into the classroom and talk about the way things used to be in our town. Successive experiences as this regarding different parts of the community will eventually begin to develop some historical perspective in the child. He comes to understand that the present has a past; that some things are as they are because of that past. Eventually, he is led into increasingly abstract and sophisticated accounts until he is ready to take on organized bodies of knowledge. Then Charles Beard's economic interpretation of American History, or Frederick Jackson Turner's frontier thesis have some significance and can be approached meaningfully.

This suggests still another principle of progressivism; that pupils learn by doing. Opponents of progressivism attack this principle vehemently. Bertrand Russell, for example, used to gleefully point out the flaw in such a system. He suggested that to study on this basis had great flaws. For example, to learn by doing "The French Revolution" would entail great danger from the guillotine, while "doing" the nebular hypothesis would take a long time indeed. His view, of course, represents a popular misunderstanding of what the progressive means when he talks about "learning by doing."

Again, the progressive was drawing from what was known in the behavioral sciences when he made his recommendation. "Learning by doing" did not mean doing the French Revolution all over again. It meant simply that the learner would do history as a historian does history. The individual would learn in that manner in which the race has learned. Viewed this way, learning by doing appears to be much less radical and not nearly so amusing as Russell made it out to be.

One other aspect of education according to the progressives needs to be considered. This is the focus on democracy, and the consequences of this. Viewing education as growth, and given the idea of growth which the progressive holds, he looks for that social system which appears to be consonant with the system he propounds. Since growth can occur only in a setting which encourages the free interplay of ideas, as well as of personalities, what is called for is a system that affords such freedom.

The connection between education and democracy may be seen in the fact that education requires free interaction, free discussion of ideas, etc. Similarly, if democracy has any meaning and is not merely formal, its meaning is shared experiences. We can judge the degree to which a society is democratic, Dewey informs us, by the degree to which there is a shared shaping of values, and by the degree to which there is freedom of interaction among members of the group and between members of the group under consideration and other groups. Such sharing of experiences and interaction with others promotes growth. Consequently, education and democracy appear to imply each other.

Beyond this, the democratic concept also leads to an emphasis on individual worth. If democracy means that we share in the shaping of values, rather than having values imposed externally, then this calls for prizing the unique contribution which each individual has to make. It also suggests that each individual be developed to the utmost in order to equip him to contribute to the expression of shared value building.

This does not, however, imply any conflict between the individual and society. The only way such conflict arises, the progressive asserts, is when we view the individual as a sort of isolated psyche. Such a view does not fit ordinary human beings, for their very humanity is bound up in shared experiences. Strip away what society contributes to an individual and you strip away his humanity. Both democracy and education, therefore, call for shared living. This is expressed in the progressive curriculum by an emphasis on shared activities through group experiences. The individual worth is measured by his unique contribution to social experiences.

If we review the position of the progressive, we find that most of the principles of his theory are suggested by the behavioral sciences. In recommending that education be active rather than passive, that the whole child be the focus of our attention, that education be the reconstruction of experience, that organized subject matter be recognized as giving direction to present educational experiences, that learning take place as a process of problem solving, in all of this the progressive is insisting that we view the child and learning the way the behavioral sciences teach us to view him rather than on the basis of wishful thinking or traditional philosophic attitudes. To this extent, progressivism may be viewed as more empirically oriented than the traditional positions.

This is not to suggest that the progressive position is not also based on values. The notion that education and democracy imply each other involves us in preference. The progressive is simply expressing the way he wishes to have both education and democracy viewed. Education is to be taken only to be a sort of free and open ended process of inquiry. Democracy is to be interpreted as fully shared experience, as equality of opportunity rather than identity of treatment. These are values which the progressive holds and must be treated as such.

But for the most part, the progressive educational theory is an empirically oriented one. The progressive is much more likely than those of the traditional position to call for data to support his position, rather than to rely solely on logic or simply to insist that his preference is enough.

V RECONSTRUCTIONISM

The reconstructionist has been friendlier toward the progressive than any other educational theorist. In fact, at least one reconstructionist, George S. Counts, is generally included as a member of both groups. Yet, there are points on which the reconstructionist does not agree with the progressive. And, similarly, there are parts of the reconstructionist position which progressives find intolerable.

Reconstructionism represents a real break with the traditional positions. Whether these call for a return to the remote past intellectually, or for a resurrection of a 19th century outlook, the task of education is regarded as one of transmission in order to guarantee continuity to the culture. In contrast to this, reconstructionists urge a view of education that involves a process of selection and rejection, correction and improvement, and otherwise altering the factors of a social order that is in the throes of decay. As a matter of fact, they point out, this is, in reality, a process that goes on anyway. Some type of social order is always maintained, an order which is not precisely and exactly like the old order, and this is accomplished through indoctrination. Therefore, there is no question of whether or not such an activity should be engaged in. The real questions with which we need to be concerned are: to what extent do we indoctrinate; and, what direction is such indoctrination to take?

George S. Counts, responding to these questions in the 1930s, concluded that education was in the grip of a conservative minority which was using the institution to serve its own ends and conserve its privileged position. In a slim little volume entitled *Dare the School Build a New Social Order?* he urged an affirmitive answer to his own question. He suggested that teachers should unite and emancipate the schools from the controls of conservative forces. They would accomplish this by facing social issues squarely and providing an education that was more democratic in that it would serve the interests of the masses.

The social order which Counts recommended was clearly laid out. It was here that he departed from the progressives. Although he was himself counted a progressive and approved of much of the progressive educational theory, he felt that the movement had failed. The failure lay in the progressive's failure to specify the goals toward which effort was to be directed. The progressives focused on ends-in-view which themselves became means to further ends, but the emphasis Counts felt, was on means. In social theory, progressives remained agnostics when the crises of the times called for commitment. They were willing to see a new social order built through education, but they would not establish what kind of new order was to be built.

Following World War II, a new voice was heard urging the reconstruction of society through education. This was the voice of Theodore Brameld. For a time, Brameld's position was regarded as largely an educational curiosity, and the movement has never become widespread. But the potential is there for Reconstructionism to become a "wave of the future." Many of the points that Brameld has made, and a number of suggestions that he has for years been urging for adoption are now being echoed by a number of dissident voices in our society. Their interests follow the lines of Brameld's theories. Urging that the schools be used as agencies of change, that there be control by the masses, that there be sweeping curricular changes, among other recommendations, a number of leaders have called for programs consistent to with Brameld's. All that is needed is for those involved to discover Brameld, and reconstructionism may become a very positive force. Here is a theory already worked out that simply awaits recognition and adoption by those for whom it is intended.

At the base of the reconstructionist theory are two central themes. The first is that education is a process of cultural transformation. The second is that we are currently in the midst of a culture crisis. Our society is experiencing a major dislocation, a dislocation of our institutions, habits, practices, and attitudes. In this crisis it becomes the role of education to apply the needed therapy. The dislocation is of such proportions that unless the remedies begin to be applied immediately and forcefully, there may be little hope for the recovery of our sick society.

The dimensions of the struggle to correct what is wrong with our society may be seen in Brameld's view that not just in our nation, or even in our society, but on a global scale there are two groups of conflicting forces. The first force consists of those who direct every effort toward the maintenance, or conservation, of the inherited structure. Making up this group are those who invest for profit, the managerial class, the military caste, the communications media, and a few other miscellaneous groups. The opposing group consists of industrial and agricultural workers, rank-and-file members of armed forces, numbers of professional workers, students, citizens of underdeveloped countries, and others, all of whom are devoted to expanding freedom.

There is much evidence of conflict, not simply between these groups, (though this conflict is the most basic), but in several areas of American culture. In science, for example, the scientist is to pursue knowledge objectively and relentlessly; yet, despite the emphasis on objectivity, his discoveries have had profound moral consequences. In economics, we have the movement toward a push-button technology and consequent displacement of workers. In human relations here is conflict between black and white, between classes, between religious groups, etc. In the arts, we find decadence portrayed and a disaffection of artists. Religions are beset with doctrinal differences despite supposed loyalties to similar codes and objects of faith. In politics, there are conflicts between nationalism and internationalism, centralization and decentralization, etc. Education being involved in all of these is also involved in the conflicts of these areas.

It must be through education that the crises are overcome. This can be accomplished only by rebuilding in new directions toward future goals and purposes. If the culture is not renewed and reshaped through education, then the culture is doomed.

Now, man is goal-seeking. That is bound into his nature. But goals are not fixed. Man decides his own destiny. The goals that man sets will determine that destiny. What is called for is the establishment of the goals that are shared by most people of the earth. Once this is established, we may then look for ways of seeking these goals.

An important aspect of man's beliefs is that they are not arrived at on a purely objective and cognitive level. Even some of his knowledge is intuitive. (The reconstructionist term for intuition is prehension.) Consequently, equally important as a center of focus is the "unrational," or man's unconscious. For this "unconscious," at least as much as his cognitive being, results in the sum total of man's beliefs and knowledge, his ideology. On the basis of this ideology, he establishes his utopia; his picture of the way the world ought to be.

This does not remain an individual matter, however. The ideals, beliefs and knowledge, and the utopia are validated by being that to which the masses give assent. This *consensual validation* is the basis on which truth is established. It is on the basis of consensual validation that we may arrive at the type of order we wish to establish and the means we may use to get there. Once we have established through consensual validation the appropriate ideals, beliefs and knowledge, we can then determine the type of social order which we hope to establish. In *Patterns of Educational Philosophy*, Brameld devotes 2-1/2 pages to an outline of the type of social order that is to be established. He lays out in some detail the economy to be established, the political system, the humane order, (what human beings are to be like), and the world order.[7] Through the use of a myth, we shall achieve affective involvement with this type of social order, i.e., we shall obtain a commitment to this specific social order.

The social order to which we shall seek commitment is one in which the factors of production and distribution are in control of the masses. The reconstructionist instructs us that the new social order must be "genuinely democratic." This means control of the resources and institutions of the culture by the working people, i.e., by the second force, mentioned earlier. All resources, cultural and natural, all institutions, all services, all industry, etc., are to be controlled by the second force.

This represents one of the areas which the progressive finds intolerable. It is not that progressives oppose such a social order as that laid out by Brameld. Many feel personally committed to just such an order. What they find reprehensible is that what Brameld offers with one hand, he takes away with the other. He promises a social order that is "genuinely democratic." To the progressive this means one in which goals and values are not predetermined and closed. Yet, one finds that Brameld has already made all the big decisions for us. He spells out precisely what we must be committed to without any room for our sharing in the shaping of these ends and goals. This is indeed a strange democracy, according to the progressive.

7. Theodore Brameld, *Patterns of Educational Philosophy* (New York: Holt, Rinehart and Winston, 1970), pp. 432-439.

In moving from the total social system to education in particular, reconstructionism calls for schools to be supported federally, with such support supplemented by state and local funds. Education is to be free from nursery school through university and adult levels. The mass communications systems are to be made a part of the educational system and placed under similar controls. Curricula, teaching, and administration are to be geared to transformative purposes of the economy of abundance, the political system, the scientific order, and esthetic patterns.

Learning, in this scheme, is regarded as goal-seeking. The goals must be transformative, not transmissive, and international as well as national. Learning will be directed at commitment to a world order, the nature of which was described briefly above. The other facet of the direction of learning will be social self-realization.

Social self-realization will be accomplished through making every child from his earliest years feel that he is helping to create his school. He will also be involved in purposeful, socially useful community enterprises. Social self-realization will be value directed. Literacy, skills, etc., are not to be ignored, but mental and physical health are also to be emphasized.

Learning shall come largely through the consideration of problems. These problems are those created by the interruption in satisfying specifiable wants. Such problems will, of course, be integral with cultural and intercultural purposes. The learner shall learn to rely on evidence in arriving at the solutions to problems. This evidence, however, is not entirely the public evidence on which the progressive relies. Also admissable is "direct" evidence, i.e., that which we know intuitively through our own personal experience. Learning comes through shared communication, through group efforts. These group efforts may include role-playing, sociodrama, group self-evaluation, etc. Among the skills and values to be learned will be ways of arriving at group consensus and the valuing of consensual validation as a test of truth and values.

Such learning shall take place, of course, through democratic persuasion. Teachers and pupils together will acquire knowledge about pressing problems, work out solutions and then act together to achieve these solutions. There will be an emphasis on commitment. This may sound like indoctrination, but the reconstructionist regards it as "education for defensible partiality." Since the goals seen by the reconstructionist are worthwhile, there is good reason to use persuasion, though some may regard this as indoctrination with propaganda. The reconstructionist not only has no objection to this but sees it as entirely defensible. Certain forms of propaganda are consistent with consensual validation.

Education will in the process of teaching skills, facts, and values, provide for the critical analysis of crucial issues such as the nature of world civilization, or what democracy means. When enough people understand the issues and meanings involved, they will come to agree that what they want is a democratic world organization as this has been portrayed by the reconstructionist. The nature of the democratic value orientation to which we must become committed is one in which man believes in himself, in his capacity to direct himself and govern himself in relation to his fellow man.

Sociological realism must also be taught to help students become more conscious of the fact of their socioeconomic position in the culture. Such knowledge will aid in preventing placing controls in the hands of a minority class which has its own interests in mind and encourages the kind of education which solidifies its own class and status interests. We will learn to see not only what our own class and social position is, but what it ought to be. We shall also learn what socioeconomic pattern we ought to believe in and support.

Even religion will be included in the curriculum. No particular religious point of view shall be imposed. All religions will be studied comparitively and critically. In addition to the standard religions, Existential Humanism will also be studied in order to teach man about his nonrational nature. Although no point of view will be required, when all positions are studied, a position something like that of the existential humanist will probably receive consensual validation.

Creativity will be taught. This will involve teaching pupils to be honest with themselves, to feel free to express their deep interests openly and frankly. There will be no room in their scheme for the authoritarian teacher. There must be room for the learner to deviate, to innovate, to be different, to create something not according to standard. Time will be provided for the pupil to search himself and express himself as he sees fit. This is not necessarily done alone, but may be achieved through group sessions such as encounter groups.

Much teaching will revolve around the teaching of values. Even skills will be developed through searching for solutions to real problems with which we are faced. One proposal is that these problems be dealt with through experimental projects in five related areas: conservation of natural resources, the class structure, sexual morality, religion, and world government.

The reconstructionist is ready to claim that his position is largely empirical. In the first place, he relies on the sciences including the behavioral sciences to develop his position. His views of the cultural, and world, crises are ontological realities. However, his view that education is transformational rather than transmissive is clearly a value judgement. The notion that we are in the midst of a culture crisis seems reasonable and supportable; there appears to be much evidence that there are dislocations in our institutions, habits, patterns, etc. But, the notion that the only solution is to make the schools agencies of transformation is a value judgement. Even more obviously in the realm of values is the view that we must work toward a particular social order, *viz.*, that specified by the reconstructionist.

As for the methods and content of education, the reconstructionist claims to be empirical, to base his recommendations on the findings of the behavioral sciences. But most of what he offers as a basis for his educational directives are based on unverified, and for the most part, unverifiable Freudian conceptualizations. These are largely metaphysical as is the "self" which the reconstructionist wants "socially realized." Therefore, most of his content and methods are really statements of preference. There simply is not the general support among behavioral scientists for the sort of methods and content which Brameld offers. The reliable findings of the behavioral sciences do not necessarily imply the directives which the reconstructionist offers. Often, the findings permit a variety of interpretations, with the reconstructionist's being only one among several possible alternatives. Much of what is offered as an explanation for what he recommends is more nearly in the nature of a rationalization of what the reconstructionist wishes to do. His theory consists very largely of value judgements despite his claims to be making empirical statements. The reconstructionist would be hard pressed to present clear and unequivocal empirical evidence for the tenents which he supports.

VI AFFECTIVE HUMANISM

The final position which we shall consider is one which, like reconstructionism, has never been widely established in our society. But, again like reconstructionism, it shows promise of becoming a meaningful force in education, and is therefore worthy of consideration. The promise it holds is not based on the strength, or logic, of its tenents. Indeed, such rational support may not even be deemed appropriate. The possibilities for becoming a force in education is based largely on the fact that this last movement has become identified to some extent with the civil rights movement. Also, a certain amount of support may result from an apparent surge of interest in our society in a sort of homely existentialism. These, rather than any particular soundness of the theory, seem to be the basis for the loyalty that the movement's disciples express.

The new movement is too new to have received a generally agreed-upon title. Advocates of the position frequently refer to it as humanism. To refer to it by this title, however, may be misleading. What has classically, or traditionally, or historically been referred to as humanism seems to be the very antithesis of the current movement. Whereas humanism has generally referred to those distinctively human characteristics of man centered about his intellect, but including creativity as well as reason, the present movement eschews rationality and order. In its place, the newer movement emphasizes raw feelings and emotion. It is this distinct difference that makes it seem grossly misleading to call the new movement humanism. In deference to the members of that group who call their views humanistic, however, the title "affective humanism" would seem to satisfy their own view and at the same time distinguish the movement from what has up to the present time been regarded as humanism.

Although a number of those writing about education in the affective humanistic vein have not established a clear or consistent conceptualization of what they are writing about, much of the theory appears to have its origin in Carl Rogers' self theory. There are a number of conceptualizations of "self" evident in the various writings. These notions appear to range from self seen as a sort of soul, to self as merely a summation symbol for an active group of processes. The sense in which the term most generally appears to be used in the affective humanist's writings, however, is as a way of denoting a person's attitudes, feelings, perceptions, and evaluation of himself as an object. In short, a self is what a person thinks of himself. This is the way the term is frequently used. However, it does not exhaust all meanings, because, as will be seen the affective humanist frequently uses the term to mean a sort of unique and inviolable entity.

The writings of Carl Rogers would be most helpful in seeing the ways in which the term "self" is used. However, there are a number of others who have also written in this area. Psychologist Abraham

Maslow is also frequently cited as a source. A number of existentialists appear also to be identified with the movement. And several writers have recently gained some prominence as affective humanists. Among these would be Paul Goodman, John Holt, J. Kozol, M. McLuhan, H.A. Otto, Arthur Combs, and Michael Polanyi. There is also a Center for Humanistic Education located at the University of Massachusetts School of Education, Amherst, Massachusetts 01002, which might serve as a helpful source of information.

Many of the educational principles of affective humanism have grown out of Rogers' client-centered therapy, or nondirective counseling. In this approach the therapist enters into an intensely personal and subjective relationship with the client, relating not as a scientist to a subject or a physician to a patient, but as a person to a person. In education, this has suggested that the teacher establish a relationship with his students which is also highly subjective and personal. Rather than following the traditional pattern of teacher-pupil relationship, the teacher establishes person to person relationships with pupils. He must regard pupils as unconditionally worthy and allow no barriers to his sensing what his pupils are feeling.

In therapy, the patient is encouraged to explore feelings within himself. This exploration may reveal strange and unknown feelings that the client himself was not aware of. He is encouraged to experience these feelings fully and completely. He is enabled to do this by the realization that he is in a nonthreatening and accepting situation.

Educational practices call for the same sort of accepting and nonthreatening atmosphere. Indeed, the purpose is even the same, since allowing these feelings to be expressed will result in altered behavior. The purpose in education, as in therapy, is a changing and freely-developing self.

Both therapy and learning are based on a number of additional principles. It is Rogers' position that every individual exists in a changing world of experiences of which he is the center. These experiences which constitute the individual's world include unconscious, or preconscious, as well as conscious experiences. Consequently, a person is the best source of information about himself. This places the therapist in the role of an enabler, or facilitator, who simply facilitates the development of insights about one's self. The teacher is cast in a similar role.

In this view learning is seen as learning how to learn. The teacher is the one who opens up this possibility. His function is to free curiousity, to enable learners to move in new directions to open the learner to the natural potential for learning that characterizes all human beings. The aim of education, then, is the facilitation of learning.

In therapy, what is significant to the client is not the world as it is, but the world as he experiences and perceives it. Reality, for the subject, is simply a tentative hypothesis which he is continuously checking. The checking is not a purely cognitive activity. The person experiences and checks as an organized whole, not simply as a mind responding to intellectual stimulation. Consequently, therapy or education, must take into account the person's perceptions and experiences if he is to be altered. It is not the therapist's or the teacher's world, (i.e., perceptions and experiences) that are relevant. The "public" world is also not meaningful; it is meaningless to talk about the way things "really" are. Further, it is inadequate to treat, or train simply the intellectual side of the individual. The individual must be treated as an organic whole in which changes in one part of the system produce changes in other parts.

In education, this suggests that it is more important to seek out, and to help the learner lay out for himself, his real perceptions of reality. What is *not* called for is the imposition of a preordered, preexistent, external reality. Also, it is an error to treat the learner as some sort of intellectual psyche. A part of the organism, and consequently of his perception of reality, are feelings and emotions. These cannot be ignored except at the expense of distorting the individual.

The individual organism has one basic tendency—to actualize, maintain and enhance the self. This is the single motivating force and the single goal of life. Self-actualization cannot take place without struggle and pain, but this can be borne because the urge to grow is strong. Growth can occur only when choices are clearly perceived and adequately symbolized.

Although this is taken from theories of psychotherapy, it has implications for education. In the first place, the motive and goal, self-actualization, underscore the need for the teacher to serve as a facilitator. The teacher must avoid imposing his own self on that of the pupil; he must not get in the way of the learner's self actualizing itself. In fact, his role is to aid this process. To interrupt, or impede, this process is to impose tension, disorganization.

Emotion accompanies and facilitates self-actualizing behavior. Self-actualizing behavior is simply the effort of the organism to satisfy its need, to realize itself. Consequently, education must encourage rather than stifle feelings and emotions. In fact, it is only when feelings are freed that growth can occur; learning comes through feeling.

Self-actualization does not, however, entail isolation, it is through interaction with the environment, and particularly as a result of evaluational interaction with others, that the structure of self is formed. There is no small voice inside the learner which guides his conduct and responses. (Some affective humanists, however, do urge that the learner be taught to listen to the small voice within himself, rather than introjecting values.) One of the ways in which the subject or learner can learn about himself is through group encounters. Such encounters are known by a number of names: T-groups, laboratory training, sensitivity training, basic encounter group, etc. Such group activities consist of a relatively unstructured group meeting in which members are encouraged to express themselves freely, explore feelings, and engage in interpersonal communication. Such encounters are reported to enable individuals to come to "know themselves." They are recommended not only for pupils, but for teachers, in order to "free" teachers to work with pupils. They are also suggested for administrators to enable them to work better with teachers. Other group activities may also be used. These may include role-playing, psychodramas, or sociodramas, group dream analysis, etc.

Evaluational interaction with others may help to develop insight in the individual that not all the values which he attaches to experiences are his own. These experiences and the values which the individual attaches to them, all of which are a part of the structure of the self, may be values experienced directly or values introjected or taken over from others, but perceived in distorted fashion as though they had been directly experienced. These distortions can be the result of inconsistency between the introjected values and the structure of the self.

Sometimes the distortions lead the individual to deny experiences as well as distort them. The denial removes the experiences from the conscious level. Consequently some behaviors are brought about by unconscious experiences and needs, even though most ways of behaving are those consistent with the self. The result may be conflict, tension, and maladjustment.

This maladjustment may arise from not treating the person as a whole person. Being forced to hide, or deny feelings by having to pretend they are not there, the person becomes distorted and does not develop as a whole person. This is what frequently occurs when we isolate cognitive from affective learning in the classroom. We drive out feelings and emotions, cause them to be hidden or denied, and produce students who are "up-tight." Those classrooms that are purely intellectual create frustrations and develop intellectual half-people who are well developed cognitively, but lack feeling in the affective domain.

Adjustment exists when all experiences of an organism are assimilated on a symbolic level into a consistent relationship with the concept of the self. Inconsistent experiences are seen as a threat and the more threats there are, the more rigidly the self-structure is organized to maintain itself. This may lead to rejection, hostility toward others, and even toward the self. Perhaps this is one of the reasons why certain groups of children, particularly those of the lowest socioeconomic class, and black ghetto children with unfeeling teachers, fall farther and farther behind other children who are not in a threatening environment that is inconsistent with their self-structures.

On the other hand, when one is consistent and integrated with the self, then one is more understanding and accepting of other selves. This factor has been seen as having significance in ending interracial conflict and partly on this basis has led to connections with the civil rights movement. This has also been seen as the key to eventual abolition of international strife and so tied affective humanism to the peace movement as well as the civil rights movement.

Moreover, it is only when the threat to the self is low that any real learning can take place. Consequently, the traditional approaches involving humiliation, devaluation, scorn, and contempt interfere with and interrupt learning rather than enhancing it.

But it is not enough simply to remove the threats in the environment and to encourage the sort of free expression that will be revealing to the individual himself and enable self-actualization to take place through self-knowledge. The tasks also must be relevant and meaningful to the child. Children will learn only as he sees the things being presented as being involved in the maintenance or enhancement of the self.

Further, the pupil cannot be involved simply in activities of "learning about." He must be significantly involved in the learning process. This means, first of all, that the pupil must be having direct experiential contact with significant problems. The problems must be practical, and personal. Thus, the affective humanist speaks of learning by doing. This sounds much like the progressive emphasis on doing, but there is a difference. In the affective humanist's concept of learning by doing, there is a tendency to reject intellectualization, to separate out doing from thinking. The progressive does not approve of this favoring the immediate acting over mediated doing. He regards such immediate (or unmediated) activity as the antithesis of what the school should be doing, *viz.*, developing intelligence.

Another aspect of being involved in learning is responsible participation in the process. Consequently, the pupil should choose his own directions, help discover his own learning resources, formulate his own problems and live with the consequences of these choices. Again there is at least a difference in the degree of meaning of such involvement between the views of the affective humanist, and the progressive who appears to be calling for the same thing. In the progressive view, the affective humanist is effectively calling for the abrogation of the teacher's role. The progressive would view the teacher as a very important resource, not only for subject matter or content, but equally for knowledge of the learning process, other resources and even for information about the pupil's own behaving. The affective humanist, on the other hand, identifying learning and knowledge with feeling and emotions, devalues the traditional role of the teacher. Rogers, in fact, confesses to having lost interest in being a teacher and feels that the outcomes of teaching are unimportant or harmful.[8]

Finally, involvement in learning, to the affective humanist, means the whole person of the pupil participates in the learning process. This means that he is emotionally as well as cognitively involved; his feelings are as much a part of the process as his intellect. It is with such an approach that, the learner comes to know that it is *his* learning that he is participating in.

Admittedly this presentation has not dealt specifically with the content of the affective humanist's educational program. This is largely because the theorists in this field talk very little about content, except for the affective content. Characteristically, writings in this area consist of testimonials concerning specific projects or activities. But, there is little talk about the place of skills like reading, and figuring, or content like history and science. The theory appears to be largely epistemological in nature, with an emphasis on knowing, rather than knowledge.

A review of the affective humanist's position reveals that it is based in large measure on the notion of an existent self. The term changes in meaning from one writer to another, and occasionally even within an article or book. But, most generally, the self, however it is portrayed, turns out to be some sort of entity whose integrity is

---

8. Carl R. Rogers, *Freedom to Learn* (Columbus, Ohio: Chas. E. Merrill Publishing Company, 1969), p. 153.

to be maintained. This notion of a self, which in some cases is potential and in others is actual, may not be precisely like a soul, but it is a metaphysical concept. No one has ever observed a self; its existence is asserted but there is no method given for verifying its existence. Indeed, none appears to be possible. Consequently, we must view as metaphysics that part of the theory which purports to give information about the self.

Those aspects of the position which deal with recommendations for what the aims of education should be are, of course, value judgments. Certain of the recommendations, such as what the teacher's and pupil's respective roles should be may be empirical in nature. That is, there may be ways of checking whether or not learnings claimed by the affective humanists really take place. However, since much of what is regarded as learning is in the area of feelings and emotions, it appears to preclude public verification. If personal and private testimony are admissable as evidence, then we may have a sort of empirical checking. In most areas, however, such data has not proved to be reliable. Consequently, there may be good reason for regarding educational directives in these areas as value judgements.

The affective humanist's rejection of intellectual or academic content in favor of affective "learnings," must also be seen as simply preferences. Consequently, his quarrels with academically-oriented teachers must be seen as simply conflicts in values. Such quarrels can be resolved only in the ways in which apparent differences in value judgments are resolved. Initially, the meaning of what is being asserted must be made clear, and following this certain claims may then be checked out.

VII

The theories which have been presented here do not by any means exhaust the theories that might be examined by the student of philosophy of education. Nor have the theories presented in the preceding five sections been dealt with exhaustively. Characteristic basic principles have been presented, enough to give a picture of the position. These have been analyzed largely on the bases of determining what type of statements are being offered.

Engaging in such analysis is only a part of what it means to do educational philosophy. Since this work represents an introduction to the philosophy of education, it may become simply a first step. One might, for example, choose to turn to the writings of the theorists themselves to enhance his own understanding of the positions. Or, he might examine the positions in greater detail with a view toward further analysis of the type we have engaged in here.

Beyond this, there is a whole field of concept analysis. It is a field which is still largely unexplored. This would involve one in examining writings in educational theory with a view to determining the meaning of terms like "learning," "teaching," "individualized instruction," etc. Some terms are so loosely used as to be meaningless and consequently require clarification. Others change in meaning from theorist to theorist and so need checking. Some are used as catch words to elicit support for particular programs or ideas. Currently terms like "innovation," "accountability," "sensitivity," and others are being used very persuasively by authors who claim to be empirical.

The presentation of the theories covered in this book was not intended to give complete and thorough view of theoretical positions. An introduction ought to be expected to do what the name implies. Nor was it intended that all the alternatives were presented in order to allow the student of philosophy of education to choose from among these alternatives his own "philosophy of education." In the first place, it is not unreasonable to hope that at this stage one will see that philosophy of education is something one *does* rather than something one *possesses*. Secondly, as for finally adopting a theoretical position that one will henceforth cling to and close out all others, it might be pointed out that G.K. Chesterton was not giving sound advice when he suggested that the purpose of an open mind like that of an open mouth was to close it firmly on something.

What it is hoped was encouraged was an openness in which one, while making up his mind, does not do so finally and irrevocably. The attitude encouraged is that it be recognized that all positions are precisely that: positions. None are final, absolute, unalterable and unquestionable Truths. Consequently what is called for, and what this book has been aimed at developing is that type of openness and criticalness which says that no evidence is so final as to render all further evidence insignificant. Equipped thus, the student of education may be ready to face the numerous and varied theories and statements about education that will consistently and constantly be offered as alternatives.

Bibliography

Acquinas, Thomas. *Basic Writings* (New York: Random House, Inc., 1945).

Adler, Mortimer. *The Conditions of Philosophy* (New York: Dell Publishing Co., Inc., 1965).

Archambault, Reginald. *Philosophical Analysis and Education* (London: Routledge & Kegan Paul, 1965).

Arnstine, Donald. *Philosophy of Education* (New York: Harper, 1967).

Ayer, A.J. *Language, Truth and Logic* (New York: Dover Publications, Inc., 1946).

Bagley, William C. *Education and the Emergent Man* (Nashville: Thomas Nelson Inc., 1934).

Barth, Karl. *Deliverance to the Captives* (London: SCM Press, 1961).

Bayles, Ernest E. *Pragmatism in Education* (New York: Harper & Row, 1966).

Beck, Clive. *Educational Philosophy and Theory* (Boston: Little, Brown and Co., 1974).

Bell, Bernard Iddings. *The Crisis in Education* (New York: McGraw-Hill Books & Education Services Group, 1949).

Belloc, Hillaire. *Essays of a Catholic Layman in England* (London: Sheed & Ward, 1931).

Berkson, I.B. *Preface to an Educational Philosophy* (New York: Columbia University Press, 1940).

Bestor, Arthur. *Educational Wastelands* (Urbana: University of Illinois Press, 1953).

Bode, Boyd. *Progressive Education at the Crossroads* (Newson and Company, 1938).

Brameld, Theodore. *Patterns of Educational Philosophy* (New York: Holt, Rinehart and Winston, Inc., 1971).

——. *Philosophies of Education in Cultural Perspective* (New York: Dryden Press, 1955).

Breed, F.S. *Education and the New Realism* (New York: Macmillan, Inc., 1939).

Brown, F.M. *General Philosophy in Education* (New York: McGraw-Hill Books, 1966).

Brubacher, John S. *Modern Philosophies of Education* (New York: McGraw-Hill Books, 1950).

Brumbaugh, Robert S. and Lawrence, Nathaniel M. *Philosophical Themes in Modern Education* (Boston: Houghton Mifflin Co., 1973).

Buber, Martin. *I and Thou* (New York: Charles Scribner's Sons, 1958).

Buchler, Justus, ed. *Philosophical Writings of Peirce* (New York: Dover Publications, Inc., 1955).

Buford, Thomas O. *Toward a Philosophy of Education* (New York: Holt, Rinehart & Winston, Inc., 1969).

Butler, J. Donald. *Four Philosophies* (New York: Harper & Row, 1951).

———. *Idealism in Education* (New York: Harper & Row, 1966).

Childs, John L. *American Pragmatism and Education* (New York: Holt, Rinehart and Winston, Inc., 1956).

Combs, Arthur, chairman. A.S.C.D. Book Committee. *Perceiving, Behaving, Becoming* (Washington, D.C.: NEA, 1962).

Conant, James B. *The Education of American Teachers* (New York: McGraw-Hill Book & Education Services Group, 1964).

Counts, George S. *Dare the Schools Build a New Social Order?* (New York: Bureau of Publications, Teachers College, Columbia University, 1952).

———. *Education and American Civilization* (New York: Bureau of Publications, Teachers College, Columbia University, 1952).

Dewey, John. *Democracy and Education* (New York: Macmillan, Inc., 1916).

———. *Experience and Education* (New York: Macmillan, Inc., 1938).

Donahue, John W. *St. Thomas Aquinas and Education* (New York: Random House, 1968).

Dostoevski, Fedor. *Notes from Underground* (New York: Dell Publishing Co., Inc., 1960).

Edwards, Jonathan. *Representative Selections* (New York: Hill and Wang, 1962).

Emerson, Ralph Waldo. *The Complete Essays and Other Writings* (New York: The Modern Library, 1950).

Finney, Ross L. *A Sociological Philosophy of Education* (New York: Macmillan, Inc., 1928).

Frankena, William K. *Three Historical Philosophies of Education* (Glenview, Ill.: Scott, Foresman and Co., 1965).

Froebel, F. *The Education of Man* (New York: Appleton-Century-Crofts, 1892).

Gilson, Etienne. *The Unity of Philosophical Experience* (New York: Charles Scribner's Sons, 1937).

Goodman, Paul. *Compulsory Mis-Education and the Community of Scholars* (New York: Random House, Inc., Vintage Books, 1966).

Green, T.M. *et al. Liberal Education Re-Examined* (New York: Harper & Row, Publishers, 1943).

Green, Thomas. *The Activities of Teaching* (New York: McGraw-Hill Books & Education Services Group, 1971).

Gruber, Frederick C. *Historical and Contemporary Philosophies of Education* (New York: Thomas Y. Crowell Co., 1973).

Hall, Calvin S. and Lindzey, Gardner. *Theories of Personality* (New York: John Wiley & Sons, Inc., 1957).

Hardie, C.D. *Truth and Fallacy in Educational Theory* (New York: Bureau of Publications, Teachers College, Columbia, 1962).

Harris, William T. *Psychological Foundations of Education* (New York: Arco Press & New York Times, 1969).

Hegel, G.W.F. *Selections* (New York: Charles Scribner's Sons, 1929).

Hobbes, Thomas. *The Citizen* (New York: Appleton-Century-Crofts, 1949).

Holt, John. *How Children Learn* (New York: Pitman Publishing Corporation, 1967).

Hocking, W.E. *Types of Philosophy* (New York: Charles Scribner's Sons, 1939).

Horne, Herman H. *The Philosophy of Christian Education* (New York: Fleming H. Revell Company, 1937).

Hume, David. *Theory of Knowledge* (Ed. by D.C. Yalder-Thompson), (Austin: University of Texas Press, 1953).

Hutchins, Robert M. *The Conflict in Education* (New York: Harper & Row, Publishers, 1953).

———. *The Higher Learning in America* (New Haven: Yale University Press, 1936).

Huxley, Aldous. *The Perennial Philosophy* (New York; Harper & Row, Publishers, 1945).

James, William. *Pragmatism* (New York: Longmans, Green, 1907).

Jaspers, Karl. *Man in the Modern Age* (New York: Henry Holt and Company, 1933).

Kallen, Horace M. *The Education of Free Men* (New York: Farrar, Straus & Giroux, Inc., 1949).

Kandel, Isaac T. *Conflicting Theories of Education* (New York: Macmillan, Inc., 1939).

Kant, Immanual. *Critique of Pure Reason* (Tr. N.K. Smith) (New York: St. Martin's Press, 1965).

Kelly, E.C. *Education for What Is Real* (New York: Harper, 1947).

Kierkegaard, Soren. *Diary* (New York: Philosophical Library, Inc., 1960).

Kilpatrick, William H. *Philosophy of Education* (New York: Macmillan, Inc., 1951).

Kneller, George. *Existentialism and Education* (New York: Philosophic Library, Inc., 1958).

———. *Introduction to the Philosophy of Education* (New York: John Wiley & Sons, Inc., 1964).

Koerner, Joseph. *The Mis-Education of American Teachers* (Boston: Houghton Mifflin Company, 1963).

Kozol, J. *Death at an Early Age* (Boston: Houghton Mifflin Company, 1967).

Lucas, Christopher J. *What Is Philosophy of Education?* (New York: The Macmillan Co., 1969).

Marcel, Gabriel. *The Philosophy of Existentialism* (New York: Citadel Press, Inc., 1961).

Maritain, Jacques. *An Introduction to Philosophy* (New York: Longmans, Green, 1930).

Marler, Charles D. *Philosophy and Schooling* (Boston: Allyn and Bacon, Inc., 1975).

Marshall, John P. *The Teacher and His Philosophy* (Lincoln, Neb.: Professional Educators Publications, Inc., 1973).

Martin, Wm. Oliver. *Realism in Education* (New York: Harper & Row, 1969).

Mason, Robert E. *Contemporary Educational Theory* (New York: David McKay Co., Inc., 1972).

Mayer, Adolphe E. *Grandmasters of Educational Thought* (New York: McGraw-Hill Book Co., 1975).

McLuhan, M. *Understanding Media, The Extension of Man* (New York: McGraw-Hill Books & Education Services Group, 1964).

Morris, Van Cleve. *Existentialism in Education* (New York: Harper & Row, Publishers, 1965).

———. *Philosophy and the American School* (Boston: Houghton Mifflin Company, 1961).

Morris, Van Cleve and Pai, Young. *Philosophy and the American School* (Boston: Houghton Mifflin Co., 1976).

Nef, John U. *The Universities Look for Unity* (New York: Pantheon Books, Inc., 1943).

National Society for the Study of Education, Forty-first Yearbook, Part I. *Philosophy of Education* (Chicago: University of Chicago Press, 1942).

———. Fifty-fourth Yearbook. *Modern Philosophies and Education* (Chicago: University of Chicago Press, 1955).

Nietzsche, Friedrich. *Basic Writings of Neitzsche* (New York: Modern Library, 1968).

O'Connor, D.J. *An Introduction to Philosophy of Education* (London: Routledge & Kegan Paul, 1961).

Otto, H.A. *A Guide to Developing Your Potential* (New York: Charles Scribner's Sons, 1967).

Ozmon, Howard and Craver, Sam. *Philosophical Foundations of Education* (Columbus, Ohio: Charles E. Merrill Publishing Co., 1976).

Pai, Young and Myers, Joseph. *Philosophic Problems and Education* (Philadelphia, Lippincott, 1967).

Pascal, Blaise. *Thoughts* (New York: Colliers, 1956).

Peirce, Charles S. *Chance, Love and Logic* (New York: Harcourt Brace, 1923).

Perry, Ralph Barton. *Present Philosophical Tendencies* (New York: Longmans, Green, 1912).

Peters, R.S. *Ethics and Education* (Oakland, N.J.: Scott, Foresman and Company, 1967).

Pius XI. *Christian Education of Youth* (New York: The American Press, 1936).

Polanyi, Michael. *The Tacit Dimension* (Garden City, N.Y.: Doubleday & Company, Inc., 1966).

Pratte, Richard. *Contemporary Theories of Education* (Scranton: Intext Educational Publishers, 1971).

Price, Kingsley. *Education and Philosophical Thought* (Boston: Allyn and Bacon, Inc., 1962).

Reid, Louis A. *Philosophy and Education* (New York: Random House, 1965).

Rich, John Martin, Ed. *Readings in the Philosophy of Education* (Belmont, CA: Wadsworth Publishing Co., Inc., 1972).

Rogers, Carl R. *Freedom to Learn* (Columbus, Ohio: Charles E. Merrill Publishing Company, 1969).

Rousseau, J.J. *Emile* (New York: Appleton & Company, 1914).

Royce, Josiah. *The Spirit of Modern Philosophy* (New York: Houghton Mifflin Company, 1898).

Rugg, Harold. *Foundations for American Education* (New York: World Book, 1947).

Russell, Bertrand. *Education and the Good Life* (New York: Boni and Liveright, 1926). (Also Avon paperback.)

———. *Education and the Social Order* (London: George Albert and Unwin, 1932).

Scheffler, Israel. *The Conditions of Knowledge* (New York: Scott, Foresman and Company, 1965).

Schopenhauer, Arthur. *Selections* (New York: Charles Scribner's Sons, 1956).

Smith, Mortimer. *Diminished Mind* (Chicago: Henry Regnery Company, 1954).

Smith, Philip. *Philosophy and Education* (New York: Harper & Row, 1965).

Stanley, William O. *Education and Social Integration* (New York: Bureau of Publications, Teachers College, Columbia, 1953).

Stephens, John M. *The Psychology of Classroom Learning* (New York: Holt, Rinehart and Winston, Inc., 1965).

Strain, John Paul. *Modern Philosophies of Education* (New York: Random House, 1971).

Thayer, V.T. *Public Education and Its Critics* (New York: Macmillan, Inc., 1954).

Thompson, Keith. *Education and Philosophy* (New York: John Wiley & Sons, Inc., 1972).

Tillich, Paul. *The New Being* (New York: Charles Scribner's Sons, 1955).

Van Doren, Mark. *Liberal Education* (New York: Holt, Rinehart and Winston, Inc., 1943).

Whitehead, Alfred N. *Aims of Education* (New York: The New American Library, Inc., 1929).

Wild, John. *An Introduction to Realist Philosophy* (New York: Harper & Row, Publishers, 1948).

Wirsing, Marie. *Teaching and Philosophy: A Synthesis* (New York: Houghton Mifflin Co., 1972).

DATE DUE

MAR 1 5 1997			

	DATE DUE		